D0490310

WITHDRAWN
FROM
UNIVERSITIES
AT
MEDWAY
LIBRARY

MW
LAC
DON

SEVEN SAILORS

By the Same Author

THE MUTINY AT INVERGORDON
THE GREY DIPLOMATISTS
WE DIVE AT DAWN
UNEASY OCEANS
MEN OF ACTION

Crown Copyright Reserved

Admiral Ramsay with General Eisenhower and Field-Marshal
Montgomery on the deck of *H.M.S. Apollo* off the Normandy
beaches.

4530909

SEVEN SAILORS

by

COMMANDER

Kenneth Edwards

ROYAL NAVY

Local Area

940
S45
942

EDW

COLLINS

14 ST. JAMES'S PLACE LONDON

THIS BOOK IS SET IN FONTANA, A NEW TYPE FACE DESIGNED
FOR THE EXCLUSIVE USE OF THE HOUSE OF COLLINS, AND
PRINTED BY THEM IN GREAT BRITAIN

∇4600051

UNIVERSITIES AT MEDWAY
2 7 APR 2007
DRILL HALL LIBRARY

COLLINS CLEAR-TYPE PRESS: LONDON AND GLASGOW
COPYRIGHT 1945

CONTENTS

PAGE

Sir Bertram Home Ramsay, K.C.B., K.B.E., M.V.O.   11
Admiral in His Majesty's Fleet

William Gladstone Agnew, C.B., C.V.O., D.S.O.   81
Captain, Royal Navy

Sir Bruce Austin Fraser, G.C.B., K.B.E.   112
Admiral in His Majesty's Fleet

Leonard Warren Murray, C.B., C.B.E.   152
Rear-Admiral, Royal Canadian Navy

Robert St. Vincent Sherbrooke, V.C., D.S.O.   177
Captain, Royal Navy

Sir Edward Neville Syfret, K.C.B.   198
Vice-Admiral in His Majesty's Fleet

Thomas Hope Troubridge, D.S.O.   217
Rear-Admiral in His Majesty's Fleet

LIST OF ILLUSTRATIONS

Admiral Ramsay with General Eisenhower and Field-Marshal Montgomery on the deck of H.M.S. *Apollo* off the Normandy beaches   *Frontispiece*

Admiral Sir Bertram Home Ramsay   *Facing Page*   24

Captain W. G. Agnew   "   97

Admiral Sir Bruce Fraser   "   112

Rear-Admiral Leonard W. Murray   "   177

Captain R. St. V. Sherbrooke   "   192

Vice-Admiral Sir Neville Syfret holds a conference with Brigadier Festing, Major-General Sturges and Captain Howson on board his flagship after the surrender of Madagascar   "   209

Rear-Admiral Troubridge with Vice-Admiral Lord Louis Mountbatten   "   224

AUTHOR'S FOREWORD

THIS BOOK is in some sense a sequel to *Men of Action*; yet it is very different from that book. *Men of Action* contained sketches of nineteen naval officers and accounts of their activities against the enemy in this war. This book deals with only seven officers. The difference has been dictated by circumstance. As the war has progressed naval actions have become more and more integrated, more comprehensive and more obviously attuned to the overriding strategy. The isolated actions of a *guerre de course* have been yielding pride of place to gigantic and closely linked operations. One might draw the analogy of the Napoleonic Wars, in which the frigate actions gradually gave way to the movements of the great fleets which culminated in the Battle of Trafalgar. In such circumstances it is inevitable that the exploits of the individual, however important, gallant and picturesque, should become to a great extent merged in the record of the great commander.

The section dealing with Admiral Sir Bertram Ramsay was read and approved by him before his tragic death in an air accident. I have thought it best to leave it untouched.

My grateful thanks are due to the officers concerned, who have given unstintingly of their time; to Admiral Sir William James, who first sponsored the book; and to Captain C. A. H. Brooking and his staff at the Admiralty, particularly Mr. D. M. Larkins, who has never failed to produce a required record at the shortest notice.

KENNETH EDWARDS

SEEND HOUSE,
January, 1945.

SIR BERTRAM HOME RAMSAY

K.C.B., K.B.E., M.V.O.

Admiral in His Majesty's Fleet

IN THE whole history of warfare no officer has ever been called upon to assume a responsibility as great as that shouldered by Admiral Sir Bertram Ramsay as Commander-in-Chief of the Allied Expeditionary Force. The invasion of Hitler's "European Fortress" has been by far the most gigantic and hazardous undertaking of all time. Its ramifications are world-wide, its complications endless, and the stakes were nothing less than the length, if not the outcome, of the war, the lives of millions, and treasure beyond counting.

The first and principal responsibility in invasion rests with the naval commander-in-chief for, except in limited airborne operations, there can be no invasion without the fighting navy and the navy of transport and supply. As Admiral Ramsay put it in the opening paragraph of his orders for the invasion of Normandy:

"The object of the Naval Commander-in-Chief is the safe and timely arrival of the assault forces at their beaches, the cover of their landings, and subsequently the support and maintenance and the rapid build-up of our forces ashore."

A man capable of undertaking a task of such magnitude without misgiving, and of carrying it through in face of the elements as well as the enemy, must be possessed of qualities beyond the ordinary. These qualities and abilities have been to a great extent the outcome of experience, which has moulded intellect and built up ability and personality to the requirements of an outstanding commander of Allied Forces ranged before the most difficult of all operations of war.

Determination is probably the outstanding factor in Bertram Ramsay's character. Close alongside this determination runs an uncompromising inability to accept defeat, in the smaller things as well as in the big things. Taken in conjunction, these two traits reveal something of the man.

Physically, "Bertie" Ramsay is a little man, but his mental stature is great—and so is his personality. Had this not been so he could never successfully have been able to ply in double harness so much of the war effort of Great Britain and the United States to the common aim.

There is in his character a streak of granite hardness which does not allow him to take kindly to compromise. He will not take a hasty or unconsidered decision, but once he is convinced of the rightness of his attitude he is immovable. He is a man who simply *will* not be beaten. It is not that he is a bad loser; he does not know what it is to lose. There are those who deprecate his apparent intractibility and inability to admit defeat; yet in 1940 Ramsay's inability to admit defeat saved the lives of hundreds of thousands of men.

That was in the black days of the withdrawal of the British Expeditionary Force and Allied Armies from Dunkirk. Night after night the evacuation had gone on. Men were so weary they could hardly stand, and damaged ships were being kept going by faith alone. Finally there came a day when it seemed that the evacuation could no longer continue and that the troops remaining on the beaches and jetties of Dunkirk would have to be left to their fate.

Bertie Ramsay, who was in command of the whole operation, refused to stop. He called for volunteer crews to man such ships as could steam, and he carried on with the evacuation until, two nights later, the whole of the British Expeditionary Force, who had not become casualties, were back on British soil. Not a single wounded British soldier had been abandoned. Ramsay's refusal to admit that he was beaten had been amply justified.

Bertram Ramsay was born at Hampton Court, Middlesex, on January 20th, 1883. Sixteen years and eight months later he was gazetted as a midshipman, and in that rank he served in H.M.S. *Crescent* on the North America and West Indies Station for nearly three years.

In the *Crescent* Bertie Ramsay lived the normal life of a midshipman of the period on that station. He learnt an enormous amount about his profession, both technically and in the art of dealing with men and taking responsibility. There was plenty of fun to be had too; and the midshipman who was destined to become the supreme sea commander of the British, Canadian and American Forces in the greatest amphibian operation in history certainly did not neglect the opportunities for fun and games which the New World offered.

Ramsay's contemporaries of those days tell some amusing anecdotes about him at this time. One is of an occasion when Midshipman Ramsay's young heart was stirred by a member of the fair sex and he determined to serenade her in true romantic fashion. Unfortunately, however, he made some slight mistake and serenaded the lady's aunt—a gentle attention which that lady certainly did not appreciate.

In due course, however, the white patches of a midshipman and the delights of the North America and West Indies Station gave place to the single gold stripe of a sub-lieutenant and much hard study for the examinations for promotion to lieutenant. Ramsay tackled the work with characteristic energy and singleness of purpose, and was duly promoted to lieutenant's rank.

It was when Ramsay was a sub-lieutenant serving in H.M.S. *Hyacinth* on the East Indies Station that he had his first experience of amphibious operations and of landing on a hostile beach. It was during the Somaliland operations, and Sub-Lieutenant Ramsay had command of a company of men from the *Hyacinth* who had to be landed through the surf from boats—a feat requiring judgment and seamanship.

Bertie Ramsay has always prided himself that he is a seaman first and a specialist second. It was to this end that he did four and a half years of the drudgery of watchkeeping, first in the *Hyacinth* and then for the first commission of the famous *Dreadnought*. That long period of watchkeeping made him familiar with every detail of his profession and with the internal administration of a warship.

As a result, Ramsay was somewhat late in becoming a specialist. He had chosen signals as his subject, and it was not until 1909 that he went through his signal course.

This step may well be considered as his first introduction to staff work, although such staff work as existed in those far-off days could not be characterised as more than the most elementary groundwork of training for the gigantic staff tasks which were to fall to Ramsay's lot more than thirty years later.

In one way, however, his specialist qualifications as a signal officer taught him something that is all-important to-day. That is the importance of communications. Without efficient and quick communications any project in modern war is apt to break down, and one can imagine no greater disaster than the failure of the all-important communications during a great invasion, involving very large forces at sea, in the air, and on land, and drawn from more than one nation.

As a signal officer, Ramsay came into contact with many important personalities, and such association taught him to be at ease with his seniors and not to hang back when he felt that he had useful suggestions to make or views to express.

After qualifying as a signal officer Ramsay was appointed to the battleship *Albemarle* in the Atlantic Fleet, where he was Flag Lieutenant to Admiral Sir Colin Keppel. Under Sir Colin Keppel, Ramsay learnt a great deal about fleet work, both while on board and during the long walks ashore on which he frequently accompanied the Admiral.

Ramsay spent a year in the Atlantic Fleet with Sir Colin Keppel, first in the *Albemarle* and then in the *London*. Then he went to the Mediterranean, where he spent the next two years as Flag Lieutenant to Admiral Sir Douglas Gamble, who commanded the Third Cruiser Squadron and whose flag flew in the *Bacchante*.

That period of service in the Mediterranean was to have two important influences on the future. It was Ramsay's first experience of the Mediterranean. He was to have much more and to become very familiar with the sudden vicissitudes of Mediterranean weather. It was this experience and local knowledge which enabled him to be confident of a sudden change in the weather and of success during the critical hours before the invasion of Sicily, when less experienced officers might have turned back on account of the deteriorating and apparently hopeless weather.

The other matter which influenced the future was to do with paint. It may seem curious in the light of the tremendous events of recent years that such store should have been set upon paint by naval officers. Rightly or wrongly, however, the Royal Navy has held for many decades that a smart ship is a "happy ship" with a contented ship's company, and that smartness breeds initiative and the power to make quick decisions in war just as the "happy ship" leaves no room for anxiety about the morale of the men in action or the monotony which is so great a part of the war at sea.

In any case there are few contemporary naval officers who will quarrel with the statement that much of Ramsay's fame as a

Commander was due to the possession of a coveted secret about paint. It did not contribute everything, but it contributed a great deal to the smartness of the smartest ship in the smartest fleet in the Royal Navy—and this at a time when Ramsay was passing through the most testing time for a naval officer of that generation—his first job as executive officer, responsible for the smartness and general efficiency of a big ship. That, however, was still in the future.

Ramsay did not gain possession of that famous secret at that early stage of his career, but he met the man who had evolved it. While Ramsay was Flag Lieutenant to Sir Douglas Gamble in the *Bacchante* the smartest ship in the Mediterranean Fleet was H.M.S. *Duncan*. Her paint was always a source of great envy to her rivals, and the *Duncan* seemed to be able to paint her sides far more often and more effectively than any other ship. The commander and executive officer of the *Duncan*, and therefore the man responsible for her smartness, was Commander James Morton, who had been one of our earliest submarine officers. Ramsay and Morton were firm friends and, although Morton steadfastly refused to part with his secret at that time, he promised to impart it to Ramsay when the latter got his first command.

From the Mediterranean Ramsay went to the Staff College, and then he went to sea again in the *Orion*. Then he again became signal officer to Sir Douglas Gamble, first in the *Dreadnought* and then in the *Benbow*.

Ramsay spent the first six months of the war of 1914-18 with the Grand Fleet at Scapa Flow. Then he was appointed to the Admiralty, where he spent the next six months re-writing the signal books of the fleet—a vitally important task and one which had to be done against time as it became necessary in the middle of a war.

It was after this that Bertie Ramsay got his first command. This was H.M.S. *M25*—one of the smaller monitors which worked off the Belgian coast, bombarding the right flank of the German armies. These monitors were based on Dover, and it was while commanding *M25* that Ramsay became familiar with that port and with the shoals and channels and tidal streams off the Belgian coast, all of which knowledge was to stand him in such good stead when he commanded at Dover during the critical period of the war.

The Belgian coast monitors were continually wearing out their guns and being fitted with other guns of different calibre. Thus at one time or another they were armed with old army bottle-nosed 9.2's, 6-inch, and 7.5's. It was great experience, for these monitors saw more action than any other ships in the Royal Navy, and they also had to contend with considerable navigational difficulties in the strong tides among the shifting shoals off the Belgian coast.

But it was not all work. The commanding officer of one of the other *M* class monitors at that time was a great friend of Ramsay's. The two had been midshipmen together in the *Crescent*. Often they went ashore together. One night they dined, in company with some other officers, and after dinner Ramsay suggested that they should have a "hare and hounds" steeplechase back to the ships to work off their dinners and regain the physical fitness on which Ramsay is so keen. After that suggestion it was inevitable that Bertie should be selected as the "hare." He was given a short start, but the others ran him so hard that they eventually came up with him while he was returning his dinner to the soil of France.

Another of the monitors was commanded by James Morton, Ramsay's friend of his early Mediterranean days, and it was at this time that Ramsay held Morton to his promise and made him tell him the secret of his paint mixture.

When he gave up the command of *M25* Ramsay, who had been promoted to Commander on June 30th, 1916, took over command of the famous destroyer *Broke* in the Dover Patrol from Edward Evans, who, as Admiral Sir Edward Evans, was to be Ramsay's Commander-in-Chief at the Nore just before the outbreak of this war, and who has played so great a part in steering London through its ordeals of air attack.

Just after the war Ramsay joined H.M.S. *New Zealand*, which carried Lord Jellicoe on his world cruise and mission to the Dominions and Colonies. On his return he was appointed commander and executive officer of the battleship *Benbow* in the Mediterranean Fleet.

Bertie Ramsay considers that his advanced career began with his appointment to the *Benbow*. In that ship he instituted a number of reforms which have become accepted throughout the Royal Navy. Ramsay was the last man to accept the theory that something must be done a certain way simply because it always had been done that way. He tackled the internal administration and routine of the ship's company and made a great many changes. One of these was concerned with the time of slinging hammocks. For no better ipanies throughipanies throughipanies throughipanies throughipanies throughipanies throughipanies throughipanies throughipanies throughipanies throughonononononononononononononononon bribery or threat. Vats of beer must have been offered to the *Benbow's* sailors, but the secret never leaked out. Once, indeed, a certain flag officer thought that he had succeeded in getting the secret out of one of the *Benbow's* officers, who told him that it lay in rubbing down the ship's side with a certain brand of furniture polish before the paint was quite dry. The Admiral returned to his flagship and sent for her commander. "I want you to paint the ship's sides to-morrow, Commander."

The Commander hesitated, and then remonstrated that the ship's sides had been painted only a day or two before. But the Admiral waved away the objection, and then remarked darkly that all the painting parties would be required as soon as the painting was finished, and that the commander was to see that each man was provided with some cleaning cloth.

The commander went off shaking his head sadly. The Admiral went ashore and bought up all available supplies of the recommended furniture polish. Next day, as soon as the painting of the ship's sides was finished, the painting parties returned to their stages armed with furniture polish and cloths.

The result was wellnigh indescribable. What had been a smart ship emerged from her ordeal a ghastly mottled greyish brown. Next day, while the fleet chuckled, the ship's sides had to be scrubbed and repainted. The experiment cost that ship nearly her full allowance of paint for three months, and somebody had to dig deep into his pockets to eke out the remainder until the next allowance could be drawn from the dockyard.

Thereafter it was recognised to be dangerous as well as disheartening to try to probe the *Benbow's* secret.

Needless to say, Ramsay was not exactly popular with some of his rivals. He has never sought popularity, and he can be devastatingly tactless at times. On one very hot afternoon in the Aegean a Greek General decided to pay an official call on the Admiral whose flag the *Benbow* wore at that time. The band was ashore, but the guard and the buglers were duly paraded to receive him. When the Admiral arrived on deck he asked the officer of the watch what bugle call he proposed to use to welcome the General. The officer of the watch gave the correct answer, but the Admiral disagreed and told the officer of the watch to ask the commander. Ramsay, who was buckling on his sword, snapped: "You were quite right, but tell the Admiral I think the Rum Call would be better."

Fortunately the officer of the watch deemed that silent discretion would serve better than literal obedience to orders.

That incident illustrated a facet of Ramsay's character. He worships efficiency. He knows all the answers and is apt to be impatient with anybody who does not. Always, when he sets himself to do a thing he succeeds in doing it better than anybody else, and he has never been known to demand that others shall do what he himself could not do. Here is an example of this.

The battleships of those days had immense steel derricks with which to hoist in and out the heavy boats which were stowed on the booms between the funnels. The four guys of the derrick were worked by hand, each guy needing twenty or thirty men to man it. The purchase and topping lift were hydraulic or electric, but could also be worked by hand. The "main derrick" as it was called was an awkward thing to work, particularly as the clearance between the boats and the funnels, searchlight platforms, and other super-structures, was very small.

One day the *Benbow* exercised "Away all boats" with an inexperienced officer working the main derrick. He was slow. Let the officer concerned take up the story in his own words: "The Commander (Ramsay) told me what he thought of my performance in unflattering but quite just terms, and repeated the evolution, ordering a very senior and experienced Lieutenant-Commander to work the derrick. He did so and was quicker than I had been. This still did not satisfy the Commander, who said he would work the derrick himself and show us how to do it. The Lieutenant-Commander was a bit peeved, and said that I had better come with him and watch the Commander find out that it couldn't be done quicker. The result was that our times were halved, and the Lieutenant-Commander suggested that we crept quietly away. I have done many years of that work since, but I have never seen so masterly an exhibition."

The man chosen to plan and command the naval side of the greatest combined operation in history needs more than technical ability. He must have vision, drive, immense organising ability, and great capacity for attention to detail. These qualities Ramsay has in a very high degree. More than twenty years ago in the *Benbow* he was showing these qualities and developing them. He knew—and said—that the secret of success lay in careful and thorough preparation for everything, and in organising so that all concerned knew that no effort would be misapplied and that no one would "get away with" a lighter share of work.

The Chief Bos'n's Mate in the *Benbow* at that time was a great character—Chief Petty Officer King. Whenever there was a really big job to be done he used to say: "That will be all right when Bertie gets on to organising it."

Three years after leaving the *Benbow*, Bertie Ramsay was back in the Mediterranean—this time as a Captain and in command of the light cruiser *Danae*. It seems almost superfluous to say that the *Danae* speedily became the smartest ship of a very smart squadron.

Bertie Ramsay believes that an officer who wishes to fit himself for high command must have considerable staff experience and must at frequent intervals undergo the various courses which keep him abreast of the latest developments, not only in weapons, but also in strategic and tactical thought. But he also holds that between such courses an officer should seek appointments at sea, and thus preserve a proper balance between theory and practice and between study and experience. One cannot help being struck by the way in which Ramsay's career since he became a captain has followed this formula.

Immediately on his promotion to the rank of Captain he went through technical and war courses lasting six months. Then he went to sea and commanded light cruisers for rather more than three years. Then, in 1927, he joined the instructional staff of the Royal Naval War College and served in that appointment for two years. His next appointment combined staff work with sea experience for, from 1929 to 1931 he was Flag Captain commanding the heavy cruiser *Kent*, an appointment which meant that he was also Chief of the Staff to Vice-Admiral Waistell, the Commander-in-Chief of the China Station.

On his return from China, Ramsay joined the instructional staff of the Imperial Defence College. He served there for two years, and was for the first time concerned on a high level with inter-Service staff work. It is worthy of remark that Ramsay's "opposite numbers" in the other Services at the Imperial Defence College were Alan Brooke, the present Chief of the Imperial General Staff, and Sholto Douglas, who is now Commander-in-Chief of Coastal Command of the Royal Air Force.

After two years at the Imperial Defence College Ramsay went back to sea in command of the battleship *Royal Sovereign*. Then, after being promoted to the rank of Rear-Admiral, he was appointed

Chief of the Staff to Admiral Sir Roger Backhouse, the then Commander-in-Chief of the Home Fleet.

In peace time there was no better appointment for an officer just promoted to flag rank than that of Chief of the Staff of one of the two main fleets. It carried with it much experience in the adminis- tration of a great fleet and in the most up-to-date methods of dealing with the manifold problems—strategic, tactical and administrative —which would face the fleet in the event of war. For this reason the appointment of an officer as Chief of the Staff of the Home or Mediterranean Fleets was regarded in the Navy as apprenticeship for more important appointments, and "marked" an officer for high command.

Ramsay's career seemed to be "set fair," but on January 11th, 1936, after having been Chief of the Staff for only a few months, he was relieved of his appointment at his own request and went on half pay.

The circumstances which led to this were in no sense scandalous. Rather should they be regarded with pride in a Service which breeds high officers who are prepared to jettison a career to which they have devoted their lives rather than abandon a principle which they feel to be in the best interests of the Service.

There is no denying that there was disagreement between Ramsay and Sir Roger Backhouse. The former was Chief of the Staff and believed that good staff work was essential, whereas Sir Roger Backhouse disliked staff work and the delegation of authority. The position became more and more difficult, and eventually Ramsay came to the conclusion that it was impossible for him to continue to serve as Chief of the Staff to Sir Roger Backhouse.

After a period on half pay Ramsay was offered an appointment as Rear-Admiral commanding the gunboats on the Yangtse River. This he refused. He felt that he could still do valuable work for the Navy, and that the Yangtse command would place him out of touch. Moreover, it was regarded as a last command and a stepping- stone to retirement into obscurity. Ramsay therefore remained at home on half pay, but, in order to keep himself up to date, he went through the Senior Officers' Technical Course in 1937 and again in 1938. Soon afterwards he was placed on the Retired List. It seemed that this most promising career had come to a premature end, and it certainly would have done had it not been for the war clouds fast gathering over Europe.

Ramsay, however, was certainly not the type of officer whose services could be dispensed with in face of a threat of immediate war. Just before the Munich crisis he was recalled to active duty—although still as an officer on the retired list—and appointed to the staff of Admiral Sir Edward Evans, the then Commander-in-Chief at the Nore. In this capacity Ramsay was sent to inspect the port of Dover and report on it with an eye to its probable use in war.

In peace time Dover was not a separate command, but was one of the responsibilities of the Commander-in-Chief at the Nore.

There were few naval officers available in 1938 who had had greater experience of the port of Dover and its approaches. From 1915 to the end of the last war Ramsay had served in that area in small ships and therefore knew it intimately under war conditions.

Bertram Ramsay was shocked at what he found at Dover when he went there again in 1938. Like everything else, Dover had been most disgracefully neglected in the years of blindness between wars. The harbour facilities were sufficient and efficient for the cross-Channel service and such small coastal traffic and fishing boats as used the port. Beyond the narrow commercial aspect, the port which geography has made the gateway of England hardly existed. As a potential war harbour it had lost most of its usefulness. The harbour was so silted up that no more than three destroyers at the most could find accommodation in all its wide space. Such defences as existed were puerile in the extreme, and provisions for rapid communications seemed to have been framed with the idea of imposing the maximum of delay upon signals of the greatest urgency.

Dover provided Bertram Ramsay with a task worthy of his impatient driving energy and immense organising ability. He threw himself into it whole-heartedly. He saw clearly that war was inevitable, for he sensed that the Munich "agreement" provided nothing but a respite of indeterminate duration, and he knew that Dover must be of paramount importance in the event of war. He realised that he had to work against time as well as the reluctance of the bureaucracy to give anybody *carte blanche* in carrying out preparations for war, however necessary the preparations and however inevitable war might seem.

Ramsay had Dover harbour re-surveyed. As a result he instituted dredging operations and certain alterations to jetties and break-waters. At the same time he examined such defences as there were and rendered an outspoken report. A lesser man might have been staggered by the requirements and tempted to curtail what he considered the minimum requirements. Not so Ramsay; his report was devastating and his requirements well judged.

Ramsay's report on the state of Dover and the requirements for its rehabilitation earned him the official thanks of the Lords Commissioners of the Admiralty. He felt it slightly ironical, therefore, to receive from the Admiralty two days later the intimation that there would be no further appointment for him—an intimation which meant his retirement after his long period on half pay.

As a result of Ramsay's report on Dover, £750,000 was spent on dredging the harbour and improving the defences between the Munich crisis and the outbreak of war. It was an outlay which has shown an incalculable dividend.

When Ramsay went to Dover that port had no means whatever of wireless communication. Years before, when the needs of economy were supreme and when the prospect of war in the North Sea and the English Channel seemed remote indeed, some staff appreciation had stated that it was considered that the established naval port of Chatham could handle such wireless traffic as Dover might require. This meant that any wireless signal to or from Dover would have to be routed through Chatham, being passed between the two ports by ordinary Post Office land telephone, telegraph, or teleprinter. Ramsay found that this sadly out-of-date view of the communications requirements of Dover still persisted—on paper—despite the radical change in the whole international situation and the obvious imminence of war in the Narrow Seas.

What happened is a refreshing instance of what men of vision and determination can accomplish in the teeth of paper recommendations.

Bertram Ramsay went to see Andrew Cunningham, who was then serving as Assistant Chief of the Naval Staff at the Admiralty. Cunningham agreed that it was imperative that Dover should have a wireless telegraphy installation. The two "got together" and the upshot was that a set was secured privately and installed at Dover while the pundits were busy thinking out more paper opposition.

Apart from his work in planning and carrying out the rehabilitation of the port of Dover, Ramsay at this time worked out the details of the mine barrages which would be required in the Straits in the event of war, and outlined the requirements for laying them.

This was a big planning task, and there is no doubt that the laying of the barrage would have been unduly delayed after the outbreak of war had it not been previously studied and planned in detail.

It is difficult to imagine the situation which would have faced us in the Narrow Seas on the outbreak of war if matters had remained as they had been at the time of the Munich crisis. In the opening stages of the war our shipping losses through U-boat attack would certainly have been far heavier and it is probable that we should have lost troops and material on their way to France. Later, we should have had to abandon a considerable proportion of our Expeditionary Force to the enemy instead of saving it—to Hitler's great disappointment. Later still, we should have had to abandon thought of maintaining our coastal traffic through the Straits of Dover; thereby imposing an additional strain upon an already overloaded inland transport system. At the same time the enemy's transport difficulties would have been greatly eased by free passage of the Straits. Moreover, England would have stood even more wide open to invasion than she did, and eventual offensive against an enemy-occupied Continent would have had to be even longer postponed. Bertram Ramsay was one of the very few men who saw ahead, thought ahead, and acted ahead during the months when England was painfully and far too slowly, dragging herself out of the clinging slime of a false Utopia.

At the outbreak of war in September, 1939, Ramsay became "Flag Officer in Charge, Dover." This was his title under the "dormant appointment" issued to him "to come into force in the event of hostilities or on receipt of orders from the Admiralty." Dover was then still a subsidiary command under the Nore. Before long, however, it was realised that it was essential for Dover to be an independent command, responsible direct to the Admiralty, and Ramsay's official title was changed accordingly to "Flag Officer Commanding Dover," or more commonly, "Vice-Admiral, Dover."

Even before this happened Ramsay had carried out a major operation of war, and had forced it through against time with his characteristic energy. This was the laying of the Straits of Dover mine barrage, composed of mines laid at different depths and closely patrolled; the object being to close the Straits to the passage of U-boats. In carrying out this task he was greatly assisted by his own forethought, for it had been he who had planned the whole operation before the war. Nevertheless, it was a big task, for the

Crown Copyright Reserved

Admiral Sir Bertram Home Ramsay

whole organisation of the mine-laying and of the establishment of the patrols, fell within Ramsay's province.

It is improbable that we shall be able to assess the full value of the Dover mine barrage until such German records as may survive are examined after the war. Certain incontrovertible facts stand out, however.

In the first three months of the war three U-boats were known to have been destroyed in the Dover barrage, and it is probable that others were damaged, if not destroyed, and that many commanding officers and crews sought to avoid the passage of the Straits. So far as is known not one single U-boat was successful in getting through.

The effect was far-reaching. Within six hours of the outbreak of war the *Athenia* was torpedoed and sunk by a U-boat in the Atlantic. It was obvious that Germany was prosecuting from the outset her sea strategy of unrestricted submarine warfare on vital British maritime trade. The moment the Dover barrage became really effective—as it did in an astonishingly short space of time— it sealed, or made too dangerous to contemplate—the southern gateway of the North Sea to the passage of U-boats. These were therefore forced to take the much longer route round the north of Scotland. The time that a U-boat can remain at sea is limited—and was far more limited in 1939 than it is to-day—so that the longer time a U-boat was forced to spend on passage to and from its operational area the shorter the time available for it to prey upon the traffic of the trade routes, and the less damage it would be likely to do in any particular voyage. Moreover, the effectiveness of the Dover barrage made the U-boats take other fairly well defined routes, and the sinking of a U-boat by H.M. Submarine *Salmon* on the edge of the German minefield off the Skaggerak in the autumn of 1939 may therefore be considered an indirect success to the Dover barrage.

Another great success which can justifiably be attributed to the Dover barrage and the patrols operating from the Dover command was the great feat of transporting the British Expeditionary Force to France without the loss of even one man. This was an achievement too often taken for granted, but history will certainly give full credit for the fact that Great Britain carried out this great operation twice in the course of just over a quarter of a century, each time with truly amazing success. Dover was not concerned with the actual outward passage of the Expeditionary Force—the main body sailed from Portsmouth and Southampton—but its safe passage was made under the shelter of the Dover barrage and the Dover patrols. Dover was subsequently the port through which many reinforcements and supplies passed to France, and through which thousands of men on leave passed to and fro. There were also all manner of important people, including the King and the Prime Minister, who were "looked after" from Dover during their crossings of the English Channel.

From the very beginning, therefore, the Dover Command was no sinecure. In many theatres of war there was an ominous lull. At Dover there was incessant activity and tremendous responsibility, but this was nothing to what was to come a few months later.

Germany attacked Belgium and Holland on May 10th. The British Expeditionary Force swung northwards to support the Belgian army. Within five days the Germans had broken through the French line. The German armoured forces were fanning out behind the allied armies.

As soon as the Germans attacked the Low Countries Ramsay, as Vice-Admiral at Dover, became responsible for the whole of the Belgian coast and the Dutch coast as far north as Imuiden in addition to the French coast on the opposite side of the Straits.

From May 10th to the end of the withdrawal of the British Expeditionary Force from Dunkirk on June 8th, all officers and men of the Dover Command worked unremittingly in an atmosphere of uncertainty, tension and danger. Hour by hour more demands were made upon them. Ramsay's resources were strained to the maximum, and his task was made the more difficult by the frequent receipt of orders from authorities who could not be conversant with the rapidly changing situation owing to the inevitable delay on overloaded lines of communication.

Ramsay rightly concentrated upon the situation as he saw it on the spot from hour to hour, and refused to be influenced by opinions and instructions which, he realised, were based upon information which had been out of date by the time it had been received.

There was a tremendous amount to do. Mine-clearance parties had to be organised at the shortest notice. So had demolition parties, which were to do as much damage as possible to the facilities of ports which would fall into German hands. There were also great naval commitments due to sudden decisions to reinforce troops in some areas and to withdraw them from others.

In the first place there was the question of Imuiden, where the Irish Guards and Royal Marines had to be landed. No sooner had this commitment been discharged than it became clear that naval demolition parties would have to be sent to destroy that port and that the troops would have to be re-embarked. So quickly did the situation change that the need for this step could not be appreciated in London, where questions of prestige and foreign policy naturally loomed larger.

No sooner had the survivors of the Irish Guards, Royal Marines and the naval demolition parties been extricated from Imuiden, and the Dutch Royal Family been taken through the minefields off the Hook, than Ramsay found himself faced with a major problem at Walcheren, the island which dominates the entrance to the Scheldt and to the port of Antwerp. So important was Walcheren that Ramsay went there himself to see what chances there were of holding the island. It was then held by four divisions of French troops, but it was immediately obvious to Ramsay that these were of indifferent quality and unlikely to stand against the scale of onslaught of which the Germans were at that time capable. He therefore informed the Admiralty that, irrespective of any political consideration, he could not foresee any possibility of a stabilisation of the situation at any point on the Dutch coast.

By this time Ramsay's command had already lost two destroyers sunk and two damaged, and it was obvious to him that his commitments would enormously increase during the next few days. Apart altogether from the loss or damage of ships there was the factor of weariness of officers and men who were operating day and night, more often than not under air attack. Ramsay could not give them respite in view of the rapidly increasing responsibilities which his command was called upon to bear; nor were any "relief crews" available.

There was no respite. A brigade had to be taken to Calais. Then a brigade had to be extricated from Boulogne. The latter step Ramsay, with his knowledge of the situation at that place, took entirely on his own initiative while the authorities in London, unaware of the fact that the Germans were already in the town of Boulogne, were considering reinforcing our troops there. Things were as bad at sea as they were on land. The extrication of the troops from Boulogne proved very expensive and that night Ramsay was faced with the fact that of his eight destroyers only one remained fit for action. The casualties and the anxiety were increased by shortage of anti-aircraft ammunition for the ships, which had to endure incessant air attacks while operating near the far shore. For some extraordinary reason the supply of this ammunition was then a military commitment, and sufficient reserves were not available close at hand to meet the sudden very heavy demands of the destroyers.

Boulogne was at this time the scene of a very gallant and quite extraordinary exploit by Ramsay's only remaining operational destroyer. This was the *Vimiera*, commanded by Lieutenant-Commander R. B. N. Hicks, R.N. After the main body of the British troops had been extricated from that port with heavy loss it was realised that a considerable number of men had been left behind. The commanding officer of the *Vimiera* volunteered to go back after dark and try to save some of these. Ramsay was reluctant to risk the loss of yet another ship, but he was still more reluctant to leave British soldiers to be killed or taken prisoner by the Germans, so he assented.

That night at dead low water the *Vimiera* crept into the harbour of Boulogne and secured alongside the wall. At that state of the tide the wall towered above her and shielded her on one side; yet there was great danger, since it was known that the entire port and its surroundings were in German hands. Providentially, however, the enemy troops were almost as exhausted as our own, and no German saw or opened fire on the British destroyer. In these queer circumstances there was paramount need for silence. For that reason the officers and men of the *Vimiera* could do nothing to stop the rush of refugees of other nationalities, so that of the 1500 men which came on board the *Vimiera* only 100 belonged to the British troops for which she had risked so much.

The *Vimiera* soon slipped out of Boulogne as silently as she had crept in, and still she was unobserved by the enemy. It was as well, for she was in no case to dodge enemy salvoes. So crowded was she that the use of only five degrees of helm gave her a list of ten degrees. There is no doubt that the ship would have capsized if full helm had had to be used.

At Dover Ramsay waited anxiously for news of this desperate venture. He walked up and down in his operations room until, at 2.30 a.m., a signal was received that the *Vimiera* was safely out of Boulogne and returning to England.

Then there was the problem of Calais, where the heroic stand of the British garrison was writing new and glorious pages in the history of the British Army. For three successive nights Ramsay's ships stood by to try to extricate the survivors. There were appeals, orders, and counter-orders before it was eventually decided that the Calais garrison would have to be left to its fate in order to cover the withdrawal of the main body of the British Army. These uncertainties were inevitable, but they added enormously to the strain imposed upon Ramsay, his staff, and his ships.

For fourteen days and nights this tempo was kept up by everybody in the Dover Command; and it was at the end of that fortnight, when officers and men were already exhausted and the number of serviceable ships had been sadly reduced, that Ramsay's command had to grapple with the far greater commitment of the withdrawal of the main body of the Expeditionary Force from Dunkirk and its neighbouring beaches. That would have been a gigantic undertaking even with fresh personnel and new and undamaged ships. Under the circumstances it was a very miracle of endurance.

As early as May 19th it was appreciated that the position of the British Expeditionary Force was becoming dangerous in the extreme, for all efforts to close the gap near Arras had failed. On that day—it was a Sunday—Ramsay attended a meeting in London called urgently to consider the question of whether it would be possible to maintain the British Expeditionary Force through the ports of Dunkirk, Calais and Boulogne, and thus hold a bridgehead on the mainland of Europe. This meeting also gave some slight preliminary attention to the problems which might arise if it proved impossible to maintain the army through these ports, in which event evacuation of the army would prove necessary. These problems were, however, then regarded as somewhat remote possibilities, as it was not thought that the necessity for evacuation would arise.

The situation in France and Belgium continued to deteriorate rapidly, and two days later another meeting was held. This was "to consider the emergency evacuation of very large forces, the necessity for air-protection, and the need of a large number of small boats to carry troops to the ships lying off-shore."

Even so, there was inexplicable reluctance on the part of our Allies to face the facts. As late as May 24th a meeting was held in Admiral Ramsay's office at Dover to decide upon the allocation of responsibilities during evacuation. There were present the French Vice-Chief of the Naval Staff, the "Admiral Nord," in whose area the evacuation coast lay, and the head of the French Naval Mission in London. After agreement had been reached and signed the French said that they would now put the agreement away in the archives as it would never be needed. They were horrified when Ramsay, with his usual directness, said positively that it was wanted at that very moment, and they averred that it would be catastrophic to contemplate evacuation. Ramsay, however, was determined that he would begin at once to withdraw base personnel and other supernumeraries so that every available facility would be at the disposal of the fighting troops when the moment came to withdraw them. The fact that Ramsay began the process in good time on his own initiative was responsible in the days to come for the saving of large numbers of fighting troops who would otherwise have had to be abandoned.

The task of organisation which followed upon the decision to be ready for evacuation was so vast that it is difficult to give any clear idea of its immensity. One can but quote facts and figures and outline some of the problems, and let these speak for themselves.

The story of that epic operation, known by its code name of "Operation Dynamo"—the lifting of the British Expeditionary Force and thousands of Allied troops from Dunkirk and its neighbouring beaches in face of the worst the enemy could do—has already been told. Here we are concerned only with an appreciation of its magnitude and of how it was handled by the Vice-Admiral, Dover, to whom hundreds of thousands of British soldiers owe their lives. The history of the British Empire is rife with examples of the devotion of British sailors to their brothers in the army. These reached their zenith at Dunkirk, not only among the "matelots" and the "grabbies," but all the way down from Admiral and staff to over-tired infantrymen.

When he is carrying out an operation Bertram Ramsay is as near tireless as any human being can be, but he had already been working day and night for a fortnight. It was fortunate that at this time Admiral Sir James Somerville visited Dover to inspect some wireless installations. He saw and appreciated the strain to which Ramsay was being subjected and telephoned to the Admiralty. As a result James Somerville remained at Dover throughout "Operation Dynamo" and worked "watch and watch" with Bertram Ramsay.

That was the initial move in a virtual duplication of the entire
staff at Dover, so that every officer had a "shadow" to deputise for
him while he snatched sleep or food. As a rule Somerville turned in
after an early dinner and relieved Ramsay at 2.30 a.m. The latter
then slept for a few hours, had an early breakfast, and again took
over. Thus there was never any cessation of work or delay in getting
a decision.

This method of working a staff proved as effective as it was new.
In it one detects Bertram Ramsay's staff experience and flair for
getting things done in a hurry.

Every available destroyer, and hosts of other craft were allocated
to Ramsay for "Operation Dynamo." It was as well, for the rate of
loss and damage to ships was high. Six British and seven French
destroyers were sunk, and so many others damaged that during the
ensuing weeks more than sixty British destroyers were under repair
in the dockyards. Minesweepers, sloops, motor torpedo boats,
naval motor launches, and even a river gunboat, were assembled.
All these naval units had to be collected, most of them from other
duties, berthed, completed with fuel, stores and ammunition, issued
with the necessary charts, and their officers "briefed."

At the same time the Ministry of Shipping "found" a large
number of suitable merchant ships and diverted them from their
current but important tasks. This meant that the organisation of
convoys, of ports, and the arrival and departure of supplies at certain
places had to be hastily altered. This affected railways and road
transport and other distributive organisations. It is not too much
to say that changes had to be made in a considerable part of the
economic structure of the country so that the emergency should
be met.

Apart from hospital ships, over ninety merchant ships assisted
in bringing off the British Expeditionary Force. As for small craft
—nobody knows exactly how many took part, but it is known that
the Port of London Authority sent thirty-four motor lifeboats and
nearly nine hundred other boats.

The responsibility for collecting the merchant shipping and
boats was that of the Ministry of Shipping, but the task of operating
them to the best advantage lay with Ramsay, the officer in supreme
command of the operation.

The organisation and operation of the merchant ships and boats
was in itself a stupendous task. If the ships and boats were to reach

their destinations and bring off the maximum number of troops with the minimum of delay and risk, they had to be provided with orders and navigational aids of which most of them were destitute. Many of the smaller vessels, in fact, had no navigational equipment whatever. The coast in the vicinity of Dunkirk, with its many shoals and strong tides, is no place for "hit or miss" methods by amateurs, particularly during a most dangerous operation in time of war, when a few wrecks might well have blocked the channels through the shoals vital to the continuance of the evacuation, and when navigational aids in the form of buoys and lights were non-existent and the hazards immeasurably increased by mines, E-boats, dive-bombing by enemy aircraft and bombardment from enemy batteries ashore. Risks had to be taken, but everything possible had to be done to reduce these risks to acceptable dimensions.

In the event, some 1000 charts were issued to merchant ships and small craft by Ramsay's staff at Dover, and more than half of these had routes laid off upon them for the benefit of vessels with insufficient navigational equipment to fend for themselves. This, in itself, was a gigantic task, but it was not one that could be dealt with and considered completed. The routes for the ships had to be continually altered on account of enemy mining and because the Germans brought up batteries of artillery which made the shorter and easier routes unusable.

Bertram Ramsay was very conscious of the fact that, apart from the employment of all possible air cover of which the Royal Air Force and Fleet Air Arm were capable, the chances of success in the most difficult task that had ever fallen to the lot of a naval commander depended chiefly on three things.

In the first place it was essential that the organisation at Dunkirk and on the beaches should be such as to ensure that there should be no avoidable delays in loading. To ensure that this requirement was fulfilled, Captain W. G. Tennant, R.N., was appointed as Senior Naval Officer ashore at Dunkirk. At the same time, a number of naval beach parties were organised at Dover and sent over to the Dunkirk area to superintend the embarkation of troops and assist in handling the boats and small craft off the beaches. Captain Tennant, in order to make himself readily distinguishable to army and navy, wore on his steel helmet the letters S.N.O. cut out of silver paper from a cigarette packet and stuck on with sardine oil. T. J. Hallet and G. O. Stephenson, both Admirals serving as Commodores, went over to help on the beaches. Off-shore Captain F. W. Bush took charge and saw that all the vessels, as they arrived, went to the places where they were most needed. As the scope of the operation grew Bush was relieved by Rear-Admiral W. F. Wake-Walker.

The second essential requirement to any great degree of success in saving the British Expeditionary Force was that there should be the minimum of congestion at the British ports of disembarkation. It was obvious that any congestion would lead to a slowing down of the whole operation, and Ramsay appreciated that speed of execution meant the reprieve of men otherwise sentenced to death. The ports were small and their facilities limited. The problem was to devise means of using those facilities to such advantage that they would, in effect, handle traffic far greater than that for which they had been built. Nor did this essential to the success of "Operation Dynamo" cease at the ports. At the ports there were both naval and civil authorities. They had to work together, and the urgency of Ramsay and "Dynamo" welded them into life-saving teams. Prevention of congestion at the British ports of disembarkation involved all manner of other problems. It would have been useless to organise the rapid disembarkation of troops from ships if those ships could not set out upon another rescue voyage for lack of fuel. The ships collected were heterogeneous in the extreme, and their requirements were diverse. Some ships wanted hard steam coal. Others wanted soft coal broken down to a certain size and "screened." There were ships wanting heavy crude fuel oil. There were ships wanting light diesel oil. There were ships wanting ammunition for Oerlikon guns and others wanting ammunition for 4.7's and even 6-inch. The requirements could be catalogued over many pages, but enough has been said to show that the supply organisation was one of great magnitude.

Supply was a tremendous problem, and it inevitably affected other problems at the ports of disembarkation. If a ship came in laden with troops and had to wait for fuel or ammunition before sailing on her next trip she might well hold up the berthing of other ships laden with weary and possibly wounded men.

In order to meet the requirements of the ships, Ramsay mobilised no less than 125 maintenance vessels of all sorts. The work that they did can best be demonstrated by the fact that, during the operation, one hundred and seventy-one British ships were given urgent repairs.

No records exist of the number of ships fuelled, stored or ammunitioned.

As to the shore-going side of the operation: suffice to say that the railway authorities co-operated so efficiently that there was never congestion sufficient to embarrass the naval authorities. No less than 670 special trains were used to disperse the men on their disembarkation at Dover and adjacent ports.

The third—and possibly the greatest requirement of success for "Operation Dynamo" was that the utmost possible use should be made of every ship, be it destroyer, merchant ship, barge or rowing boat. Ramsay, with his wide knowledge, appreciated that herein lay the manifestation of one of the greatest and most essential principles of war—economy of force. Clausewitz put his theories on paper and the world studied them, but Ramsay had to put them on the shifting tides between the sand banks—and the world was thankful.

The organisation of evacuation would have been greatly simplified if it had been possible to work to a prepared time-table, but circumstances ruled out such a possibility. A time-table might have been possible if all the ships and vessels involved had been capable of the same performance; if the tides stood still and navigational hazards immolated themselves; if the enemy had allowed the ships to do exactly as they liked when they liked; and if "Operation Dynamo" could have been nicely rehearsed. None of these conditions obtained.

Ramsay and his staff, however, were very far from leaving things to chance or to the caprice of the enemy. Everything possible was done and every conceivable contingency allowed for. Officers spent every hour of the day and night plotting the routes for the various ships, but the plans remained fluid and the routes subject to instant alteration, so that the enemy could never steal a march by producing a hazard for the countering of which no provision had been made.

For instance, during the early stages of the evacuation ships went to Dunkirk by way of the south-western channel through the sandbanks, but there was no delay when the enemy made this voyage impossible by dominating the channel by shore batteries. The armada of salvation shifted its course almost automatically to the north-western channel, and when this became unusable owing to the enemy's gunfire, the ships changed their courses and navigated the central Zuydecoote Pass. The length of the round trip from Dover to Dunkirk had been doubled, but the traffic went on.

It is as well to remember that Ramsay and his staff had only five days in which to produce the gigantic and many-sided organisation necessary for the withdrawal of the British Expeditionary Force. The meeting at the Admiralty "to consider the emergency evacuation . . ." had been held on Tuesday, May 21st. "Operation Dynamo" began at 6.57 p.m. on Sunday, May 26th. In these five days Ramsay and his staff had built a great organisation out of practically nothing—an organisation designed to carry out an operation for which there was no precedent.

The saving of the British Expeditionary Force from Dunkirk —and of a large number of Allied troops—has been described as a miracle. It seemed like a miracle at the time, and it seems like one when viewed in retrospect. One cannot, however, dismiss it as such. The saying that God helps those who help themselves has in it much truth, and Dunkirk was certainly a triumph of tenacity and of faith which transcended human fallibility and physical limitations. Men went far beyond the breaking point—and still went on. Such things do not happen without the deployment of terrific driving force, and in such a case men must always look to a leader. Ramsay was not alone—Somerville and the whole staff were keyed to the same pitch—but it was Ramsay's drive which animated them all. One of his staff officers at that most testing time has said that Ramsay never seemed tired; never seemed to be carrying a terrific weight of responsibility; never flinched from an instant decision involving thousands of lives; never found it difficult to devote time and trouble to the smallest detail.

Day after day, almost hour by hour, it seemed that the evacuation would have to be abandoned, yet "Dynamo" went on invincibly and the numbers of men saved continued to rise far above anything that even the most optimistic had dared to hope.

A signal from the Admiralty brought "Operation Dynamo" to an end at 2.23 a.m. on June 3rd. In seven days, twenty hours and thirty-four minutes, more than 335,000 men had been saved. And this had been done where it had been hoped to save only a small number—forty or fifty thousand at most.

"Operation Dynamo" was at once a negation and a justification of Bertram Ramsay's tenets of faith. It was quite impossible for that operation to have that careful planning and preparation by which Ramsay set so much store. At the same time, "Dynamo" could never have achieved a tenth of its success had it not been for the keenly analytical staff-trained mind, the practical experience, the driving force, and the inherent inability to accept defeat.

When it was all over the duplicate staff at Dover was dispersed. Men gave themselves up for a short time to the unbelievable luxury of rest and relaxation. Not so Bertram Ramsay. From May 10th to June 4th he had been under a ceaseless strain of responsibility, such as few men have ever been called upon to bear, yet on the first afternoon that he could leave his headquarters he did not relax. He went to Sandwich to play golf and, astonishing as it may seem, he played better than he has ever played before or since. He went round Sandwich that day in 78, and he had never been round any course in less than 82.

There was no respite from responsibility for Bertram Ramsay. Dover had become a port right in the front line, separated from the Germans by only twenty-two miles of sea and subjected to frequent heavy air attacks at a few seconds' notice.

The ever-present question was whether the Germans would immediately follow up their advantage and attempt the invasion of England while her defences were chiefly makeshift; the British Army was largely disorganised and almost wholly without equipment; and the Luftwaffe had scarcely disputed superiority over the Royal Air Force. There were plenty of indications that Germany was preparing for invasion of the British Isles as the next step towards world domination. Britain stood alone, facing a foe vastly superior in numbers and equipment, who had seized every strategic advantage provided by the coast of Europe from Northern Norway to the Spanish frontier. It was not so much a question of whether the Germans would invade as when they would invade. Mr. Winston Churchill said: "We shall fight on the beaches, we shall fight on the landing grounds, we shall fight in the fields and in the streets, we shall fight in the hills." At Dover Ramsay was acutely conscious of the fact that his command stood between the inviolability of British soil and the realisation of the grim words of the Prime Minister. Theorists might point to the Humber, to Ireland, or to Scotland as likely places for the Germans to choose for invasion. Ramsay had no illusions. There might be feints, but his staff training and analytical brain told him that the first requirement of the Germans for invasion on a grand scale would be the seizure of a port as close as possible to the mainland of Europe.

Dover, therefore, had to be considered as the gateway to England, and preparations for its defence were rushed forward without an instant's delay. The defences were not, of course, the sole responsibility of the Vice-Admiral. There was a garrison commander at Dover in charge of the military. It was essential that there should be the closest co-ordination between the military and naval commands, and this was at once achieved. There was no denying the fact, however, that Dover's chief value to the enemy would be as a port, and the port and harbour were the responsibility of the Vice-Admiral.

In these more secure days one is apt to forget the terrible dangers of the summer of 1940 and the urgency of preparations to meet those dangers. At Dover they demanded every atom of Ramsay's tireless driving energy, while his clear thinking proved an ever-present blessing to those who worked with him. An officer who served on his staff at Dover through this anxious period has said of Ramsay: "He drives by personal leadership and example, never sparing himself, but at the same time taking less out of himself than most, because of his level temper, which I have never seen ruffled. He has wonderful judgment and refuses to be swayed by higher influences. I remember so well how he was at times badgered from higher quarters to do this, that or the other, but feeling that he—the Man on the Spot—was right, how admirably he resisted all pressure to do something silly suggested by higher authority."

Dover is a little town which, with its harbour, is dominated by high cliffs on either side. The easterly one has at its top the famous Dover Castle, and is honeycombed by galleries, begun by prisoners of war during England's last threat of invasion during the Napoleonic Wars, and considerably enlarged in this war. It is in this hollowed-out cliff that the Vice-Admiral, Dover, and his staff have their offices. Outside the Admiral's personal office is a gallery cut in the rock, for all the world like the Admiral's stern walk in one of the older battleships. On this balcony were mounted powerful binoculars trained on the French coast and pairs of Lewis guns always loaded—sign of the instant readiness essential at Dover.

The plan for the holding of Dover in the event of enemy attacks and landings in force was threefold. Firstly, there were the defences of the neighbouring beaches, where steel scaffolding interlaced with barbed wire and mines and dominated by batteries and machine-gun posts stretched for many miles. Secondly there was the defence of Dover itself. All arrangements were made to hold the two heights dominating the town and harbour to the very last, even should they be completely cut off from help from inland. To this end ammunition supply and all manner of stores and provisions were collected and stowed underground. It was resolved that, even if the tide of German invasion should sweep far inland, those two heights should be held and continue to deny to the enemy the use of the port. Thirdly, every imaginable precaution was taken to ensure that Dover Harbour would prove unusable to the enemy even if it were taken, and to guard against any possible surprise attack.

To these ends Ramsay—and with him all under his command—laboured unremittingly. One of the vulnerable spots was the dock from which the cross-Channel train ferry used to run in times of peace. The dock itself was not demolished, but the approach to it was blocked by enormous tank traps and very heavy barbed wire entanglements. In order that the railway approach could be blocked at a moment's notice a railway truck was filled with concrete and wheeled almost into position. Then explosive charges were fitted to its wheels. Thus in order completely to block the railway approach to the train ferry dock, the dock station, and the railway jetty, all that had to be done was to push the truck a few yards and fire the charges which would blow off the wheels.

Demolition charges were also fitted to cranes and other harbour installations; additional obstructions were planned and made ready at the harbour entrance; and strong points were built to command the entrance and all the jetties where ships or landing craft might try to come alongside.

All this work had to be pushed forward against time and despite continual interference from the enemy. The Germans were continually dive-bombing the harbour, shooting down barrage balloons and *strafing* working parties. That they did so with comparative impunity, apart from the anti-aircraft fire from batteries all round the harbour was no fault of the Royal Air Force. A German fighter could *strafe* a working party in the Dover area within about eight minutes of taking off from an airfield in occupied territory. Dive-bombers, given time to gain height, would be able to attack in less than twice that time. The conditions did not give the Royal Air

Force fighters much chance of interception, particularly in those days when radiolocation was of far shorter range and less accurate.

In Dover there is a place of worship at the entrance of which there is a plaque which announced that the building was badly damaged by a bomb in 1917. That plaque remains—but the building has again been badly damaged by a German bomb. There is something about that plaque which is indicative of the spirit of Dover —Britain's Front Line Town, as it has so often been called.

Ramsay naturally came into close contact with the military authorities during those anxious days, and it was at this period that he first found himself working in conjunction with Bernard Montgomery—now "Monty" to the whole world—who was then the General Officer Commanding-in-Chief, South-Eastern Command. They got on exceedingly well together. They were queerly assorted. In their single-mindedness, their forcefulness and their "drive" they were very much alike. In another way, however, it would have been difficult to find two more dissimilar men. The Irish General believed in courting the limelight as a greater inspiration to his troops. The Lowland Scot Admiral would have done almost anything to avoid the slightest suggestion of personal publicity.

One of the results of the attention that the Luftwaffe gave to Dover was to make the harbour untenable for destroyers without risking unacceptable losses. Thus Ramsay found that the sea-going part of his command dwindled rapidly to a flotilla of "light coastal forces"—that, in those days, meant early-type motor torpedo boats.

Dover was, in fact, the cradle of the "light coastal forces" in this war, and Ramsay nursed them with great tenderness and at the same time brought them up hard. The whole of his irresistible desire to get at the enemy was at that time centred on those boats, and on the better boats—both of the torpedo boat and motor gunboat classes—which began to come into service. They went minelaying, patrolling, and on sweeps designed to intercept and attack enemy convoys creeping up the French coast, but they never went out on any operation or patrol the plan and operation orders of which had not been personally studied by the Vice-Admiral. Nor, while they were at sea, did the Vice-Admiral ever leave the operations room, and relays of boats were before long at sea for many successive nights whenever the weather promised good hunting and reasonable conditions.

There was a day—or rather a night—at Dover which showed how Ramsay felt for his motor torpedo boats and what store he set upon their ability to get at the enemy. Bertie Ramsay is a typical Lowland Scot, reserved to a degree and finds it almost impossible to show his feelings. On the night in question the motor torpedo boats from Dover were out on an operation which promised them an important target for the first time. In the operations room the duty officers were tense and silent, thinking of what was happening towards the other side of the narrow "no man's water." Suddenly a signal was received which announced tersely that the enemy had been attacked and sunk. The astonished staff in the operations room were regaled by piercing fox-hunting calls from the usually emotionless Admiral!

At that time, too, Bertie Ramsay had upon his shoulders the responsibility for the most dangerous part of the voyage of our own coastal convoys. These ran backwards and forwards between the Thames estuary and the more westerly Channel ports, and in the Straits of Dover they ran the gauntlet of air attack, bombardment from shore batteries, mines and E-boat attack. The convoys were composed almost entirely of little coasters, but they were as valuable as vessels several times their size. Had the coastal trade been forced to cease its voyages, the war potential of Great Britain would have slumped. The greatest danger to the coastal trade lay within the precincts of the Dover Command, and the greatest responsibility for ensuring that it should not suffer crippling losses rested upon the Vice-Admiral, Dover. The trade went on, and the credit for that feat must be shared between the indomitable men who manned the little coasters and the men who wrought so well for their greater safety.

Little by little the Dover Command began to take on a new character. The danger of imminent invasion was receding, and England was beginning, not only to breathe again, but to cherish hopes of taking the offensive. Dover was, of course, in the forefront of this change. Naturally, it still had to be incessantly on the lookout for attack by air or sea or by shelling, and for attack upon the coastal convoys in the Straits, but it came gradually to take a more offensive part in the war. This grew from small beginnings. At first there were just those few small motor torpedo boats. Then there came motor gun-boats and more powerful and efficient motor torpedo boats. Dover began to operate a striking force worthy of the name. By this time, too, Dover had been equipped with the finest radar sets available, and with gun batteries capable of worrying the Germans. Among these must be listed the two 15-inch guns mounted on the personal direction of Mr. Winston Churchill, and affectionately christened "Winnie" and "Pooh." They were manned by Royal Marines, made a most satisfying noise, and must have made the Germans wonder what was going to happen next. There were also most efficient batteries of 9.2-inch, 8-inch and 6-inch guns. The fire of these batteries were controlled from a room next to the naval operations room, and having a communicating door so that there could be the closest co-operation between the shore battery fire and any naval units at sea. So close was this co-operation, in fact, that the plot of light coastal forces or other units at sea was laid upon the great semi-circular table in the gunnery control room. This table was divided into hundreds of squares and upon it the fall of every shell fired could be plotted.

In the operations room at Dover there was always on duty an officer of the Royal Air Force acting as Air Liaison Officer. He was in instantaneous telephonic touch with the headquarters of No. 11 Fighter Group and with air stations in the vicinity from which striking forces and reconnaissance units were working. Thus the closest possible touch was maintained with such units of the Royal Air Force as would be operating in the Dover Command area.

Out of the close co-operation of the Navy and the Royal Air Force in the Dover area there was evolved a method of getting over the difficulties imposed by the German "port-hopping" technique when passing convoys through the eastern part of the English Channel and the Straits of Dover. This technique consisted of making a quick dash from one port to the next and sheltering there until the radar reports showed that the British light coastal forces had returned to harbour. This technique, of course, added greatly to the time taken by the convoy to make the passage, but the Germans presumably argued that it was better to lose time than ships and cargoes.

In those days the Germans had marked air superiority on their side of the English Channel and the Straits of Dover. The cost of sending Blenheims and similar aircraft across the Channel on reconnaissance had become prohibitive and unproductive. The special stripped Spitfires of the Royal Air Force Photographic Reconnaissance Unit were coming into service, but they were all needed to cover more distant and more important objectives. So there came into being in the Dover area the "Jim Crow."

The "Jim Crow" was merely an ordinary fast and well-armed fighter aircraft manned by a pilot who had been given some special training in reconnaissance work and particularly in recognising the type and approximate size of ships. These "Jim Crows" could make sneak spying raids over the French coast harbours and "get away with it." Their reconnaissances were visual and not photographic, so that their reports were instantaneous. They could see and report a ship or ships in a particular port and often judge whether they were about to sail. Thus they enabled the light coastal forces to set out to the attack earlier and with far greater chance of success, for the time-lag between the German convoy putting to sea, being detected and reported, and the motor torpedo boats setting out was eliminated.

In the Dover area there was also another form of co-operation between the Royal Navy and the Royal Air Force which paid dividends the value of which cannot be assessed in ordinary terms. This was—and is—the Air Sea Rescue Service. This service operates all round our coasts, far out into the Atlantic and the Bay of Biscay, and in the Mediterranean, but it was in the Dover area that it came into being, and it was in that area that it did its most concentrated and effective work.

At first the Air Sea Rescue Service was formed entirely of high-speed launches, manned partly by sailors and partly by personnel of the Royal Air Force, but was under the operational control of the naval commander—that is, under Ramsay's control in the Dover area.

If a pilot baled out over the sea, or an aircraft crashed into the sea, the air station concerned would at once telephone the Air Liaison Officer in Vice-Admiral, Dover's operations room. Within a few seconds high-speed launches were dashing out to the position indicated. It was the same system, in reverse, as the Navy asking the Air Force for fighter cover, a reconnaissance, or an air striking force. Later, Walrus amphibian aircraft of the Fleet Air Arm were employed on more distant rescues, and saved valuable lives which must otherwise have been lost. During Ramsay's command at Dover, that is up to April, 1942, a total of 179 airmen were saved from the sea in the Dover Command. Of these 39 were Germans.

Towards the end of Bertram Ramsay's term in command at

Dover there occurred an incident which stirred Service and public opinion throughout the world and led to an official legal inquiry by a court set up by His Majesty's Government. This was the success of the German battle-cruisers *Scharnhorst* and *Gneisenau* and the cruiser *Prinz Eugen* in running the gauntlet of the English Channel and the Straits of Dover from Brest to Germany.

The inquiry instituted by the Government was presided over by Mr. Justice Bucknil, and the Admiralty and Air Ministry were represented by Vice-Admiral Sir Hugh Binney and Air Chief Marshal Sir E. Ludlow Hewitt respectively. As Mr. Winston Churchill stated in the House of Commons:

"The only questions which are open are:
"*First*, why was their (the German ships') movement not detected shortly after daylight?
"*Secondly*, was the contact and the liaison between the Coastal Command and the Admiralty, and also between the R.A.F. Commands and the Admiralty as close as it should have been?"

The inquiry was held in secret and its findings have been kept secret, as Mr. Churchill said they would have to be. That was essential, since the first point on the agenda would, amongst other things, raise questions of the range and reliability of types of radar equipment, while the second point would entail detailed examination of inter-Service and inter-headquarters communication systems. Such information would, of course, be of immense value to the enemy. There are other facts, however, which cannot help the enemy, and which at least help to clarify events which have come to be regarded as a mystery within which there is an element of stigma to both Services.

The *Scharnhorst* and *Gneisenau*, both modern battle-cruisers of 26,000 tons, and with a fast turn of speed, had lain in Brest since March, 1941, when they were hounded into port after a brief career of attempting to raid our Atlantic convoys. They had been joined in May, 1941, by the heavy cruiser *Prinz Eugen*, which had sailed from Bergen in company with the great battleship *Bismarck*, but had saved herself by abandoning her consort shortly before the *Bismarck*'s destruction by the English fleet in the Atlantic. Only once between their arrival at Brest and their spectacular dash up-Channel in February, 1942, had any of those three ships left Brest harbour. This was the *Scharnhorst*, which paid a brief visit to La Pallice, presumably in order to carry out some repairs or trials at a greater distance from British air bases.

During the ten months that the *Scharnhorst* and *Gneisenau* had been in Brest that port had been attacked by R.A.F. bombers on every favourable occasion. This was done at the instigation of the Admiralty, which was not unnaturally nervous of the presence of so fast and powerful a German squadron in a strategetic position on the flank of our convoy route to Gibraltar, South America, South Africa, and the East, and within striking distance of our great North Atlantic convoys.

Mr. Churchill stated in the House of Commons that 3299 bombing sorties had been made against Brest in this time, and that 4000 tons of tombs had been dropped on the port at a cost of 247 Air Force personnel and 43 aircraft.

It was known that serious damage had been done to the ships in some of these raids—one of the battle-cruisers, for instance, had to have a new main propeller shaft sent from Germany. At the same time it was appreciated that repair work was being rushed forward so that, over a period, it kept pace with the damage sustained. Moreover, early in 1942, there was reason to believe that the speed of repair to these ships was outstripping the rate of damage.

These facts were well known to the Admiralty, and as a result the opinion was formed that the German ships might be expected to move from Brest early in February, in spite of the somewhat exaggerated reports circulated of the damage caused to them by our bombing raids. Nor did the Admiralty discount the possibility of the ships trying to break through the English Channel and Straits of Dover and so reach the major German dockyard ports. This was underlined by the Prime Minister when he stated in the House of Commons on February 18th, that:

> "The Admiralty did not consider that an attempt to run through the Channel would be an impossible operation under the conditions that prevailed, and this was certainly much less to be apprehended than that they should break out into the trade routes or into the Mediterranean."

A few days before the German ships actually left Brest the Admiralty had ordered a submarine reconnaissance. The importance of accurate knowledge at this stage is stressed by this action in sending a submarine to carry out a mission of such extreme danger. The submarine concerned was the *Sealion*, commanded by Lieutenant Ian Colvin. This ship penetrated the Rade de Brest in the hope of being able to attack with torpedoes one or more of the ships while exercising or undergoing trials preparatory to sailing. The penetration of the Rade was a feat of great gallantry, but unfortunately none of the German ships had left the inner harbour on that day. The *Sealion* was to have penetrated the Rade again on the day that the German ships left Brest, but her orders were immediately cancelled when the *Scharnhorst*, *Gneisenau* and *Prinz Eugen* were sighted in the western approaches to the Straits of Dover.

Vice-Admiral Ramsay had given a great deal of thought to the problem of the three German ships. He had come to the conclusion that the German ships from Best would probably try a dash up-Channel. Two of the factors that led him to this conclusion were that the Germans would, particularly after the *Bismarck* fiasco, desire to keep their ships as close as possible under the protection of the Luftwaffe, and that the Germans would have the initiative in being able to choose their time and date of their voyage in accordance with the state of the moon, tide and with meterological information which they would be receiving from Eire and also from weather-reporting trawlers sent out into the Atlantic for the purpose.

Having regard to the probable speed of the German ships, Ramsay considered that they would be likely to leave Brest soon after nightfall in order to slip through the submarine cordon off Brest in the dark hours and make as much easting as possible up the Channel under cover of night. He therefore considered that the Germans could be expected in the neighbourhood of Cape Barfleur at dawn.

Ramsay spent the night of February 11th in the operations room at Dover, expecting all the time to receive a signal to the effect that the *Scharnhorst*, *Gneisenau* and the *Prinz Eugen* had been detected in the western part of the English Channel. But hour after hour passed and no signal came. February 12th dawned grey and cheerless and still there was no signal. Ramsay was at last forced to the conclusion that he must have been wrong in his expectations. In his own words, his reaction was, "Well, if it's not to-night it must be to-morrow night."

Ramsay did not show it, but he felt uneasy. He was not satisfied that his calculations and instinct had proved wrong. Then things began to happen which proved even more puzzling. There had been considerable activity by enemy small craft during the night and there had been indications of fishing boats or other small craft. Moreover, aircraft reported the presence of a number of small craft off the French coast. Staff officers were inclined to think that there could be no connection between these reports and the expected move of the three big German warships from Brest. If these had moved they should have been detected and reported well over three hours before—at dawn at the very latest.

Ramsay, however, was not reassured, and he was definitely worried despite the fact that the usual dawn air patrols had been flown and had reported nothing. Yet the visibility had been, and remained, tricky. There was a lot of low cloud and one could not be sure from one moment to the next whether one could see five miles or only three.

Then suddenly there came a report which galvanised the whole of the Dover Command into quick action. Group Captain Victor Beamish, who commanded one of the air stations in the Dover area from which the "Jim Crows" operated, had decided to carry out a reconnaissance on his own account. He took off in a fighter and before very long he sighted the big German ships steaming up-Channel.

Nobody, and least of all Ramsay, then had time to wonder why the enemy had not been detected and reported earlier. The time lag in their detection had given them more than three precious hours of grace, and the Germans were making high speed to put that grace to the best possible account. There is little doubt that the German Admiral Ciliax must have wondered why he had not already been attacked.

There was much to be done and practically no time left in which to do it. Immediately on receipt of the enemy report the motor torpedo boats roared away from Dover with their throttles wide open. Ramsay was bitterly conscious as he ordered those motor torpedo boats to sea that he was almost certainly signing the death warrant of their crews. Those small and intensely vulnerable craft had always been considered as a night striking force, and he had to send them against powerful German warships in broad daylight. Moreover, the time lag had been such that the motor torpedo boats would be prevented from attacking from a position ahead of the fast-steaming enemy, and that meant that they would be under fire from the enemy's guns for much longer before being able to fire their torpedoes. The sortie of the motor torpedo boats was, in fact, in the nature of a forlorn hope. They were old boats and in the weather conditions prevailing they could make good no more than 23 knots. The German ships were reported to be steaming at 29 knots. As it turned out, however, the motor torpedo boats attacked with the utmost gallantry and all of them survived. It was thought that at least one of their torpedoes had found its mark, although there was no sign of a reduction in the speed of the enemy.

Ramsay was thinking and acting with almost incredible rapidity. He had two other striking forces at his disposal, but time was desperately short for their deployment owing to the late reporting of the enemy. One was a squadron of Swordfish torpedo-carrying aircraft of the Fleet Air Arm, which was based in Kent. The other was a flotilla of old destroyers, which was based at Harwich. The Swordfish aircraft had been sent to the Dover Command at Ramsay's personal request to provide a striking force for this very purpose, for he realised that the torpedo-carrying Beauforts of the Royal Air Force, having more distant commitments, would be too far away to meet a sudden emergency in the Straits of Dover. The flotilla of destroyers had been put under Ramsay's operational control, although they normally belonged to the Nore Command. They were based on Harwich so as to be in a good position ahead of the German ships as they emerged from the Straits of Dover, which would greatly increase their chances of getting in their attack. This positioning of the destroyers was important because they were old and comparatively slow ships and would not have a margin of speed over the enemy. The destroyers were, in fact, Ramsay's main striking force.

It will be seen that the dash of the German ships up-Channel and through the Straits of Dover had been foreseen and that all possible steps had been taken to deal with the situation that would arise, including extensive mine-laying. There had been nothing wrong with the planning, but things went wrong because of the fatal delay in the detection of the enemy.

As soon as the motor torpedo boats were clear Ramsay ordered the Swordfish aircraft to attack. The squadron of old and slow Swordfish was commanded by Lieutenant-Commander Esmonde, who won the V.C. in this attack but lost his life, as did nearly the whole of his squadron.

The arrangements made by Ramsay had included the provision of an escort of sixty fighters of the R.A.F. for the Swordfish, and Ramsay thought that this escort had in fact been provided. In fact, however, Esmonde, who was imbued with the emergency caused by the late sighting of the enemy and anxious to attack without any delay, took his squadron of Swordfish into the air with an escort of only twelve fighters. Had he waited five minutes he would have had his full escort of sixty fighters, which should have been able to ensure that the Swordfish were able to press their attacks home. As it was the escort of only twelve fighters was quite unable to deal with the situation, since the German ships had forty fighters over them the whole time, and the Swordfish squadron was virtually wiped out.

Apart from the heavy bombers of the Royal Air Force, there now remained only the destroyers. These were under the command of Captain C. T. M. Pizey, R.N., in the flotilla leader *Campbell*.

Providentially Captain Pizey's destroyers were not in Harwich harbour when the German squadron was reported. They were at sea doing exercises. This fact saved nearly an hour of the three hours lost by the delay in detecting the German squadron on their way up-Channel, and was alone responsible for their ability to get in an attack.

Even so they had very little time to spare because of the shortness of the day. It was 12.30 when Captain Pizey received the signal that the enemy heavy ships were passing Boulogne, and he set off at once at 28 knots—the highest speed of which his ships were capable in the weather conditions prevailing. It was blowing hard from the westward and there was quite a considerable sea and swell. At the time the destroyers set out the visibility was about four miles. This lengthened to about six miles during their voyage across the North Sea, but had again shortened to four miles before contact was made with the enemy.

The destroyer flotilla consisted of only six ships, the *Campbell*, *Vivacious*, *Worcester*, *Mackay*, *Whitshed* and *Walpole*. Unfortunately the latter ship had engine trouble and had to turn back, so Pizey was left with only five very elderly destroyers to pit against the infinitely more powerful modern German ships. Nor could he hope to achieve surprise, for in the early afternoon a Junkers 88 on reconnaissance flew over the flotilla. Shortly after that the bombing began. Pizey's destroyers were bombed steadily for about three-quarters of an hour, but, providentially, no ship was hit.

At 3.30 in the afternoon the flash of a gun was seen to starboard. The destroyers turned towards it, and as they turned across the wind they began taking green seas over their bridges. It was no weather for fighting exposed hand-worked guns, but the enemy was at once engaged. In a few minutes it was realised that there were at least seven German destroyers of powerful modern type, and beyond them the shapes of the *Prinz Eugen*, *Scharnhorst* and *Gneisenau* were made out.

The British destroyers turned to attack the big ships, and they pressed home to within 3800 yards of the enemy battle-cruisers before firing their torpedoes. Why they were not all blown out of the water by the enemy's big guns is a mystery. As it was, only the *Worcester* was hit. She survived miraculously after being hit by an 11-inch shell, a 5.9 inch shell and a 5.1-inch shell, and was eventually brought safely back to harbour.

Having fired their torpedoes the destroyers turned away under cover of smoke screens and made their way home through a series of spectacular but fortunately ineffective bombing attacks. It was impossible for them to assess the results of their attack. Explosions were heard and at least one brilliant flash was seen before they were enveloped in their own thick black smoke. It was certain, however, that the enemy sailed on to German ports, and so the world read in the newspapers of next morning—it was Friday the 13th of the month—that the incredible had happened in that the German ships had successfully made the passage of the English Channel, the Straits of Dover, and the North Sea.

It was a bitter pill, and for nobody was it more bitter than for Bertram Ramsay. He had been right in his deductions and in his calculations and his planning had been wisely directed to making the best possible use of everybody and everything at his disposal, but things had gone wrong owing to the German squadron not having been detected earlier in the Channel.

It subsequently became clear that the *Gneisenau* had been so damaged during this passage, either by mines, torpedoes, or bombs, that she remained inoperative and dismantled at Gdynia, and that damage had also been sustained by the other German ships. In the long view, moreover, the Prime Minister was quite right when, having pointed out that the constant air attacks on Brest had been a "very grievous substraction from the bombing effort against Germany," he said:

"I should like to state that in the opinion of the Admiralty, with which I most cordially concur, this abandonment by the Germans of their position at Brest has been decidedly beneficial to our war situation.

"A threat to our convoy routes has been removed and the enemy has been driven to leave his advantageous position. The diversion of our bombing effect, which though necessary, was so wasteful, is over, and heavier scale attack on Germany is now possible in which the near misses will hit German and not French dwellings.

"Thirdly, both the *Scharnhorst* and the *Gneisenau* have received damage in their passage which will keep them out of action for some time to come, after which they will have to be worked up in gunnery and other practices.

"Before they can again play any part in the war the Royal Navy will be reinforced by various important units of the highest quality; and a similar strengthening process is going forward in the Navy of the United States.

"Whatever smart of disappointment or annoyance may remain in our breasts that the final forfeit was not exacted, there is no doubt that the naval position in the Atlantic so far from being worsened, is definitely eased."

Vice-Admiral Sir Bertram Ramsay—he had been made a Knight Commander of the Order of the Bath in June, 1940, for his brilliant conduct of the withdrawal from Dunkirk—did not stay at Dover long after the *Scharnhorst*, *Gneisenau* and *Prinz Eugen* episode.

There was absolutely no connection between the dash of the German squadron and Ramsay's departure from Dover. It was due solely to the fact that he was wanted for a more important task.

The United Nations were beginning to move towards the offensive. Up to that time there had been a number of combined operations and commando raids, and there had even been the "reconnaissance in force" at Dieppe. All these, however, had had only limited objectives. Now something much bigger and more permanent was being considered. Those concerned with recommendations for such an undertaking were under no illusions as to the magnitude of the task. Its ramifications would be legion, and it would demand the most skilful and careful planning.

There was no man better fitted for such a task than Bertram Ramsay, with his organising ability and driving force, his experience and staff training, and his genius for far-sighted but detailed planning.

One would have thought that, after the prolonged strain of the Dover Command, Bertie Ramsay might legitimately have expected some leave. He got none. A temporary successor was found to take over the Dover Command—for the Admiralty at that time expected that he would be able to return there on completion of his special task.

This special task was none other than the study of the problems involved in certain large-scale combined operations. Ramsay was the naval representative on a high-level planning staff which had to consider certain outline plans for effecting a breach in Hitler's "West Wall."

The task of setting up a staff capable of examining certain proposals and working out detail plans for operations involving the sea, land and air forces of two nations was by no means easy. Officers of ability in this work were hard to come by, as were also the material needs of a staff. When Ramsay arrived from Dover all he found was a dusty empty room with a telephone sitting forlornly in the middle of the floor. There were not even tables and chairs, much less charts, books of reference, and the rest of the paraphernalia essential to detailed planning.

In the late summer of 1942 Ramsay was in Scotland witnessing some combined operations training exercises when he received a hasty summons from the Admiralty. He flew south at once, and by ten o'clock that night he was in conference in the Admiralty with Admiral of the Fleet Sir Dudley Pound, the then First Sea Lord.

It had been decided by the War Cabinet that French North and West Africa were to be invaded by forces of the British Empire and the United States.

It was a brilliant conception. It would meet the American insistence upon taking the offensive. It would divert large German forces from the Russian front and tie them down at a distance from their bases, so that additional strain would be put upon their transport systems. It would put an end to the long ding-dong struggle in Libya. It would give new impetus to the resistance and sabotage movements in enemy-occupied territory. It might put Italy out of the war. It promised to open the Mediterranean and at the same time reduce the requirements in the Eastern Mediterranean—a combination of two factors which would release a large quantity of shipping for other duties—and since shipping was the limiting factor in the final invasion of Europe, it would be a definite step towards that end.

The operations against French West Africa were to be entirely an American commitment mounted direct from the United States. Most of the troops to be landed on the Mediterranean shores of French North Africa were to be American, but the naval forces in this area were to be almost entirely British and this part of the operation was to be mounted from the United Kingdom.

Ramsay was appointed naval Commander-in-Chief, Expeditionary Force—an appointment which carried the acting rank of full admiral and which was naturally kept secret at the time. He was given two months to plan and mount the operation. In this work he was ably assisted by Admiral Bieri of the United States Navy, who is now Deputy to Admiral Ernest King, Chief of Naval Operations and Commander-in-Chief, United States Fleet, who is the American equivalent to our First Sea Lord.

It was a gigantic task. It had to be done against time, and everything had to be begun from the very beginning. There were no precedents upon which to draw; no past experiences of an operation of this type, even on a small scale. Ramsay and his staff worked very long hours, with meetings and discussions going on far into every night, and after some weeks it still seemed that no real progress was being made. Every time they thought one aspect of the problem had been dealt with some new difficulty would crop up. It seemed very disheartening, but Ramsay's tireless driving energy never slackened.

In an invasion, the primary task of the Navy is to ensure that the Army and, in a long-distance operation, the Air Force, are delivered at their destinations safely and at the right time. The same applies to all their equipment and supplies. For an operation as large and as far away as the invasion of North Africa these primary requirements involved a very large quantity of shipping, and, of course, the deployment of powerful naval covering forces. It must be remembered that the Italian Fleet was then "in being" and, on paper at least, constituted a powerful threat. Risks could not be taken either with the Italian Fleet or with the Vichy French warships, for the reaction of their crews was an unknown quantity.

Every morning Ramsay held a meeting of his staff. At this meeting all the other Ministries and Departments involved were represented. These were many, for the requirements of such an operation were so large and varied that they impinged upon most of the activities of the nation.

The Ministry of War Transport was required to supply the shipping. This was not a simple matter of allocation, for ships cannot be kept idle while an operation is pending. They must continue with their ordinary tasks until the last possible moment, and their voyages so arranged that the suitable vessels will not all be at the other side of the world when they are needed for loading for the operation. The Ministry of War Transport had to work out the shipping which would be needed to carry what the Navy, Army and the Air Force required, and say what ships would be available. Such things as speeds, fuel requirements and sea-keeping endurance had to be taken into account in making these calculations. Everything had to be most carefully dovetailed, not only with other aspects of the operation, but with the general economic life and war effort of the nation.

The first necessity was the military plan, for the military requirements are always the largest. The Army Commander had to work out how many troops and what types of troops he required for the initial assault and for each phase of the operation. Then these requirements in men, guns, tanks, vehicles, stores, ammunition and rations had to be translated into terms of ships.

The next problem was planning the loading of the ships; and here there is always the basic difficulty that it is a physical impossibility to load any ship to meet all military requirements. All manner of compromises have to be reached, and these have to be based upon the fundamental law that the "first in"—whether man, vehicle or box of stores—is not the "first out" but the "last out." Thus the loading plan has to be a complete inversion of the military requirements.

As far as possible, too, certain things must be transported together.

That was one of the bitter lessons learnt during the Norwegian campaign, when the anti-aircraft guns for Namsos were loaded in one ship and their ammunition in another. The latter was sunk, with the result that the troops ashore at Namsos, suffering very heavy air attacks, received the guns but no ammunition to fire from them. That lesson had been well learnt, and it has been developed in the light of more modern needs. Not only had guns and ammunition to be shipped together, but there were all sorts of other things which it would have been folly to ship separately, even though the need to load them in the same ship involved several other problems. Thus, it was felt that a cargo ship laden with motor transport should also carry petrol for the initial requirements of the vehicles, and the drivers and crews of the vehicles. On the face of it, that seems simple common sense, but the simplicity disappears when one realises that ships suitable for carrying motor transport have no accommodation for passengers and no storage for highly volatile and inflammable motor spirit. These things had to be built into ships without interfering with other shipyard work, without taking ships off the trade routes for a day longer than absolutely necessary, and without interfering with their normal carrying capacity.

In the event, most of the petrol was carried cased because this made handling easier and quicker, particularly since it would be necessary to establish dumps ashore; but the average supply ship laden with motor transport had to be fitted to accommodate the crews of the vehicles—approximately 200 men.

At Ramsay's daily meetings there were often as many as thirty or forty officers and officials round the table. Ramsay asked each in turn if they had any points or problems to raise. He said after the operation had been completed that it was a tremendous relief if at these meetings even one person said "there is nothing to-day." Those meetings were invaluable. They resulted in all concerned knowing exactly what was going on. There was no confusion or overlapping as is bound to occur in an organisation which works in a series of watertight compartments. Ramsay saw to it that the minutes of these meetings were circulated without delay, so that the decisions taken could be acted upon at once.

Naturally, with big meetings and so many people involved on both sides of the Atlantic, security—that is, the preservation of secrecy—became a big problem. In the event, however, even Ramsay was surprised at how well the secret had been kept, observing that many thousands of troops, sailors, airmen, shipyard workers and all manner of others were involved. Code words were, of course, extensively used, but sometimes these themselves led to trouble. On one occasion the naval officer in charge at a small port in the United Kingdom reported that some strange packing cases had been delivered to him and he did not know what they were or what to do with them. It turned out that they were labelled with the code word for their destination abroad, but this code word was identical with the name of the small British port.

It is absolutely certain that the enemy had no inkling of our intention to invade French North and West Africa on anything approaching the scale employed. The preservation of that secrecy is the more remarkable when one reflects that the United Kingdom is a small area close to enemy aerodromes, so that it can be reconnoitred and photographed whenever the weather conditions permit —as they usually do in the late summer. Moreover, the enormous convoys involved had to voyage down to Gibraltar—a distance of more than 1000 miles through a U-boat infested sea and with enemy air bases on its flank—and then pass through the narrow Straits of Gibraltar, with the binoculars of Nazi agents on both sides.

It is considered that one of the chief reasons why the Germans did not appreciate the destination and size of our expedition was that they had become deluded by their own propaganda. Month after month the German staff as well as the German public had been fed with fictitious figures of Allied shipping losses concocted in Dr. Goebbels' Propaganda Ministry. These figures had only to be examined, as they doubtless were examined by the German staff, to prove conclusively that the Allies did not retain sufficient shipping to mount so gigantic an overseas undertaking at such a great distance from the point of departure. It is possible that German propaganda was one of the most important factors in preserving the secrecy of our intentions.

Almost every department of the Admiralty was concerned in the preparations for the North African landings, yet very few officers, by comparison, knew why it was that they were asked to supply this, that, or the other. As soon as the military requirements were sufficiently known for a convoy to be made up—on paper—consideration had to be given to how much naval stores of each type could be taken in the same convoy. At the same time the number of landing craft needed had to be worked out, in conjunction with the numbers available and the means of getting them to their destinations. The landing craft, of course, needed specially trained crews, while other specially trained officers and men were wanted to form beach parties, communication parties, repairing staffs, and so on.

Apart altogether from crews of the ships employed, the naval personnel involved amounted to over eight hundred officers and between seven and eight thousand men. Complete staffs had to be ready to take over the administration of occupied ports, and full repair, supply, and fuelling staffs had to be formed and made ready to take over without delay. One of the first necessities in invasion is the seizure of one or more ports, but it is not much good seizing a port if there is no organisation to make immediate use of it.

The supply problem was enormous. Many different types of ships and many different types of landing craft were involved. Many of these had differing fuel requirements, often as regards quality as well as quantity. Moreover, here was a problem that had to be dealt with well ahead, for most of the fuel had to be secured from the other side of the Atlantic.

Ramsay realised early in the planning stage that great importance would have to be placed upon the speed of handling the ships at their destinations. The faster the "turn round" the smaller would be the shipping requirements in the later stages of the operation, and the smaller would be the chance of losing ships and cargoes, and of having ports and channels blocked by wrecks. No ship is ever so vulnerable as when it is lying off a port waiting to enter and unload, and it was obvious that the Germans would concentrate numbers of U-boats in the Western Mediterranean and strong squadrons of the Luftwaffe at the Sardinian air bases in order to attack our shipping. Ramsay knew that the enemy appreciated that shipping was the Achilles heel of any invasion carried out by the United Nations.

Quick unloading and "turn round" of ships would, of course, depend upon the labour available. Ramsay did not know if local labour would be available at the ports of destination. The Foreign Office did not know. Nobody knew. The secret reconnaissance carried out by parties landed from submarines had elucidated much information of great value, but they had not been able to form any reliable estimate of what would be the temper of the local population, particularly among the dock labourer and stevedore classes, when the Luftwaffe reacted as it was bound to do.

All the time that the planning was going forward, training was being carried out and rehearsals were held. To rehearse an operation like the French North African landings means doubling the already enormous amount of work which has to be done, but rehearsals are an absolute necessity if one is to be quite certain that everything is "going to be all right on the night." They reveal small weaknesses in the planning and in the organisation in time for them to be corrected. It is far from easy to stage, in secret, rehearsals for so large an operation, particularly when it is desired that enemy air reconnaissance shall not notice that anything out of the ordinary is toward, but this was done.

The weather also took a hand. It frequently made necessary the postponement of exercises and rehearsals. Then the weather, combined with the fact that certain ships were not available early enough, led to a postponement of the operation itself. As the time for the sailing of the convoys again approached, the weather again began to deteriorate, yet after that initial postponement the operation went forward according to plan as if it had been run by a railway company in peace time jealous of the reputation of Bradshaw.

Ramsay had also to consider the purely naval commitments, and these were far from easy of fulfilment. The naval planning organisation had to think of two main phases. The first was the safe conduct of all the large convoys in secrecy and safety through dangerous waters and a narrow strait so that every man and every item of equipment should be at the required place at the very moment they were required by the Army and the Air Force commanders. The second phase was the protection of that shipping after the initial assault, when there could be no further question of surprise or secrecy, and when a very strong reaction from the enemy was to be expected. Such a reaction might involve the employment of the main body of the Italian Fleet and possibly units of the French Fleet, certainly it would mean counter attack by large forces of U-boats and aircraft.

One of the many problems involved in the first phase of the operation was the use of large numbers of small convoy escorts. It was naturally desirable that these escorts should have sea-keeping qualities and fuel endurance similar to the ships in convoy, but this was far from being the case. Many of the escorts were incapable of covering the whole distance at the necessary speed. An even larger number of escorts had therefore to be found and allocated to the operation, and a careful programme of reliefs between them worked

out so that all the convoys should have full protection throughout
the voyage. A complicated fuelling programme had also to be
worked out and the necessary fuel provided at the fuelling points.

There was also the need to provide a minesweeping force to
precede the assault convoys during the latter stages of their approach
to their destination. This involved the building up at Gibraltar of
a reserve of operational minesweepers and crews, for it would have
been quite impracticable for the minesweeping force to have accompanied the convoys from England.

The Straits of Gibraltar presented a great difficulty. There
geography imposed a hazard which to the seaman's eye, was at
least as formidable as any likely to be posed by the enemy. The
greatest armada in history had to be conducted in safety and secrecy
through a narrow strait, the shores of which were plentifully
sprinkled with sharp-eyed enemy agents, while fishing craft which
were strongly suspected of being in enemy service were frequently
upon its waters.

The convoys destined for North Africa, together with their
escorts and covering forces, formed an armada of some 8000 ships,
of a wide diversity in type and performance. Some were manned
exclusively by officers and men with many years of experience at
sea in the Merchant Navy—experience which made them value
sea-room and have a profound distrust of crowds of ships in narrow
waters. Others were manned by men, endowed with matchless
courage and keenness, but who nevertheless might be considered
"enthusiastic amateurs."

Imagine a very important road junction, completely unlit, when
unprecedented traffic has to pass in one direction without any traffic
control to stop vehicles wishing to pass either through that junction
in the opposite direction, or across that junction. Even on land one
would not be surprised if such conditions produced accidents. In the
Straits of Gibraltar there was every possibility of chaos and collisions. Ships without lights are less visible than vehicles without
lights, and their courses and positions are likely to be more variable.
Moreover, ships, although they may be able to check their way by
going astern, have no brakes, and if their way is off they are not
stationary but drifting at the mercy of tide, current and wind.

Men who have spent a lifetime at sea have averred that the
passage in the Straits of Gibraltar by all those great convoys without
one collision or one ship lost or damaged through taking the shore

was one of the greatest feats of seamanship of all time. It certainly was, but one must concede that the success of that passage was a reflection of the triumph of the planning of that expedition.

Adequate air cover was a pre-requisite of success, and it was obvious that in the approach and the initial stages of the landings such air cover could only be provided by the Fleet Air Arm, operating from aircraft carriers in the offing, for they would be out of range of shore-based fighters.

The responsibility laid upon the Fleet Air Arm was therefore immense. There is no time when an amphibious force is so vulnerable to air attack as when troops are being landed; when the situation ashore is often far from clear; when the landing craft are plying to and from between the ships and the shore; and when ships are lying off awaiting their opportunity to discharge troops, vehicles or stores. Nor was the protection of the initial landing the only responsibility of the Fleet Air Arm. They had to take the offensive against French airfields, to prevent aircraft operating from them against our ships and troops, and to help in their early capture so that the shore-based air force could "move in."

The personnel of the Fleet Air Arm performed prodigious feats of gallantry and endurance, and accomplished everything demanded of them within the time-table laid down in the plan. This had had to be very carefully worked out, and heavy calls made upon men and material because of the shortage of available aircraft carriers at that time.

In the North African operation there were two naval Force Commanders. One was Rear-Admiral Sir Harold Burrough, who was in command of the Eastern Task Force which had to carry out the landings in the Algiers-Bougie area. The other naval force commander was Rear-Admiral T. H. Troubridge, who commanded the Western Task Force charged with effecting landings in the Oran area. The movements of the forces under Burrough and Troubridge had to be co-ordinated, not only with the fleet which was to cover the landings, but with expeditions which were being assembled in the United States for the assaults on Casablanca and Dakar.

As the planning stage of the North African operations drew towards a close the naval commitments increased and it became clear to Admiral Ramsay that the naval forces involved would amount to a very large and powerful fleet. Ramsay was very conscious of the fact that he had never been at sea in command

of a fleet and that a great expedition and fleet under the supreme
sea command of an officer with no sea experience in flag rank
might cause comment. After giving the matter considerable
thought Bertram Ramsay consulted Admiral of the Fleet Sir Dudley
Pound, who was then First Sea Lord. As a result it was decided to
ask Admiral Sir Andrew Cunningham, who was then head of the
British Admiralty Delegation in Washington, to take supreme
command at sea, with Ramsay as his deputy.

This necessitated other changes in the appointments of flag
officers, among them the appointment of Admiral Sir Percy Noble
to take over in Washington from Sir Andrew Cunningham and
Admiral Sir Max Horton to relieve Sir Percy Noble as Commander-
in-Chief, Western Approaches. This left the submarine command
vacant, and this was assumed by Captain Claude Berry, with the
acting rank of Rear-Admiral.

Admiral Ramsay at once flew to Washington to discuss the
detailed plan with Admiral Cunningham. Time was short. Admiral
Cunningham's appointment as Commander-in-Chief of the Expeditionary Force was not made until November 1st, 1942—and the
landings in French North and West Africa took place on November
8th. The full responsibility therefore remained with Bertram
Ramsay throughout the planning and preparation of the expeditions, and only passed to Andrew Cunningham on the sailing of the
fleet and convoys. Naturally, the appointment of the new
Commander-in-Chief of the Expeditionary Force was kept secret
until after the landings had taken place.

When the Allied landings in French North and West Africa
became an accomplished fact the headquarters of Sir Andrew
Cunningham, as supreme naval commander, were established in the
first instance at Gibraltar. Most of Ramsay's time, however, was
spent in England, where he had to represent Cunningham's needs
and point of view on many questions to the Admiralty, looking
after the interests of the forces under Cunningham's command,
and co-ordinating his requirements with those in other theatres of
war.

Towards the end of the Tunisian campaign, and almost as soon
as the final overwhelming defeat of the Axis forces in North Africa
was assured, Sir Bertram Ramsay was selected by Sir Andrew
Cunningham to examine and expand the plans for the invasion of
Sicily. It had already been decided that Sir Andrew Cunningham

was to re-assume the title of Commander-in-Chief, Mediterranean, on completion of the Tunisian campaign, and that the Commander-in-Chief in the Eastern Mediterranean should then be styled Commander-in-Chief, Levant.

An outline plan for the invasion of Sicily had been prepared and sent to the Mediterranean. Ramsay had had nothing to do with its preparation and it had never been intended as a war plan, but only to serve as a basis for discussion of the problems involved. It was not surprising, therefore, that this plan was found on examination to be impracticable.

Some time was lost in the examination of this outline plan and in obtaining the decision that it was to be scrapped and that planning would have to be begun again. This in no way delayed the actual invasion of Sicily, but it did delay the start of the detailed planning and made it necessary for Ramsay and his planning staff to carry out their work at higher pressure and in reduced time in order that the detailed plan would be ready as soon as the man-power and material resources required for the operation could be collected. There was some further delay due to the time taken to extricate General Montgomery from his immediate responsibilities in the field. General Montgomery had been nominated as the British Military Force Commander for the invasion of Sicily, and Ramsay, who had always held that the planning of an operation without reference to the Force Commanders was worse than a waste of time, was reluctant to proceed with planning the military aspects of ship-loading, landing craft, beach requirements, bombardments and supporting fire from the ships without full discussion with the Force Commanders.

The planning was difficult, apart from the need for working against time, and Ramsay went to Cairo for a period of intensive work on it. It was the first projected invasion of territory known to be in enemy hands, and it was to be carried out by both British and American forces of all three arms. Provisions had to be most carefully made, therefore, for inter-Allied as well as for inter-Service co-operation.

The scale of the planning of the invasion of Sicily is best illustrated by the fact that, even in the initial stages of preparing the plan, provision was made for nearly 2000 vessels to take part in the first assault. In the event, some 2500 ships and landing craft took part in the assault, while the operations as a whole entailed no fewer than 3266 ships, vessels, and craft of all types. These ranged from battleships and aircraft carriers to landing craft and motor torpedo boats; from large merchant ships of the liner type used as transports to the little ships carrying stores and fuel. Nor were the British and United States the only flags concerned. Units of the Royal Canadian and Royal Indian Navies took part in the widespread naval operations covering the landings, as did also ships of the Dutch, Polish and Greek Navies.

The problem of collecting the enormous quantity of transport shipping and landing craft required was immense, and required time to solve, as ships had to be collected from most of the major convoy routes of the world. The loading of the ships, too, had to be carefully considered and worked out so that every unit landed would have everything it needed in the order in which its requirements would be felt. The loading task can be appreciated when one recalls that on July 29th President Roosevelt announced that the initial force landed in Sicily consisted of 160,000 men, 14,000 vehicles, 600 tanks and 1800 guns. To these figures must be added the needs of the men in equipment, rations and water, of the vehicles and tanks in fuel and oil, and of the weapons in ammunition. Moreover, it must be borne in mind that President Roosevelt's figures applied to the initial landing only, and took no account of the subsequent "build up."

The topography of the Sicilian coast provided other problems for the planners. In the Mediterranean there is no appreciable rise and fall of the tide. Thus the slope of that part of the beach upon which landing craft will ground, and the depth of water off-shore are constants. On the face of it, these facts would appear to facilitate an amphibious operation. The mere fact that they are constant, however, added to the complications in planning the Sicilian operation. There could be no question of ships going closer to the Sicilian shore for a few hours at high tide in order to facilitate and accelerate the process of unloading off the beaches.

The very gradual shelving of most of the Sicilian beaches presented other and more difficult problems. Landing craft have to be designed and built for a particular slope of beach. The idea of an Allied invasion of Sicily had come after such craft as were available had been designed and built for the northern European beaches, which are of far greater gradient than those of southern Sicily. The result was that these craft, which were quite capable of placing their bows against the dry part of the average beach in north-west Europe, could not approach within a hundred yards or more of a Sicilian beach. This entailed the provision of improvised methods of unloading, such as the construction of pontoon bridges or piers, and the special equipment for these bridges had to be prepared and collected, together with trained personnel capable of assembling it in the minimum time under fire.

In the invasion of Sicily, too, there was need for very strong naval covering forces. These had to be of sufficient strength to be able to deal with the main units of the Italian Fleet, should they emerge from Taranto or come south through the Straits of Messina. Moreover, these covering forces had to operate close to enemy air bases and outside the range of our short-range shore-based fighters, which necessitated the provision of an adequate aircraft carrier force. Experience off North Africa had shown the capabilities of the enemy in counter-attacking with U-boats, and account had to be taken of the fact that the operations would be carried out in waters known to be heavily mined and close to enemy E-boat bases. To these factors affecting the degree and composition of the naval forces required had to be added the fact that the south-eastern coast of Sicily contained fortified ports guarded by heavy gun batteries. It was clear, too, that the navy would be called upon by the army for a great deal of supporting gunfire, particularly along the east coast.

The assault on Sicily was a joint Anglo-American operation, and it was planned on the basis of two main groups, one British and one American, working in co-ordination but in different sectors of the Sicilian coast. The commanders of these two groups were:

BRITISH

Sea—Admiral Sir Bertram Ramsay.
Air—Air Vice-Marshal Harry Broadhurst.
Land—General Sir Bernard Montgomery.

AMERICAN

Sea—Vice-Admiral Henry K. Hewitt
(Commanding the U.S. Naval Forces in the Mediterranean).
Air—General Karl Spaatz.
Land—General George Patton.

For the initial landings the British forces were responsible for the assault on thirteen beaches, spread along about thirty-seven miles of coast from Cape Murro di Porco, just south of Syracuse on the east coast of Sicily, round Cape Passaro, the south-eastern point of Sicily, to a point on the south coast about seven miles west of Cape Correnti. Along the southern coast of Sicily from the British left flank, the United States forces were responsible for the assault on eleven beaches spread over a distance of about thirty-eight miles from Cape Scalambri to a point six miles west of Licota. Thus no less than twenty-four landings from the sea were entailed.

In order to control and cover the landings at so many different points, both the British and American commands were divided into three Assault Forces. From west to east these Assault Forces were commanded by the following officers:

AMERICAN

Rear-Admiral Richard L. Conolly.
Rear-Admiral John L. Hall, Jr.
Rear-Admiral Alan G. Kirk.

BRITISH

Rear-Admiral Thomas H. Troubridge.
Rear-Admiral Sir Philip L. Vian.
Rear-Admiral Roderick R. McGrigor.

It is worthy of note that the commander of the most easterly United States Assault Force, that is, the one adjacent to Bertram Ramsay's sector of responsibility was Rear-Admiral Alan Kirk. This was the first collaboration under invasion conditions between two men who were to work together even more closely when planning and carrying out the invasion of North-western Europe.

The invasion of Sicily involved special problems of approach. Geography made it necessary for the Assault Forces to be assembled in Algerian and Egyptian ports. The direct approach to Sicily was out of the question from both assembly areas, but more so from that in Algeria since, if an assault force was to arrive off the beaches at the right time it would have to run the gauntlet of the Sardinian Channel by daylight and, apart from the danger of attack, there was the certainty of it being observed and reported, so that all possibility of surprise would vanish.

These and other considerations made it necessary to evolve a method of indirect approach. To this end an assembly area for both the Eastern and Western Assault Forces was established well south of Malta. Thus it was that the Western Assault Forces, on sailing from their bases of assembly in French North Africa, passed through the Sardinian Channel by night and rounded Cape Bon, steaming southwards, down the narrow mine-swept channel known as the Tunisian War Channel and passing the ruins of Carthage, whence Sicily had been invaded more than 2000 years before. Thus it spent the daylight hours under the fighter umbrella which could be provided from the recently captured airfields in Tunisia, while prying enemy reconnaissance would have been justified in assuming that it was bound for Tripoli or Alexandria.

From the assembly area both groups of Assault Forces made a direct approach to Sicily past Malta and under fighter cover provided from that island.

During the actual invasion of Sicily Admiral Sir Bertram Ramsay was afloat in his headquarters ship H.M.S. *Antwerp*, but after the initial assault he made his headquarters ashore in Malta, although he was still afloat for most of the time, visiting the beaches daily in fast craft such as destroyers and motor torpedo boats.

Bertie Ramsay was afloat in his headquarters ship H.M.S. *Antwerp* during that memorable night of July 9th, which was to see the first landings successfully carried out before dawn. It was a night full of intense anxiety for all concerned. This was not solely the inevitable human reaction to the knowledge of embarking upon a hazardous operation and being on the threshold of history in the making. Deeper anxiety was caused by a sudden and unexpected deterioration in the weather.

On the afternoon of July 9th, when most of the warships, transports, supply ships, and landing craft making up the great armada of invasion were already north of Malta, a storm arose. By 2.30 that afternoon the Mediterranean waters were being kicked up into vicious seas by a 30-knot wind. The small ships were making heavy weather. The "light coastal forces" were travelling half submerged in spray. The lives of those in the landing craft became a hell of discomfort. Even destroyers were "taking it green," and big transports were responding to the surge of the sea.

Many people thought that the expedition would have to turn back, and were appalled at the prospect. All possibility of securing the advantages of surprise would be lost; the whole of the forces would have to be refuelled before the operation could again be "laid on"; men who had already been cooped up for long days in crowded troopships would have to remain in them even longer; and morale would inevitably slump, while the invasion could be far more hazardous when it did eventually take place. Against these factors had to be set the danger of damage to craft and casualties owing to weather and surf on the beaches if the expedition went on and the weather did not improve, to say nothing of the fact that seasick troops cannot be expected to fight well the moment they are put ashore.

Strangely enough, the man who was least anxious was the man chiefly responsible—Admiral Sir Bertram Ramsay. He was certainly worried on the score that the bad weather would inevitably upset some of the intricate time-tables of invasion "according to plan" and might necessitate a slight postponement of "H hour"—the actual time at which the first waves of the Assault Forces were to "touch down" on the beaches, but he had complete faith in an improvement in the weather. His long experience in the Mediterranean had taught him how quickly gales arise and subside in those waters, usually resulting in a complete change in the weather at about sunrise or sunset. He thought at first that the weather would change with nightfall, but when it blew even harder he became more than ever certain that it would change before dawn. So great was his faith in this that when his ship called at Calafrana in Malta in the afternoon—and many hours before the gale reached its height —Ramsay sent a message to Admiral Cunningham to the effect that he had no doubt at all in the weather moderating and had complete confidence in being able successfully to carry through the operation.

The weather changed suddenly about an hour before midnight. The phenomenon was well described by the American naval officer detailed by Rear-Admiral Kirk, U.S.N., to keep his men informed of the situation over the internal broadcasting system of the flagship. He said:

"Then suddenly a little while ago, the miracle occurred. No matter where you may be stationed, you must have felt it. The wind died down almost as abruptly as it had started. Look over the sides now in the faint light left by a storm-clouded quarter moon, which is nearing the horizon, and you will find the Mediterranean still choppy, still tossed by a heavy surf, but, compared to what it was only a short time back, as quiet as if God had put His hand on it. This ought to be the best of good omens."

So the early hours of July 10th saw the ships still steadily approaching the coasts of Sicily, their crews determined and steadfast, remembering the words of two Special Orders of the Day issued by the men under whom they served. One was from the Commander-in-Chief, Admiral Sir Andrew Cunningham, and read:

"We are about to embark on the most momentous enterprise of the war—striking for the first time at the enemy in his own land.

"Success means the opening of the 'Second Front' with all that implies, and the first move towards the rapid and decisive defeat of our enemies.

"Our object is clear and our primary duty is to place this vast expedition ashore in the minimum time and subsequently to maintain our military and air forces as they drive relentlessly forward into enemy territory.

"In the light of this duty great risks must be and are to be accepted. The safety of our own ships and all distracting considerations are to be relegated to second place or disregarded as the accomplishment of our primary duty may require.

"On every commanding officer, officer, and rating rests the individual and personal duty of ensuring that no flinching in determination or failure of effort on his own part will hamper this great enterprise.

"I rest confident in the resolution, skill and endurance of you all to whom this momentous enterprise is entrusted."

The other, from Admiral Sir Bertram Ramsay, was:

"To all ranks and ratings of the Eastern Naval Task Force.

"The capture of the island of Sicily has been decided upon in order to facilitate the passage of Allied shipping through the Mediterranean and as a further stage in the defeat of the Axis Powers. We are therefore about to take part in a combined operation, the success of which will have a far-reaching effect on the future course of the war. It is well known that com-

---

bined operations are among the most difficult and hazardous operations of war, requiring the closest co-operation of all arms and services and a high degree of individual gallantry, determination and resource.

"Awkward and unexpected situations will arise and we must expect and accept casualties, but there must be no slackening of effort.

"You must continually bear in mind the fact that the Army are helpless and entirely dependent upon us until we establish them on shore. We did not let them down when they were retreating at Dunkirk, in Greece, or Crete, and we will not let them down when they are advancing.

"We have the inestimable advantage on this occasion of being associated with the veteran troops of the Eighth Army, and with the Canadian Army; we have overwhelming strength in the air; we are on the crest of the wave while the enemy is in the trough, and we have the opportunity now to hasten his downfall.

"I count, therefore, on every man to do his utmost.

"Good luck to you all and God Speed."

Tens of thousands of eyes had as their first sight of Sicily the lurid glow of fires well inland, started by the Allied bombing attacks. Offshore, submarines which had approached submerged by daylight and carefully fixed their positions, acted as navigational marks for the approaches to the beaches. Overhead roared further waves of bombers, and of aircraft carrying parachute troops and towing gliders.

Long before dawn on July 10th boats left the transports and felt their way secretly into the beaches. They had a difficult job and a heavy load of responsibility. It was for them to mark the beaches for the arrival of the assault craft, but to avoid detection until the very moment of arrival of the first flight of the invading forces.

"H hour" had had to be postponed by one hour owing to time lost by many of the small craft in the gale, but when the time came for the assaults the great landings went entirely "according to plan." That is synonymous to saying that the plans were well and truly laid, with due consideration to the smallest details and the possibilities of the unexpected. No better testimony of the excellence of Ramsay's planning of this operation could be found than the fact that the last minute postponement by an hour of "H hour" had no

other effect upon the carrying out of the plan and did not interfere
in the slightest degree with the successful conduct of the operation.
This is a tribute, too, to the communications system worked out as
part of the plan. With "triphibious" forces belonging to two
nations and spread along seventy-five miles of enemy coastline,
rapid and efficient communication presents all manner of difficulties. A good plan will iron out these difficulties, and here
Ramsay's training as a signal officer had given him invaluable
experience. Had there been any fault in the planning of the whole
operation, or had there been delay or breakdown in communications
between the various task forces engaged, the last-minute necessity
for the postponement of "H hour" would have led to costly confusion. There was no confusion. The plan was excellent and so
was its execution.

Before daylight on that fateful July 10th the guns of the warships
thundered into action, their shells silencing the shore batteries
which replied to their fire, blacking out the inquisitive searchlights,
and in general making the enemy "keep his head down" during the
assault. Along the southern coast of Sicily were strung out the
transports and landing craft of the three American task forces, and
the assault here was supported by the guns of United States cruisers
and destroyers. At the south-eastern corner of Sicily, and round
it off the coast running north to the Straits of Messina, was the
British inshore support of cruisers and destroyers known as "Force
K," and the heavy metal of "Force H," ranging right up to the
16-inch gun battleships *Nelson* and *Rodney*, to deal with the heavily
defended Sicilian ports and guard against intrusion by the Italian
Fleet.

At the same time, to act as a diversion and to discourage any
Italian attempt to attack the left—American—flank of the invasion,
the Italian naval and air base of Cagliari, at the southern end of
Sardinia, was subjected to a heavy bombardment from the sea,
while Palermo, the base in Northern Sicily, was battered from the
air.

While the armies drove inland, the Navy's primary duty of
getting more troops and their supplies and vehicles ashore continued
without a break, although surf still hampered the work on some of
the beaches. At the same time, many bombardments were carried
out by naval vessels at the request of the military authorities.

The invasion of Sicily was an accomplished fact, although much hard fighting lay ahead before the Allies secured complete control of the great island. On July 11th General Eisenhower, the Supreme Commander of the Allied Forces in the Mediterranean theatre of operations, sent the following message to all ships of the Allied navies:

"In the Sicilian operation the United States and Royal Navies have again proved that, even while engaged in operations covering the seven seas, they can plan and successfully execute vast and intricate movements in support of land operations, and can do this despite obstacles of distance, weather and enemy opposition. In this theatre the skill of the Allied Naval commands and staffs, under the leadership of Admiral of the Fleet Cunningham, and his principal Lieutenants—the American Vice-Admiral Hewitt and the British Admiral Bertram Ramsay—are reflected in the precise timing and perfect technique displayed on the beaches of Sicily, where there were landed hundreds of ships and boats whose ports of origin were scattered over half the world. Their comrades of the Air and Ground Forces unite in an enthusiastic ' Well done.'"

It is worth noting that the salient points to which General Eisenhower alluded in this message—planning, precise timing, perfect technique, and the widespread points of departure of the ships and other craft employed, are, in the last analysis, implicit in the first—the good planning of the operation by Bertram Ramsay and his "opposite numbers" in the United States forces and their assistants.

There was a certain inexorable quality about the march of events after the successful invasion of Sicily. Sicily was completely conquered after some very hard fighting. The Italian mainland was successfully invaded at several points. Italy was knocked out of the war. Admiral of the Fleet Sir Andrew Cunningham reported that the surrendered Italian Fleet lay under the guns of Malta.

On October 25th, 1943, Admiral Sir Bertram Ramsay was appointed Allied Naval Commander-in-Chief for the next and greatest of all operations—the assault upon Hitler's "European Fortress" from the north.

No man, and least of all Ramsay, had any illusions about the magnitude and difficulty of the task. Had he not studied the question in detail when called from Dover to consider a large-scale operation across the English Channel ? He did not have to begin the planning of the invasion from the beginning, however. A tremendous amount of preparatory work had already been done, dating from as far back as eighteen months before.

The study of the administrative probems involved in invasion had begun as long ago as May, 1942, with the formation of what was then known as the "Round-Up Planning Staff." This did a lot of very useful work, although its activities were soon afterwards diverted to the needs of "Operation Torch," as the North African landings were officially styled. Most of the "Round-Up Planning Staff" were also required for this operation, but a skeleton had remained. This was placed under the Commander-in-Chief at Portsmouth, Admiral Sir Charles Little, as it was appreciated that the Portsmouth Command would have the greatest share of responsibility in any invasion of the Continent across the English Channel. This nucleus staff became known as the "X" staff. It worked at Norfolk House in St. James's Square, London, although it was part of the Portsmouth Command. At that time the head of this "X Staff" was Commodore J. Hughes-Hallett, but he was relieved by Rear-Admiral Creasy, who was later to be Admiral Ramsay's Chief of Staff.

The choice of the sector of the French coast to be invaded was made as early as January, 1943, by a panel of officers of the three Services. Ramsay was one of these officers, although he was then serving as Deputy Commander-in-Chief to Sir Andrew Cunningham. Throughout the preliminary period, in fact, Bertram Ramsay worked very close to the planning staff at Norfolk House.

The outline plan for the invasion of the Normandy coast was ready by July, 1943, and was submitted to the Combined Chiefs of Staffs of Great Britain and the United States and was approved by them at the Quebec Conference. Once approval had been secured to the outline, detailed planning was pushed ahead.

At that time the Commander-in-Chief at Portsmouth was still the Allied Naval Commander designate for the invasion. When Ramsay was appointed Allied Naval Commander, Expeditionary Force—with short title A.N.C.X.F.—he took over the "X staff," but very soon found that he had greatly to increase it in the light of his experience in planning the North African landings and the invasion of Sicily, and he had to form an American section, since the invasion was to be a joint British-American operation.

The preparatory work which, apart from the obvious administrative bodies, involved the Ministry of War Transport, the Ministry of Supply, the Movement Directorate of the War Office, the United States Transportation Corps, the United States War Shipping Administration and many other organisations, proved invaluable. Nevertheless it was, in sum, only a small part of the vast and detailed planning and organisation which was essential before the prospect of "D day" could be viewed with any equanimity. It cannot be too strongly emphasised that failure on that day, to which any one of hundreds of different factors might have contributed, would certainly have greatly lengthened the war, and might even have had a profound influence upon the outcome. These hundreds of factors had to be examined and weighed day by day by Ramsay and his co-planners, while they were engaged upon the greatest feat of organisation in history. It has been said that Jellicoe, as Commander-in-Chief of the Grand Fleet at the Battle of Jutland, was the only man who could have lost the last war in an afternoon. A similar responsibility—perhaps an even greater responsibility— rested upon Ramsay day and night for months.

During the planning stage Ramsay found himself continually confronted with all manner of difficulties. A lesser man would have been daunted or diverted from his main purpose by so much consideration of detail and would have been unable to see the wood for the trees.

Among the major problems was the difficulty of meeting the requirements in ships, and particularly in escort craft, until very late in the preparatory stage; choice of the time of day or night at which to deliver the initial assault; and the fact that the Americans were unaccustomed to detailed planning.

The first difficulty naturally held up the planning, for it would have been useless to lay down instructions for certain ships if those ships were unlikely to be made available. It was aggravated, moreover, by the fact that the naval requirements inevitably increased as the plan grew, and particularly when General Montgomery relieved General Paget as the Commander of the 21st Army Group and said that he wished to deliver the assault on a wider front. To do the Admiralty justice, they were trying to reach some sort of compromise between the naval requirements for invasion and those of other theatres of war. They felt that it would be disastrous to promise A.N.C.X.F. so many escort ships for invasion purposes that the ocean convoys would be insufficiently protected, and at the last moment find themselves faced with an increase in U-boat activity or the escape of surface raiders into the Atlantic. Moreover, in the initial stages of the planning it was agreed that the whole of the naval responsibility for the invasion should be British, and that no United States naval forces would be available.

The original outline plan had been for the assault to be delivered in daylight. Ramsay, with the experience of the invasion of Sicily fresh in his mind and the achievement of surprise in that operation, was at first reluctant to abandon the obvious advantages of a landing in the dark before dawn. Very soon, however, as he studied the special problems involved in the invasion of Normandy, he realised that the advantages of delivering the assault by daylight far outweighed those of a landing in the dark. Chief of these was the need for the full deployment just before the assault of the over-powering air and naval superiority possessed by the Allies in order to help to crack the "hard crust" of the German anti-invasion defences. The military authorities, however, continued to favour a landing in the dark, and the Royal Air Force commanders seemed reluctant to commit themselves. It was only when the Germans installed the anti-invasion obstructions on the beaches between high and low water marks that final agreement was reached, for these obstructions, to which explosive charges were attached, made it essential to land at low water and by daylight.

The American attitude towards a cut-and-dried plan made out in great detail was implicit in the training of officers of the United States Forces. As one American Naval officer remarked to Admiral Ramsay: "I'm not used to being tied down to all this detail. In our navy we tell an officer to do a job and let him get on with it in his own way." That summed up the problem. The Americans were used to broad directives rather than detailed plans. It was not until Ramsay had pointed out that in an operation of this sort a plan with full details was essential because the movement of one force off the coast of Normandy would affect the movements of convoys coming from the Clyde or the Thames, and even ocean convoys in the Atlantic, that the Americans appreciated the necessity for detailed planning. Even then they were apt to consider that they were being given too many detailed orders and not enough latitude.

Habit dies hard. Nevertheless, there are few, if any, American naval officers who, in the light of experience on D day and after, hold the same view.

Bertram Ramsay has himself said that the first duty of an Admiral is to select a good Chief of the Staff. Ramsay selected Rear-Admiral Creasy, who had been head of the "X staff." They had served together before in this war, for Creasy, in H.M.S. *Codrington*, had commanded the destroyer flotilla working from Dover for three months before the withdrawal of our troops from Dunkirk. George Creasy joined Bertram Ramsay as his Chief of the Staff on October 25th, 1943—the day that Ramsay assumed the title and responsibilities of Allied Naval Commander, Expeditionary Force, and he proved a tower of strength and an unremitting worker throughout the anxious months of planning.

When General Dwight Eisenhower was appointed Supreme Commander for the invasion of Western Europe, he found the planning far advanced, and he brought to his new command that driving energy and passionate belief in co-operation which had characterised his period in Supreme Command in the Mediterranean theatre of operations.

On the first occasion that he visited Norfolk House he assembled the combined British and American staffs in the big conference room. To them he said: "We are not Allies. We have plenty of Allies among the United Nations, but we who are to undertake this great operation are not Allies, we are just one indivisible force with all its many parts more closely integrated than has ever been the case in any force before." General Eisenhower was certainly not decrying the value of the other United Nations, the armed forces of many of whom had served him so well in the Mediterranean theatre of war and were going to serve him so well farther north, but he instilled into the staff and into the troops, ships' crews, and air crews, allocated for the invasion of North-west Europe a spirit of mutual confidence and dependability that transcended co-operation.

Even with the best and most efficient staff in the world it required the alert brain, the quick grasp of essentials and the great organising ability of a Bertram Ramsay to keep constantly in touch with all the vast ramifications of the plan in the making and to see that each one of the thousands of parts would work, not only independently, but in perfect co-ordination with all the other working parts. For an ordinary man twenty-four hours in the day would have been insufficient, and even then fatal snags would have remained. Not so with Bertie Ramsay. His ability and his long staff training combined to economise both time and energy and to eliminate snags before they grew to menacing proportions. Officers on Ramsay's staff will tell you that he has the most astonishing flair for being able to dissect and examine even the most complicated proposals in less time than it takes the average man even to read them through, and to pick almost instantaneously upon any fallacies or weak spots. "It is quite useless, and sometimes even dangerous, to put up to Bertie Ramsay anything which is not worked out in every detail and is not absolutely watertight."

Sir Bertram Ramsay lived in Sloane Street during the initial planning stage of the invasion. Every morning he walked past Buckingham Palace and along the Mall to Marlborough Gate, where he turned up towards his headquarters in Norfolk House.

Ramsay used to reach his office before 9.30 every morning and at once settle down to go through his signals. Then, at 10 a.m., he held a meeting with the heads of departments of his own staff, after which he usually had to attend a series of *ad hoc* meetings which frequently used to occupy almost the whole of the rest of the day. He had, of course, to keep in very close touch with Admiral of the Fleet Sir Andrew Cunningham, the First Sea Lord, and with Admiral Harold Stark, Commanding the United States Naval Forces in the European Theatre of War, as well as with officials of the Ministry of War Transport and other Ministries and Departments.

It was the rule rather than the exception for these meetings to keep him busy until after 5 p.m., when he would return to his office with the knowledge that he had not had a chance of dealing with any of his papers, which had been accumulating steadily on his desk throughout the day and the previous night. It was then that Ramsay's powers of concentration and speed of working stood him in such good stead. It was seldom that he had not finished the paper work within three hours and was thus able to leave his headquarters by 8 p.m. Ramsay believes in leisure as well as in work. He plays hard when he is not working hard, and he used whenever possible to take Sunday off to play golf.

At fairly frequent intervals Ramsay had to attend meetings of the Chief of Staff's Committee in which, under the chairmanship of the Prime Minister, is vested the higher direction of the war.

Although so deeply occupied with the planning and staff side of the preparations for the invasion of north-west Europe, Bertram Ramsay never neglected the personnel or material sides of these preparations. Very frequently he attended trials and demonstrations of new invasion methods, or of weapons or craft specially designed for invasion, and he attended in person every large-scale exercise held to test the progress of the training of the assault personnel. As the prevalence of German air reconnaissance over Southern England and the need for preserving secrecy made it necessary, until the final stages, for these exercises to be held in northern Scotland, this entailed many hours of travelling—hours which had to be made up on return to headquarters after the exercise. Usually, Ramsay used to go north by a night train after a full day's work at his head-quarters, and return by night after the exercise, going straight to his office from the station on arrival in London.

The date initially chosen for D day had to be postponed one month owing to the expansion of the assault area to meet General Montgomery's views, but even the complications involved in a 40 per cent increase in the front to be attacked were overcome, and the initial Inter-Service Plan was completed on February 1st, 1944. Once the Inter-Service Plan was ready the outline Naval Plan went ahead. It was only delayed by doubts as to the availability of suffi-cient ships to ensure to the extended front the degree of protection and support that Admiral Ramsay considered essential. Even so, it was ready by the middle of February, and the more detailed Naval Plan was completed within another fortnight. That left a month for the working out of the manifold time-tables and dovetailed details which made the Naval Plan fit in accurately with the plans of the other Services, and for the preparation of the Naval Operation Orders.

It may be thought, as some of the Americans thought, that too much emphasis had been placed upon the preparation of a plan and of orders which gave in detail the movements of every vessel and of its cargo or duty, route and timing, during the approach to the enemy's coast prior to the initial assault and for days there-after. Nobody would, however, be disposed to question Bertram Ramsay's determination to leave nothing to chance in the greatest amphibious operation of all time, and one upon which hung the future of the world. Mr. Winston Churchill paid tribute to this careful and detailed planning when he said in the House of Commons on D day: "Thus far the commanders who are engaged report that everything is going according to plan—and *what* a plan!"

Bertie Ramsay was reinstated on the Active List of the Royal Navy on April 26th, 1944, and confirmed in the rank of full Admiral on the following day.

This is not the place to detail the complexities which were harmonised into composition of the plan, or to set out the epic story of the invasion. To do so would require a volume in itself. Let it suffice to quote here the Order of the Day issued by Admiral Ramsay to all under his command on the most momentous day in modern history:

> "It is to be our great privilege to take part in the greatest amphibious operation in history—a necessary preliminary to the opening of the West Front in Europe, which in conjunction with the great Russian advance, will crush the fighting power of Germany.
>
> "This is the opportunity which we have long awaited and which must be seized and pursued with relentless determination. The hopes and prayers of the Free World and of the enslaved peoples of Europe will be with us and we cannot fail them.
>
> "Our task in conjunction with the Merchant Navies of the United Nations and supported by the Allied Air Forces is to carry the Allied Expeditionary Force to the Continent, to establish it there in a secure bridgehead, and to build it up and maintain it at a rate which will outmatch that of the enemy. Let no one underestimate the magnitude of this task.
>
> "The Germans are desperate and will resist fiercely until we out-manœuvre and out-fight them, which we can and will do. To every one of you will be given the opportunity to show by his determination and resource that dauntless spirit of resolution which individually strengthens and inspires and which collectively is irresistible.
>
> "I count on every man to do his utmost to ensure the success of this great enterprise which is the climax of the European war."

*   *   *   *   *   *

It was after the above had been written and had received the approval of Sir Bertram Ramsay that, on the second day of 1945, the cause of the United Nations suffered most grievous loss. On that day Admiral Sir Bertram Ramsay was killed in an aircraft accident while leaving Paris for a conference in Brussels. With him in the aircraft died Commander George W. Rowell, who was the Admiral's Staff Officer, Planning, and had contributed mightily behind the scenes; Lieutenant D. M. Henderson, Admiral Ramsay's Flag Lieutenant; and the crew of the aircraft—Lieutenant-Commander Sir George Lewis, Bt. and Petty Officer Telegraphist D. L. Morgan.

If it were possible to find solace in face of such tragedy it should be found in the realisation that Ramsay had wrought so well that the triumph which he had built for the cause of freedom was beyond the reach of Death.

Admiral Sir Bertram Ramsay and those who had died with him were laid to rest in the soil which they had done so much to liberate. In London a Memorial Service was held in Westminster Abbey. An account of that Memorial Service, written by the Author for the *Daily Telegraph and Morning Post*, is here reprinted by permission of that newspaper.

A TRIBUTE

Leaders of the Armed Forces of the Realm, representatives of the Empire, and of every free nation joined yesterday in a farewell tribute at Westminster Abbey to Admiral Sir Bertram Ramsay, whose service in the cause of freedom and liberation will stand high in history.

It was Admiral Ramsay who, to use his own words, "built a bridge to France" across which the mounting tide of the forces of Liberation would pass to the European Continent.

What Philip of Spain failed to do, Napoleon could not do, and Hitler dared not do, Admiral Ramsay, as the Supreme Allied Commander at Sea, succeeded in doing so well that nearly 100 per cent of the Allied assault troops and their supplies arrived safely in France.

In the Abbey the high vaulted roof was shrouded in winter

gloom when the Dean and Chapter, in their robes of sable and gold, passed up towards the High Altar.

On one side were ranged the high officers of the Board of Admiralty, the Air Council, and the Army Council, with representatives of the War Cabinet, headed by Mr. Attlee, Deputy Prime Minister. On the other side were representatives of all the nations whose forces have joined to carry out the ideal for which Sir Bertram Ramsay wrought so well and paid the final forfeit of greatness.

Near the corner of the north transept one could not help noticing the marble figure of a woman prostrated with grief over a pile of sandbags—an unconscious commentary upon the sorrow of the civilised world faced with devastating war.

The service began with quotations from the Scriptures, sung by the choir. Then followed a part of Psalm 107, that stirring extract which begins:

" *They that go down to the sea in ships and occupy their business in great waters . . .*"

It was sung softly and beautifully until the notes of the organ made the great vaults tremble as the music swelled to the triumphant words:

" *And so He bringeth them unto the haven where they would be.*"

One of the most moving moments of the Abbey Service was the reading by the Dean of Westminster, Dr. de Labilliere, of that time-honoured naval prayer, to which so many naval heroes in our long history have sailed forth to honour or to glorious death:

" *Preserve us from the dangers of the sea and from the violence of the enemy ; that we may be a safeguard unto our most gracious Sovereign Lord, King George, and his Dominions and a security for such as pass on the seas upon their lawful occasions.*"

In those words there is compressed a tradition of service, humanity and high endeavour which never fails to stiffen shoulders wearing naval uniform.

The Lesson was read by the Rev. B. G. Beale, Royal Navy Senior Chaplain, Combined Operations H.Q.

There followed the short prayer of the Order of the Bath, the hymn "Abide With Me," written by Henry Lyte when Britain was last in mortal danger, and then the Blessing.

The well-known words of the Blessing were varied by the Dean, and included the words "May He give you courage, victory and peace." They seemed essential rather than additions to the well-known formula.

After the Blessing there was sung, kneeling, the "Contakion of the Departed," composed by Birbeck, and at the words "Whose sorrow and pain are no more; neither sighing, but life everlasting," the light in the Abbey suddenly increased. The sun had broken through the clouds and was flooding the vaulted roof and marble floors with a sudden golden light.

There must have been many who thought that it must be a promise of the completion of Admiral Ramsay's great work as well as a manifestation of the faith of those who knelt.

The Last Post, then the stirring notes of the Réveillé, and a half-muffled peal of bells. The officers in uniform went out of the peaceful Abbey to give of an even greater best to the cause which that short memorial service had interpreted to them so vividly.

Admiral Sir Bertram Ramsay had been buried in a foreign field ; in his service he had achieved mightily, and in his passing he had greatly inspired those who follow. It was just part of the endless tradition of the Royal Navy.

WILLIAM GLADSTONE AGNEW
C.B., C.V.O., D.S.O.

Captain, Royal Navy

WHEN one considers the careers of naval officers who have played prominent parts in this war, it is noticeable how often there is a distinct relationship between war exploits and some period of service or training in peace. This argues that there was little .wrong with the training of the Royal Navy in the years before this war, although so much of it had to be done in what might be called skeleton form in obedience to the dictates of economy. In this connection it is worth remembering that after the first notable surface action of the war—the Battle of the River Plate in December, 1939—Rear-Admiral Harwood remarked particularly in his official despatch that there seemed little wrong with the peace-time training of the Navy.

This link between training in peace and execution in war is very marked in the case of Captain William Gladstone Agnew. It is marked in play as well as in work. Bill Agnew was known on nearly every rugby football ground in England as a tireless bustling forward, for ever urging his men on to greater efforts and with his red face and fair hair—it is grey now—always close to the ball. In war he has been the same—a tireless cruiser captain always on top of the enemy and hounding him with almost demoniac energy, urging his men always to greater efforts and in so doing earning among them a most enviable position of trust and respect.

Agnew's most triumphant action in this war, after which he was immediately created a Companion of the Order of the Bath, was a night action. So were many other actions in which he has been concerned. It is as a cruiser captain in daring close night actions that Agnew is chiefly famous, and again, there is in his pre-war career a period of service and training which has led directly to this.

He is a gunnery specialist, and his first appointment as gunnery officer of a capital ship was to H.M.S. *Queen Elizabeth* in 1931. The *Queen Elizabeth* was the flagship of the Mediterranean Fleet, and the

Commander-in-Chief at that time was Admiral Sir Ernle Chatfield, now Lord Chatfield.

There had at that time been a complete reversal of policy in the Admiralty with regard to night action, and Admiral Chatfield had had much to do with securing this change of policy. Up to that time it was clearly laid down by the Admiralty that night action was to be avoided except by small ships such as destroyers. There was nothing faint-hearted in this. All the tactical experts were agreed that there was a greater risk in night action than in day action, and the bigger the ship the bigger and less justifiable the risk. From this arose the feeling that night action would always be the weapon of the weaker force, and that, while destroyers might well seek night action in the hope of scoring torpedo hits on heavy ships in a close range encounter, night action should be avoided by larger and more valuable ships.

This policy had ruled for decades, and then it was completely reversed. The Admiralty agreed that cruisers and battleships should seek, instead of trying to avoid, night action.

There was good reason for this change of policy. Admiral Chatfield and others felt that the Royal Navy in any future war would have to deal with enemies which would seek to avoid action whenever possible—a theory which was supported by the fact that most other navies—and certainly those of the Continental Powers—were being provided with inordinately fast ships. In these conditions action might never be joined, for our faster adversaries would in all probability be able, by reason of their superior speed, to carry out their policy of avoiding action. The only chance, therefore, of bringing them to close action lay either in crippling ships by air attack or forcing a daring night action. It was felt that in the latter event the superior training and steadiness of the British sailor under the exciting and confusing conditions of night action would outweigh the risks entailed.

Thus it was that the Mediterranean Fleet under Admiral Chatfield embarked upon a programme of manœuvres which were designed to probe every problem involved in night action, and to train the personnel of the Fleet to a high degree of efficiency in this most difficult of all naval operations.

This programme of exercises and manœuvres, begun by Admiral Chatfield, was further built up by his successors as Commanders-in-Chief, Admiral Sir William Fisher and Admiral Sir Dudley Pound.

The result was a fleet and a personnel trained to a hair. Human nerves are apt to be stretched at night in war-time when there is prospect of sudden encounter with the enemy. Lookouts are apt to think that they are "seeing things," and officers and men are tempted to act excitedly when the galvanising order "Alarm bearing . . ." is given; or when the first star shell bursts high in the night sky or the first searchlight beam stabs the darkness. Night action at sea has its peculiar and very strong psychological effects. Training could combat these dangers, and did so. The training given by Admirals Chatfield, Fisher and Pound, and by the officers under their command was directly responsible for the outstanding night victories of Admiral Sir Andrew Cunningham at the Battle of Matapan, of Captain Stokes off Cape Bon, and of Captain Agnew south-east of Cape Spartivento.

Agnew, as Gunnery Officer of Admiral Chatfield's flagship, had of course been concerned with this new conception of training in night fighting from the very moment when the Admiralty policy had been altered. He was a young and immensely keen gunnery specialist, and would have been less than human had he not been imbued with the fascination of building a new technique.

Bill Agnew learnt self-reliance at a very early age. He was at the Royal Naval College, Dartmouth, when war was declared in 1914. When he went to sea he joined the old battleship *Glory* which spent a year on patrol in the waters off New York, during which time the ship was based on Halifax, Nova Scotia. It was a dull job, but one full of discomfort.

After a year off New York the *Glory* went to the Dardanelles, and arrived there a month before the Suvla landings. During the landings at Suvla and during the subsequent withdrawal of the troops from that part of the Gallipoli peninsula, Midshipman Agnew had charge of a picket boat. There could have been few more gruelling baptisms of fire than standing at the exposed wheel of a 45-foot steamboat during these operations.

Agnew was soon to see action in a different theatre of war. After the Dardanelles campaign he was appointed to the new battleship *Royal Oak*. The *Royal Oak* was commissioned for the first time on May 1st, 1916, and thirty days later, after a period of feverish "working up," she was present at the Battle of Jutland.

Then in March, 1917, came promotion to the rank of Sub-Lieutenant, and Agnew was duly appointed to the destroyer *Victor*, which was employed on patrol and convoy escort duties in the Western Approaches to the British Isles. His time in the *Victor* was short, however, and ended when that ship was seriously damaged in collision. That was the first of three collisions which Agnew was to experience. For the rest of the 1914-18 war he served in the destroyer *Skilful* in the Harwich Force.

When the war came to an end Agnew went to Cambridge University under the Admiralty scheme for providing something in the nature of a "finishing school" for the large number of naval officers whose general education had been rudely interrupted by the fact that they were required for immediate service at sea.

Bill Agnew will tell you that it seems to him in retrospect that he spent the next three years playing rugby football. He got his first Navy Cap in 1920, and after coming down from the university he served successively in the Royal Yacht *Victoria and Albert*, the destroyer *Rob Roy* in the Portsmouth Defence Flotilla, and in the *Alexandra*, which was then a sort of " second string " to the Royal Yacht. During all this time he was playing football regularly.

In the summer of 1922, Agnew, then a Lieutenant of three years seniority, again went to sea in earnest. This was as a watchkeeping officer in the light cruiser *Delhi*. He spent a year in that ship in the Home Fleet.

In 1924 Agnew was nearly twenty-six years of age and had nearly five years seniority as a Lieutenant. It was high time he specialised if he were going to do so. He had for some time been keen on naval gunnery and had forwarded his name as a candidate for specialisation in this science. In 1924 he was selected and went to the Royal Navy's premier gunnery school at Whale Island, Portsmouth, to undergo his qualifying course. In this he was successful, and after qualifying he remained at Whale Island for a time as Field Training Officer before going to sea again—this time in the light cruiser *Durban*. In that ship he served for more than two and a half years, first on the China Station and then on the North America and West Indies Station.

It was an interesting commission, but there was little scope for a keen young gunnery officer, full of the sense of modern development, for this ship had only six old hand-worked six-inch guns and no anti-aircraft armament worthy of the name. Yet those years broadened his mind, gave him wider experience of the world, and sent him back to Whale Island in 1929 full of pent-up energy.

Agnew is one of those men who always find it difficult to discover adequate outlet for their energy. Take the case of his games. He had already at that time earned fame as a rugby footballer and had also played for the Royal Navy at cricket and tennis. While he was serving in H.M.S. *Durban* he fell sick and the doctors diagnosed a perforated gastric ulcer. They gave him back his health but told him that he must never again play rugby football. His reaction was typical of the man and of his exuberant need for violent exercise. He persuaded the doctors to allow him to play hockey—a game which he had not hitherto played seriously. When they agreed he took up the game, and very soon he was playing in first-class matches and representing the Navy at this game also.

His pent-up energy affected his work no less, and when he left the *Durban* and went back to Whale Island it was not slow to show itself. He was at that time employed in what was called the "Instruction Production Section" of the staff—a panel of officers who worked out training programmes, courses of lectures, and all the other matters concerned with turning out better gunnery officers and better gunnery ratings than any other navy in the world. His energy, keenness and the standard of his work at Whale Island secured for him the coveted appointment of Gunnery Officer of the *Queen Elizabeth*, flagship of Admiral Chatfield, in the Mediterranean Fleet in June, 1931. In that ship he served for eighteen months, during which time he was intimately connected with solving the problems of night action and the development of the navy's gunnery to meet the change in Admiralty policy.

Agnew came back to England in the *Queen Elizabeth* in November, 1932. The ship was due for a large refit, and Agnew was promoted to Commander at the end of that year—proof of the good work he had done in a fleet flagship during a critical transition period in the Navy's gunnery history.

As a young commander Bill Agnew served his term in the Admiralty—in that section of the Training and Staff Duties Division which has since become the Gunnery Division of the Naval Staff. After that he went back to H.M.S. *Queen Elizabeth*. That ship was again the flagship of the Mediterranean Fleet, but by now the Commander-in-Chief was Admiral Sir Dudley Pound. Agnew joined the *Queen Elizabeth* as Executive Officer of the ship in March, 1936, and served in her in that capacity for just over a year.

It was a gruelling time. The Abyssinian crisis had discovered rents rather than chinks in our armour. The Home Government had produced White Papers and set in motion the ponderous machinery for repairing the material gaps. Meanwhile our sea officers threw themselves into the task of producing an efficiency among the personnel of the Royal Navy which would make up for the material deficencies. Too much had been left almost too late, and even then circumstances seemed to conspire against the uninterrupted and urgent training of the Fleet. Opportunities for training were curtailed by the problems arising out of the Spanish Civil War, in which the British Mediterranean Fleet had to "keep the ring" to prevent a spread of the conflict, and to act in obedience to the dictates of common humanity.

The result, of course, was a system in the Mediterranean Fleet which gave little rest to either officers or men. A programme of practices and manœuvres was worked out which was designed to make the greatest possible use of every minute at sea and of every gallon of oil fuel. Whenever ships were in company not a moment of the day or night, nor a mile of sea, was wasted.

It can well be appreciated that life in the Mediterranean Fleet at that time was strenuous. It was a forcing-house in which energy was currency and lethargy a passport to half pay. And it would be difficult to find any officer in the whole of the Mediterranean Fleet to whom that applied more directly or forcibly than to the commander and executive officer of Sir Dudley Pound's flagship, the *Queen Elizabeth*. That officer was Bill Agnew.

It was a job that would have broken many men. It did not break Agnew; and yet anybody with an insight into naval affairs might well have interpreted his next two appointments as indications that he had failed and was being gently relegated to the "shelf."

After more than a year as commander and executive officer of the *Queen Elizabeth*, Agnew was appointed to command the sloop *Deptford* in the Persian Gulf. Rightly or wrongly the Persian Gulf had been regarded in the past almost as a sort of "penal settlement" where officers who had "blotted their copybooks" could serve out their time for pension.

Admittedly, Agnew did less than a year in command of the *Deptford* in the Persian Gulf, but when he left that ship in 1938, after being promoted to Captain, he was given an appointment which, in the eyes of the initiated, seemed little better. This was to command H.M.S. *Pegasus*. The *Pegasus* was one of those freak ships which was a product of the eternal conflict between Treasury parsimony and the desire of the Royal Navy to experiment and evolve better weapons and better means of using existing weapons.

Until the launching of the famous aircraft carrier *Ark Royal*, the *Pegasus* had borne that name. There can have been few ships more unsightly and more apparently unseaworthy. Her one spindly funnel and her untidy upperworks were right aft. The rest was a flat deck, broken only by strange and unsightly trellis-work structures—the aircraft catapults with which she was for ever doing trials and tests. Her appearance was clumsy, and so was her performance, for she had only one screw, not much power, and a shape which invited every wind of heaven to jest with her.

When war was declared, the old *Pegasus* was wanted at Rosyth, and Agnew took her there. There he left that ship and crossed over to Belfast, where the Peninsular and Oriental liner *Corfu* was fitting out as an armed merchant cruiser, and he took command of this ship. Here again was a rather curious appointment. Agnew was a very young man, only just turned forty, and most of the armed merchant cruisers were commanded by officers of much greater age, who had retired from the Navy but had been called up again on the outbreak of war.

The next six months were gruelling ones for Agnew. The *Corfu* was detailed for the Northern Patrol throughout that interminable winter. She was at sea for long periods right up in the Arctic, where the spray froze all over her as it fell and where the only day was an hour or so of murky twilight. There was plenty of danger too—the gallant *Rawalpindi*, an armed merchant cruiser from the same line as the *Corfu*, had gone down fighting impossible odds in those same waters and many armed merchant cruisers had fallen victims to U-boats—but no action came the way of the *Corfu*. It was just a long winter of utter discomfort.

Then, in the early summer came relief. The *Corfu* was detailed to escort convoys to and from Freetown. It was a change in every sense—from the Arctic in winter to the tropics in summer.

For three months the *Corfu* carried out these duties, and then Agnew experienced his second collision. The big armed merchant cruiser was escorting a convoy homeward bound from Freetown, and by night she was stationed ahead of the convoy, chiefly to prevent outward bound ships which were sailing independently from running into the convoy in the dark. It was a very dark night, with torrential tropical rain which reduced visibility to practically nothing, and the first Agnew or anybody knew was the crash of the collision. The *Corfu* had come into collision with the small aircraft carrier *Hermes*, which was withdrawing from the abortive Dakar operation.

For some minutes nobody in either ship knew what they had hit. Agnew's first act was to switch on the *Corfu's* navigation lights in order to warn the convoy to keep clear. An officer of the *Hermes*, seeing the bright steaming light of the *Corfu* high above him in the darkness, reported to his captain that the enemy was firing star shell! One of the *Corfu's* officers, arriving hastily on the bridge and looking down on to the flight-deck of the *Hermes*, which appeared to him as a wide expanse of asphalt with a white line running down the centre, ejaculated "Good Lord! Have we hit Regent Street?"

The *Corfu* had her forward holds flooded, but was able to steam under her own power. The *Hermes* was not seriously damaged. Agnew took the *Corfu* back to Freetown to be repaired and then he left her.

On October 1st, 1940, Bill Agnew took over command of the light cruiser *Aurora*. It was the beginning of one of the most eventful commissions any ship has ever had.

The *Aurora*, a 5250-ton cruiser armed with six 6-inch guns, was then lying at Sheerness. Much of the Battle of Britain had just been fought over the heads of her crew, for they had been stationed at Sheerness as part of the naval dispositions taken to guard against the invasion of England, which then seemed imminent.

Gradually the danger of invasion receded and the warships which had been at "anti-invasion stations" around our coasts went back to more orthodox tasks. The *Aurora* went back to the north and joined the main body of the Home Fleet. Thus Agnew experienced his second winter in the far north, escorting convoys, patrolling and so on. It was dull, uneventful slogging in the dark and the cold.

At last, however, the winter fell away and then came those few hectic days which formed the whole sea-going career of the German battleship *Bismarck*. Apart from hard steaming, Agnew and his men had little part in that operation. The *Aurora* was one of the cruisers detailed to escort the new aircraft carrier

Victorious on her dash towards Greenland in order to get within aircraft striking range of the *Bismarck*, and then it fell to the *Aurora* to escort the damaged battleship *Prince of Wales* back to Iceland. That was all.

A few days later, however, the *Aurora* was at last to have some action on her own account. Again she was up in the Arctic, this time with the cruiser *Kenya* in company and upon a more specific mission than the everlasting patrolling. It was known that supply ships had been ministering to the wants of U-boats at sea in order to save the latter the trip back to harbour, and that one of these had been working south of Greenland. The *Aurora* and *Kenya* were out to find and sink her.

The weather was foul and the first things they found were two ships' lifeboats crowded with forty-four survivors from a torpedoed merchant ship. Those men had spent nine days in their open boats before they were picked up by the cruisers. They were to witness the Royal Navy taking vengeance on the Germans for the loss of their ship.

It was shortly before nine o'clock one morning that the *Kenya's* Walrus aircraft, which had been searching ahead of the cruisers, reported a suspicious ship about eighteen miles away. The cruisers closed at high speed, and they found the German U-boat supply ship—a big tanker of about 10,000 tons—in the act of fuelling two U-boats, which lay alongside her. It was not long before the cruisers' guns set her on fire, and they then closed in and finished her off with torpedoes. What happened to the two U-boats nobody knows, but their mere presence sent the crew of the supply ship to their deaths, since there could be no question of trying to pick up survivors with U-boats in the vicinity. And so back to Iceland, through a blizzard and much pack ice, to land the Merchant Navy survivors.

It was soon after this that "Force A" was formed under the command of Rear-Admiral Philip Vian. It consisted of the cruisers *Nigeria*, which wore Admiral Vian's flag, and *Aurora*, and the Tribal class destroyers *Tartar* and *Punjabi*. The Arctic farther north than ever was to be the scene of "Force A's" operations. The force went first to Iceland and then sailed for Spitzbergen.

Spitzbergen was known to have valuable coal mines, but it was not known whether the Germans had landed there or occupied it after their conquest of Norway, and it was desired to find out.

Apart from the coal, Spitzbergen might have become an important link in the chain of German weather reporting stations. The mines had in peace time been worked largely by Russians, but there had also been many Norwegians on the islands.

"Force A" approached Spitzbergen very cautiously, keeping a sharp lookout for aircraft or anything in the least suspicious, but all was peaceful. Leaving the smaller ships to patrol the entrance to the fiord, the *Nigeria* and *Aurora* went in and landed parties to contact the local authorities and discover what had been happening in this remote settlement, which had been completely cut off from the rest of the world for so long. The colony had been living from hand to mouth and had not been molested by the Germans, although it sent weather reports by wireless to the mainland of Norway and these were, of course, used by the Germans.

Having completed the reconnaissance of Spitzbergen, the cruisers kept a rendezvous with an oil tanker and then sailed south-ward on another operation which had been planned to dovetail in with the Spitzbergen reconnaissance. This was to be a bombard-ment from the sea of the oil storage tanks and installations at the north Norwegian port of Hammerfest, while carrier-borne aircraft attacked the Norwegian airfields to prevent interference from the Luftwaffe.

Such an operation would have been feasible only in low visibility, and the visibility was extreme, with that crystal quality that exists in the Arctic in summer. Moreover, the cruisers were sighted by a German long-range reconnaissance aircraft as they approached the coast. It was clearly out of the question to press on with the pro-posed bombardment of Hammerfest, but Rear-Admiral Vian was not the man to do nothing. He turned north, and carried out a bombardment of the wireless station on Bear Island, midway between northern Norway and Spitzbergen, which was an impor-tant weather reporting station working for the Germans.

Next day "Force A" had another try at Hammerfest, but again it was spotted by German air reconnaissance, so that the bombard-ment had reluctantly to be abandoned, and the force returned to the United Kingdom.

It was not long, however, before Agnew and the *Aurora* were back in the Arctic. On August 24th "Force A" again arrived off Spitzbergen, and the warships had with them the transport *Empress of Canada*, carrying supplies, Norwegian Commando troops and detachments of the Royal Canadian Engineers, the Saskatoon Light Infantry and the Edmonton Regiment.

This time the object of the visit was to deny to the Germans the products of the coal mines. It was clear that the enemy would need fuel in the winter for his garrisons in northern Norway and for the prosecution of the war on his northern front against the Russians, and it was considered probable that he would seize Spitzbergen in order to obtain this fuel near at hand. Moreover, if the Spitzbergen supplies were denied to him, he would be forced to transport from Germany all the fuel for the North Russian front and his garrisons in Norway, and this would impose a further heavy strain upon his already extended transport organisation. The mines and their machinery were therefore to be destroyed, and also the very large stocks of coal which had been mined during the period when Spitzbergen had been totally isolated. The miners, and indeed all the inhabitants, would then be deprived of their livelihood, so they were to be removed from Spitzbergen. The Russians were to be taken to Russia and the Norwegians were to be brought back to the United Kingdom, where they would be enrolled in the Norwegian forces.

The troops and engineers were duly put ashore to undertake the work of destruction. While the Russians were embarked and taken to their home country in the *Empress of Canada*, Agnew in the *Aurora* was engaged in rounding up the people from the outlying settlements, mostly Norwegian trappers. While carrying out this task Agnew took the *Aurora* into waters that had never been disturbed by the passage of a warship, and to the most northerly human habitations in the world. He brought the settlers back to the main township, where they were picked up by the *Empress of Canada* on her return from Russia. Finally, the demolitions were carried out. All the mine-working machinery was destroyed and some 450,000 tons of stacked coal and 270,000 gallons of fuel oil, petrol and grease was burnt.

During the Spitzbergen operation the Germans were successfully hoaxed. The wireless station at Spitzbergen had been in the habit of transmitting weather reports to the German authorities in Norway. As soon as "Force A" arrived on the scene the wireless station was taken over, but it did not cease to transmit weather reports to the Germans. In fact, the weather was crystal clear throughout the operation, but the Spitzbergen wireless station repeatedly told the Germans that it was shrouded in fog, so that not even a German long-range reconnaissance aircraft put in an appearance. Only when "Force A" left was the wireless station destroyed, and the ships could then hear German stations frantically calling Spitzbergen and demanding an explanation of its silence.

The *Empress of Canada* and the captured ships steamed on to England, but once these were out of the danger zone "Force A" turned and headed back towards North Norway. Close to the North Cape there is a deep and broad stretch of water known as Mageroy Sound. Here ships skirting the Norwegian coast have to leave the shelter of the off-lying islands and traverse a stretch of open water. It was here that Admiral Vian determined to strike at the enemy and round off a highly successful mission.

For once the weather played into his hands. There was mist and rain from low clouds as the *Nigeria* and *Aurora* approached the Norwegian coast, and the German air reconnaissance was inoperative. By midnight on September 6th the ships were about thirty miles off the coast, and they closed rapidly into Mageroy Sound, at action stations and with every man on the alert.

It was just after 1 a.m. when the shadowy outline of a ship was sighted on the port bow. The turrets swung round, only to swing back a few seconds later. Another ship had been sighted on the starboard hand. The latter was obviously a warship, and was soon identified as the German cruiser *Bremse*.

It was a matter of moments before the British cruisers opened fire. The range was short and the German was taken completely by surprise. She stood up to five broadsides and then turned away, seeking refuge in the darkness.

Meanwhile other ships had been sighted. Things were happening very quickly—so quickly that it was almost impossible for anybody to know exactly what *was* happening. Only good training prevented a confusion which might have been disastrous.

The first vessel sighted turned out to be an armed trawler, which was followed by a large supply ship. No sooner had these ships been identified than a German destroyer appeared. It was heading straight for the *Aurora* at high speed. Collision seemed inevitable, and collision might have been serious, for the British ships were many hundreds of miles from their nearest base and the weather was deteriorating. As it happened, the two ships narrowly avoided collision and the German destroyer passed close down the *Aurora's* port side. As she passed she was raked fore-and-aft by pom-poms and other short-range weapons. Then, as she fell astern, she was hit amidships by a salvo of four-inch shells. She swung suddenly to starboard, and Agnew was quick on the *Aurora's* helm, for it looked as if she might fire torpedoes, but at that moment the *Aurora's* after six-inch gun turret scored again on her. She drifted away, listing heavily.

During this phase of the action it appeared that the *Bremse* was engaging the *Aurora* with her five-inch guns, but Agnew's ship was certainly not hit. The next target was the armed trawler. She was finished off with a single broadside, and then Agnew again sighted the *Bremse* and opened fire on her. At least three of the *Aurora's* broadsides hit before the German again disappeared in the night.

It is probable that no connected and coherent account of what happened in the next few minutes can be compiled unless and until German records fall into our hands. As far as can be ascertained, another German destroyer put in an appearance and was fired at and badly hit by the *Nigeria*, and a supply ship was hit at very close range and left sinking and on fire. There was smoke everywhere. As the *Nigeria* emerged from a smoke bank she rammed something —probably the remains of the German destroyer which had been so roughly handled by the *Aurora*. The *Nigeria* sustained serious damage to her bows—serious, that is, when one considers the weather and the distance from a repair base. At about the same time the *Bremse* blew up and sank. It seems probable that she was hit by a torpedo fired by the second German destroyer and intended for the *Nigeria*.

It had been Agnew's first real night action, and it had been a good night's work, but the engagement had to be broken off on account of the damage to the *Nigeria's* bows. She was brought safely home to England and repaired, but her passage home caused no little anxiety.

One can well imagine that Agnew and his men had had enough of the Arctic, but they fully expected to spend at least another year in the far north. Suddenly, however, their sphere of operations was changed, "navy fashion," by the receipt of a terse signal in the early hours of a Sunday morning.

"*Aurora* take *Penelope* under your orders and proceed with all dispatch to Gibraltar."

There seemed to be something almost unreal about a signal like that to ships which were expecting to take part in a North Russian convoy operation in the Arctic in a few days' time, but there was certainly nothing unreal about the job they were to do.

So, early on a Sunday morning, the *Aurora* and *Penelope*—ships whose names were to become household words—slipped quietly away from the northern base of the Home Fleet and set course southwards.

The two cruisers arrived at Gibraltar after dark, spent some busy hours fuelling and loading stores for the beleaguered island of Malta, and slipped away from Gibraltar again before dawn, thus avoiding the prying eyes of the many German agents on the Spanish shores of Gibraltar Bay. Soon after leaving Gibraltar Agnew's force was joined by the destroyers *Lance* and *Lively*.

Those four ships—*Aurora*, *Penelope*, *Lance* and *Lively* formed "Force K" which was soon to prove a terrible scourge to Rommel's supply lines and gain fame throughout the world.

"Force K" was to be based on Malta and operate against the enemy's supply lines across the Mediterranean to his armies in North Africa. The British submarines and aircraft had been doing sterling work in preying upon these supply lines, but in spite of all they could do General Rommel was continuing to receive fairly considerable reinforcements and supplies. The Admiralty had decided to take the risk of basing a force of small cruisers and destroyers at Malta in the hope that surface ships, in conjunction with the submarines and aircraft, would result in much greater losses being imposed upon the enemy's sea-communications across the Mediterranean. Events were to show that the Admiralty's decision was fully justified.

Agnew's "Force K" had an uneventful voyage to Malta, a fact which seemed rather to give the lie to the tales they had heard of the war in the Mediterranean, but there was certainly no tendency to relax and take things easy.

Malta is strategically in the midst of the short sea routes across the Mediterranean. It was realised therefore that quick action would be required as soon as the presence of enemy ships at sea were reported or suspected; the more so since the enemy had adopted the expedient of running troops across in destroyers instead of transports in order to minimise the risk.

It was not long before the first alarm came. "Force K" quickly raised steam and slipped out of harbour on a Saturday night. Three enemy destroyers carrying troops had been reported at sea. Agnew swept the waters ahead of the reported position of the enemy, but "Force K" found nothing, and returned to Malta in the morning after having spent a night at action stations.

Again on the following Saturday night "Force K" put to sea in a hurry in quest of the enemy—and found none. It was disappointing, but Agnew and his men were by no means disheartened, and they bore the taunts of the submarine crews good-humouredly when these referred to them as "Saturday night sailors."

The time in harbour was far from wasted. While officers and men drilled themselves to an ever higher pitch of efficiency and examined and re-examined material to make sure that nothing would fail in a sudden emergency, Bill Agnew and the other captains held frequent and long counsel. Agnew knew enough about night action to know that success goes to the man who thinks and acts quickest. There is less than no time for drill-book methods, correct signal procedure, or complicated manœuvres, and yet drill and procedure, remain important as safeguards against confusion. What is even more important, however, is that each commanding officer shall know the mind of the Force Commander, instinctively think as he does in any given situation, and know what is required of him in all conceivable circumstances. It was this close communion of thought which Agnew and his captains strove to build up while in harbour, and to this end the commanding officers of the four ships of "Force K" used nearly always to lunch or dine together when in harbour in addition to holding long conferences.

As luck would have it, the next occasion when Agnew took his ships to sea in quest of the enemy was also a Saturday night. It was the third Saturday night in succession that there had been an alarm. It was to prove a case of "third time lucky."

It was the evening of Saturday, November 8th. The *Aurora*, *Penelope*, *Lance* and *Lively* slipped out of harbour in a hurry, having had to collect some of their men from the cinema while steam was being raised, and Captain Nicholl of the *Penelope* only just caught his ship after she was under way. Air reconnaissance had reported an enemy convoy of six supply ships escorted by four destroyers in a position about forty miles east of Cape Spartivento, at the "toe" of Italy, and steering towards Benghazi.

Once clear of the boom guarding the entrance to the Grand Harbour, "Force K" increased speed to 28 knots, steering north-east.

It was a bright moonlight night, with a half moon well up in the sky and a light wind. Conditions could hardly have been better.

Midnight came and went. Men were beginning to think that "Force K" were going to draw yet another blank. Agnew had announced his intention to turn back at 1 a.m. if nothing had been sighted. To be caught by daylight in those waters would be to invite most unwelcome attentions from the Luftwaffe, and this it was no part of "Force K's" duty to do.

Then suddenly, at forty minutes past midnight, a look-out reported darkened ships on the port bow. In a few moments they were clearly discernible, and it was seen that they were about seven miles away and steering south. The position was about 100 miles east-south-east of Cape Spartivento.

Agnew made one of the only three signals which he found it necessary to send to the other ships of his force, so well had the commanding officers profited by their association and study of tactics while at Malta. The signal was for alarm, to let them know that the enemy had been sighted, and on what bearing. Then he made his second signal—for a reduction of speed from 28 to 20 knots in order to reduce the chance of ships' bow waves, stern waves or wakes being seen by the enemy.

Meanwhile Agnew led "Force K" round to the northward in order to reach a position where the enemy would be silhouetted against the moonlit horizon, while the British ships would have a dark horizon behind them. As the range closed gradually and the enemy became more clearly defined against the moonlight it was seen that the convoy consisted of eight large supply ships, with four destroyers as escort. The prize was even greater than had been reported by the reconnaissance aircraft.

Having achieved what might be termed the "moonlight gauge," Agnew led round in order to attack the escorting destroyers, which were stationed astern of the convoy on account of the conditions of light. Incredible as it may seem, the enemy was still blissfully unaware of the presence of British warships. Agnew had closed to within five miles of the enemy destroyers when his lookouts reported more darkened ships to the north-westward. Here was a surprise. Had the enemy laid a trap and sent heavy cruisers to sea to cover the passage of this obviously important convoy? If the ships now sighted turned out to be 8-inch gun cruisers "Force K" would be in a very awkward position indeed.

Captain W. G. Agnew

Crown Copyright Reserved

It was a moment for cool thinking, particularly since Agnew
had already committed his force to an attack on the first group of
ships sighted and could not disengage without making another
signal, which might well betray the presence of his force. So he
held on towards the destroyers astern of the eight-ship convoy, and
as he did so the ships to the north-westward were identified as two
large supply ships escorted by two destroyers. "Force K's" luck
was evidently "in." It seemed that the two convoys had been about
to join up for the final stage of the voyage to Benghazi when the
British ships arrived on the scene.

At three minutes to 1 a.m. Agnew opened fire at the nearest
destroyer with the *Aurora's* foremost turrets. "Force K" had been
in sight of the enemy for seventeen minutes without being detected,
and had shortened the range to 5700 yards before opening fire. The
Aurora's first salvo hit with all four shells. That unfortunate
destroyer received two more salvoes of 6-inch shells. Within forty
seconds she was heavily on fire and sinking by the bows.

Meanwhile the action had become general. The *Aurora's* 4-inch
armament had opened fire on the ships to the north-westward, as
had also the destroyer *Lively*. One of the destroyers in this group of
ships was certainly heavily hit, but it was difficult to assess results
at that time owing to the flash of the main armament guns of the
cruisers and the speed at which events were happening closer at
hand. Almost as soon as the *Aurora* opened fire on the first destroyer
the *Penelope* engaged another destroyer and quickly reduced her to
a sinking wreck.

Thus within a minute or two, and probably before the enemy
had begun to realise what had happened, two destroyers had been
sunk and a third so heavily hit that she could be considered out of
action.

Agnew's ships then turned their attention to the ships in convoy.
Ship after ship was engaged at close range and sunk, blown up, or
set on fire. One broadside was enough for most of the ships. One
10,000-ton tanker was obviously laden with petrol. A broadside
turned her into a blazing torch. Another of the enemy ships was
obviously laden with ammunition. On being hit she blew up with
so violent an explosion that men between decks in the *Aurora*
thought that their own ship had been torpedoed. The exploding
ammunition from that ship produced a most spectacular firework
display stretching thousands of feet up into the night sky. The only

S.S.   G opposition put up by the convoy escorts was by one destroyer, which tried to close our ships and fired torpedoes (they were easily avoided), and another which fired its guns spasmodically from a comparatively safe distance and with no effect.

Forty minutes after opening fire Agnew made his third signal to the ships of "Force K." It was a terse order: "Do not waste ammunition." There was the cool and trained gunnery officer restraining the exuberance of those under his command even in the moment of complete victory.

As Agnew led "Force K" back towards Malta he could count eight ships blazing and so low in the water that there could be no prospect of saving them. Two more had been sunk outright, and it was subsequently established and announced by the Admiralty that three destroyers had been sunk and two seriously damaged.

Thus "Force K" under Agnew's leadership had snapped up two convoys under the noses of the two powerful *Trento* class 8-inch gun cruisers which were supposed to have been covering their passage, had sunk every one of the supply ships in both convoys, and sunk three and damaged two of the six escorting destroyers. "Force K" had received not a casualty nor a scratch to its paintwork.

Small wonder that Mr. Winston Churchill at once sent the following message to the Admiralty : "Many congratulations upon this most important and timely action which gravely interrupts the enemy's supply lines to Africa and impedes his long boasted offensive against the Nile valley. Pray convey my congratulations to all concerned." Next day it was announced that Agnew had been created a Companion of the Order of the Bath for this model and successful action.

"Force K's" task with the enemy convoy and its escorts was completed forty minutes after opening fire, and as Agnew steamed away he could see the fires from a distance of twenty-five miles. The Royal Navy, however, had not finished. The surface ships had to be back at Malta by daylight, but as they went on their way a signalling lamp suddenly stabbed the darkness.. It was the famous submarine *Upholder*, commanded by Lieutenant-Commander M. D. Wanklyn, who, after winning the V.C. and the D.S.O. and two bars, was later to lose his life with his whole crew. The *Upholder* had watched the night action from a distance and was closing in to finish off any damaged ships which looked like floating, or attack any ships which came to the assistance of the virtually annihilated convoy. In the morning she attacked two destroyers and torpedoed both of them. One of them was seen to sink.

Only the enemy's records can assess the degree to which Agnew's action wrecked Rommel's plans in North Africa, but it is certain that his sea-borne supply lines had received a blow from which they never fully recovered.

In the third week of November the Desert Army was about to launch an offensive, and "Force K" was detailed to make a series of diversions in the enemy's rear. They "trailed their coats" in the Central Mediterranean to no mean tune. They steamed about off Pantellaria. They sent out long extracts of verse by wireless to make the enemy think that there were large forces in the vicinity. They took some empty merchant ships to sea as if to make a landing behind the enemy's lines. But none of this led to any clash with the enemy. It was not long, however, before Agnew's ships again drew blood.

On a Sunday evening "Force K" was ordered to sea to intercept a convoy of two oil tankers escorted by destroyers which had left the Piræus bound for Benghazi. The report of this movement came from the Admiralty—proof that Whitehall is not always so out of touch with events as some critics would have us believe.

It was obviously impossible to make this just a night raid. The distance was far too great. Agnew accordingly set about deceiving the enemy, and the whole of the next forenoon "Force K" steamed steadily south-east as if the ships were merely on passage to Alexandria. Only when they were to the east of the Piræus-Benghazi line did Agnew turn north, spread his ships five miles apart in line abreast, and begin his search for the enemy. Even so, the British ships were spotted by an enemy reconnaissance aircraft, but the situation was saved by the effrontery of a telegraphist in H.M.S. *Lively*. He answered the aircraft's call as from a shore station, jammed the signal, and then acknowledged its receipt—again pretending that he was an enemy shore station. Then he ordered the aircraft to keep wireless silence and send no more signals—and was obeyed. It was just that sort of barefaced bluff that "Force K" indulged in—and got away with. No wonder it worried the enemy so much!

At 4.30 that afternoon the *Penelope* sighted the convoy in the neighbourhood of Crete. The *Aurora*, on the far wing of the sweep, did not get within range before the *Penelope* and the destroyers had set both the oil tankers on fire and left them in a sinking condition, abandoned by their escort of two destroyers who had made off at high speed as soon as they saw what they were up against. The *Aurora* was attacked by a few aircraft, but these did no damage, and "Force K" again returned in triumph to Malta.

The exploits of "Force K" were already producing a strong reaction on the part of the enemy. This took the form of sending stronger covering forces to sea whenever they were trying to run convoys across to North Africa. It was true that "Force K" had snapped up two convoys almost under the noses of a covering force of two Italian 8-inch gun cruisers, but one could not do that often. To meet the threat of the stronger Italian covering forces, therefore, the Admiralty reinforced the surface ships based on Malta by two more 6-inch gun cruisers and two more destroyers. This force was known as "Force B" and consisted of the cruisers *Neptune* and *Ajax* and two destroyers of the "K" class.

On November 30th "Force K" and "Force B" sailed in company from Malta to try to intercept an enemy force which was reported to contain at least one battleship. It was perhaps fortunate that the British ships failed to make contact with this greatly superior enemy force, but the trip was far from sterile. Agnew's force went on alone to investigate a report from an R.A.F. Wellington of an enemy supply ship off Benghazi. "Force K" duly found and sank her just after midnight. She turned out to be the *Adriatico*, laden with ammunition for Rommel's army.

Having sunk that ship close to the shore near Benghazi, Agnew hauled off in order to be well clear before daylight as heavy air attack was to be expected. On the way back to Malta, however, he received a report of an enemy tanker and destroyer near the Kirkennah Banks, off the Tunisian coast. Agnew was then operating in broad daylight in waters where enemy air attack in strength could be expected, but he was not the man to ignore the chance of inflicting more damage on the enemy's sea communications, and he led his force off to the west-north-westward at 28 knots to investigate.

Once again Agnew was on the point of abandoning the search when three fighters were sighted "orbiting" in the distance. ("Orbiting" is a term which means flying round and round in order to indicate some object below them); Agnew continued to close and soon saw the tanker and the destroyer. The latter, the

Aviso da Mosta, put up a most gallant defence, steaming up and down between the British ships and the tanker when she might have been able to make good her escape. Her resistance was futile. She was blown up by salvoes from the *Aurora* and *Penelope*, and the tanker was then shelled and set on fire. It turned out that the tanker had already been damaged by air attack.

Agnew's next job was to sail from Malta to meet a convoy coming to the island from the eastward and take over the job of escorting the fast supply ship *Breckonshire*, which carried a great deal of petrol for Malta's aircraft, on the final lap of her voyage to Malta. The *Breckonshire* and other ships were being escorted from Alexandria to the rendezvous south-east of Malta by the cruisers *Naiad* and *Euryalus* and ten destroyers under the command of Rear-Admiral Vian.

Agnew met the convoy at 8 a.m. on December 16th, and it continued on its voyage escorted by both Agnew's and Vian's ships. All the forenoon there were sporadic air attacks, but they did no harm. In the afternoon the Luftwaffe redoubled their efforts, and there were a series of concentrated high level bombing, dive bombing and torpedo bombing attacks, but the defence put up proved too much for them and the only casualties were among the aircraft. Then, just as dusk was falling, ships were reported to the northward. They proved to be two battleships, three cruisers and about fourteen destroyers. By all the rules of warfare the convoy and its escort of four small cruisers and a dozen destroyers should have been annihilated, but the Italians were reluctant to press their advantage and obviously determined not to risk night action. They fired a few shells at long range and then made off, just as Rear-Admiral Vian, having ordered Agnew to screen the convoy, hauled out with his two cruisers and most of the destroyers to attack the enemy. No further contact was made with that powerful section of the Italian fleet and, after surviving further air attack next morning, Agnew brought the *Breckonshire* and her consorts in triumph to Malta.

Triumph, however, was short lived. Within a few hours "Force K" again put to sea, this time to be met by tragedy. On this occasion "Force K" consisted of the cruisers *Neptune*, *Aurora* and *Penelope* with the destroyers *Lance*, *Lively*, *Kandahar* and *Havock*, and was under the command of Captain Rory O'Connor in the *Neptune*, who was senior to Agnew.

The force steamed fast to the southward in pursuit of a convoy

escorted by cruisers and destroyers which had been reported off
Tripoli. It seemed that the enemy was trying to slip an important
convoy through, knowing that "Force K" had been preoccupied
with the Malta convoy to the south-eastward.

The weather was bad, with a sea which made the cruisers uncomfortable and the destroyers much more so. All went well,
however, until the force was about fifteen or twenty miles off
Tripoli. Then suddenly there was an explosion in the *Neptune*,
ahead. Almost immediately the *Aurora* was shaken by an explosion.
Then there was a third explosion from the *Penelope*. The force had
run into a minefield. The *Neptune* drifted helpless and a moment or
two later she hit another mine. The *Aurora*, listing heavily and down
by the bow, turned 180 degrees to get out of the field. The *Penelope's*
mine had exploded in her paravane and she was only very slightly
damaged. It was already obvious that the *Neptune* was virtually a
total loss. The destroyer *Kandahar* went into the minefield to take
off survivors, but before she could reach the *Neptune* she also struck
a mine and was crippled.

It was a terrible situation for Agnew, aggravated by the fact
that Rory O'Connor of the *Neptune* was one of his greatest friends.
Yet to allow any other ship to enter the minefield in the hope of
being able to save life would have meant the almost certain loss
of yet another ship and her company. Destroyers asked permission
to try and take survivors off the *Neptune* and *Kandahar*, but Agnew
had to harden his heart and refuse. Soon afterwards the *Neptune*
struck another mine and slowly turned over and sank. It was later
established that there was only one survivor from her gallant
company. Agnew had no alternative but to set course for Malta.
To be caught with a damaged ship in those waters in daylight would
have been suicidal. The destroyer *Jaguar* was sent to the scene of
the disaster and found that the crippled *Kandahar* had providentially
drifted clear of the minefield. She was able to save many of her
crew before sinking the wreck and making off.

The *Aurora* was placed in dry dock in Malta on December 22nd,
1941. Within a matter of days the great Luftwaffe "blitz" on Malta
began. Despite frequent interruptions due to air-raids the repairs
to the *Aurora's* bottom went ahead, while all the crew not employed
on board lent a hand anywhere and everywhere in the defence of
Malta. So it went on until March, when the Luftwaffe redoubled
its efforts following Rear-Admiral Vian's epic action of fighting a

convoy through to Malta despite continued attempts at interference by the Italian battle fleet and heavy cruisers and the Luftwaffe. By that time the repairs to the *Aurora's* bottom were all but complete, but all thought of repairs had to be abandoned, for two 500-pound bombs hit the inside of the dock in which the *Aurora* was lying. The damage to the ship was not severe, but the dock gate was damaged and the dock began to flood. Nothing could be done about it as the pumping machinery had been wrecked. The only thing that could be done was for divers to try to plug the remaining rivet holes in the ship's bottom, as well as the many splinter-holes made by the bombs. The *Penelope* was in dock and in no condition to put to sea at that time, but Agnew was convinced that to remain would only mean the almost certain loss of the *Aurora*, and there was nothing to be achieved by her retention at Malta.

Apart from an attack by nine torpedo-bombers—which was fought off without damage—and bad weather, the voyage to Gibraltar was uneventful. So was the voyage back to the United Kingdom, where the ship spent the next three months refitting, and Agnew and his crew were able to get a little badly needed rest and relaxation.

When the *Aurora* was again fit for sea Agnew took her to Freetown, where she was engaged on convoy escort duties and on carrying out a whole series of bombardment practices in secret. In the midst of this work Agnew paid another visit to the Mediterranean. This time the *Aurora* had been detailed to form part of the escort for the aircraft carrier *Furious* on one of her "club runs"—taking fighter aircraft of the R.A.F. to the Central Mediterranean and flying them off to land at Malta.

It was not long after this that the reason for those bombardment practices at Freetown became clear. The *Aurora* was detailed to be part of the naval forces to take part in the Oran part of what was known as "Operation Torch"—which was the code name for the Allied invasion of French North Africa.

While the cutters *Walney* and *Hartland* made their heroic dash at the boom at Oran under a murderous fire, the *Aurora* opened fire repeatedly at French batteries and searchlight positions. Agnew's main task, however, was to patrol off Mers-el-Kebir to prevent any French destroyers from making a sortie and interfering with our shipping.

At dawn a French destroyer of the *Aigle* class emerged from

Mers-el-Kebir. She was at once engaged by the *Aurora* and was rapidly put out of action and set on fire. Agnew then ceased fire, nor did he open fire again when a second French destroyer emerged from the harbour and approached the burning wreck of the first, which was then on the point of sinking. He considered that this destroyer was about to take off survivors from the first, and this she did. Having done so, however, she turned and fired three torpedoes at the *Aurora*. While Agnew turned away to avoid the torpedoes he had no alternative but to open fire on this destroyer despite the fact that she had a large number of helpless survivors on board. In a matter of minutes the *Aurora* had set fire to this ship and driven her ashore.

For the rest, Agnew's activities in "Operation Torch" were confined to standing by to bombard as required by the military authorities ashore. In fact this entailed the firing of only ten rounds before the French surrendered and fighting ceased. Yet there was plenty of need to keep a sharp lookout, for in twenty-four hours the *Aurora* had no less than fifteen torpedoes fired at her from U-boats.

When the situation at Oran was well in hand, Agnew took the *Aurora* back to Gibraltar, and his next job was to take Admiral Sir Andrew Cunningham, the Commander-in-Chief, on a visit to Oran and Algiers. After taking Sir Andrew Cunningham back to Gibraltar, Agnew returned to Algiers, where the *Aurora* hoisted the flag of Rear-Admiral Cecil Harcourt as flagship of the Twelfth Cruiser Squadron. This squadron, with two destroyers, was known as "Force Q" and was our advanced striking force in the Western Mediterranean. It was based on Bone, which was made unpleasant and unhealthy by continual enemy air attacks, and its task was to harry the enemy's sea communications in the Sardinian and Sicilian channels.

It was not long before "Force Q" was in action. It left Bone on the evening of December 1st and swept to the eastward at 27 knots in search of an enemy convoy which had been reported. It was a night of rain and low visibility, and during the approach it was realised that two E-boats were shadowing, but the speed of the force was too great to allow them to reach an attacking position in that weather. Having reached the convoy route "Force Q" turned to the northward and reduced speed soon afterwards to 20 knots.

At ten minutes past midnight ships were sighted ahead, and a moment or two later Agnew opened fire on a destroyer at a range of 1800 yards. The *Aurora's* first broadside hit, and the destroyer rolled over and sank. Meanwhile the other ships of the force had opened fire on various targets which appeared. There was a confused action, during which Agnew's *Aurora* again distinguished herself by her devastatingly accurate fire. Among other exploits, she put seven successive broadsides into a 7000-ton troopship packed with luckless German troops. In all, three enemy destroyers and four supply ships, at least two of which were troopships, were sunk or left burning hulks beyond hope of salvage.

It had been a highly successful action, and one which must have done a great deal towards relieving the pressure on our hard-pressed troops fighting their way along the Algerian coast towards Tunisia.

For the next three months "Force Q" operated in those waters, but did not have any luck. In order that the crews should have a little rest the force was divided into two, one half going to Algiers to rest while the other half was based on the much-bombed port of Bone.

On March 12th Agnew in the *Aurora* led the cruiser *Sirius* and the destroyers *Lightning* and *Loyal* to sea in quest of a convoy which had been reported off Sicily. The enemy were expecting the British force to put to sea, and had laid a trap for it. The first thing that happened was a determined torpedo-bombing attack by two waves of aircraft, but none of the torpedoes took effect. Then, soon after 10 p.m., E-boats put in an appearance, and soon afterwards the destroyer *Lightning* was hit by a torpedo and disabled. The *Loyal* was detailed to stand by her, while the cruisers went on in search of the convoy. The cruisers were on two more occasions engaged by E-boats, but these were driven off each time by accurate gunfire. Finally Agnew gave it up and turned to see how the *Lightning* was faring. He found that she had been hit by another torpedo and had sunk, but that most of her crew had been picked up by the *Loyal*. He headed back for Bone. It had not been a good night.

Early in May, 1943, there was a re-shuffle among the senior officers in the Mediterranean. This was necessitated by the sudden illness of Vice-Admiral S. S. Bonham Carter, who was commanding at Malta. Rear-Admiral A. J. Power, who was commanding a cruiser squadron in the Eastern Mediterranean took over the command at Malta, being relieved in his cruiser squadron by Rear-Admiral Harcourt. Sir Andrew Cunningham asked, and received, permission from the Admiralty to give the command of the Twelfth Cruiser Squadron, thus left vacant, to Bill Agnew. So Agnew became Commodore commanding the Twelfth Cruiser Squadron, with his Broad Pendant flying in H.M.S. *Aurora*.

One June 7th Admiral Sir Andrew Cunningham, the Commander-in-Chief of the Allied Naval Forces in the Western Mediterranean, and General Dwight Eisenhower, Supreme Commander of the Allied Forces in the Mediterranean Theatre of War, embarked in H.M.S. *Aurora* at Bone. The *Aurora* sailed at once and turned eastwards along the old familiar "tramlines" to the Sicilian Channel. Off Bizerta at dawn she was joined by the destroyer *Troubridge* and shaped course for Pantellaria, the strongly fortified enemy island in the Central Mediterranean. Off Pantellaria the *Aurora* joined the main force, consisting of the cruisers *Newfoundland*, *Orion*, *Penelope* and *Euryalus* under the command of Rear-Admiral Harcourt. From the bridge of the *Aurora* General Eisenhower and Admiral Cunningham witnessed the attack on the island, first by dive bombers, then by naval bombardment in which the *Aurora* took part, and finally by a heavy bombing attack by a large number of Flying Fortresses. Then Agnew took his distinguished visitors back to Bizerta.

The following morning the *Aurora* left again, this time to take part in the final assault on Pantellaria. As it turned out the *Aurora* had nothing to do. So effective had been the "softening up" process that white flags of surrender were run up almost as soon as the assault troops reached the beaches.

Agnew then took the *Aurora* to the island of Lampedusa to carry out a bombardment of its northern coast. The chief target was a fort and battery in the vicinity of the lighthouse, which formed a very convenient aiming mark until a shell from the *Aurora's* second broadside knocked the top off it! Next day Lampedusa duly surrendered, and Agnew took his ship back to Algiers.

While the *Aurora* was lying at Algiers the King passed through the port on his way to visit the First and Eighth Armies, and he inspected the companies of all ships in the port. Little did Agnew or his men then realise that they were to be singled out in the very near future for the greatest honour which can fall upon any of H.M. ships.

On June 17th Agnew took the *Aurora* to sea from Algiers. Her destination was Tripoli, where she arrived on the 19th. There the King came on board in the destroyer *Eskimo*, and the *Aurora* sailed at once for Malta with an escort of destroyers. It was not only an honour; it was a tremendous responsibility for Agnew. The Central Mediterranean had been to a great extent cleared of the enemy, but Sicily and southern Italy were still in enemy hands, and harboured large Luftwaffe squadrons as well as E-boats, U-boats, and the still powerful Italian battlefleet. Moreover, the Sicilian coast is only some sixty-five miles from Malta.

It was an uneventful trip and the Sunday of June 20th dawned bright and clear. That morning the *Aurora* steamed proudly into the Grand Harbour at Malta between the bomb scarred battlements and cities. At her foremast-head fluttered the Royal Standard. The King stood on a platform in front of the bridge where he was in full view of the cheering multitudes which crowded every point of vantage on both sides of the harbour. Below him the white-clad crew of the *Aurora* "manned ship," standing rigidly at attention but conscious that they were playing a part in one of the most moving scenes in history. The King-Emperor had come, in war-time and through peril and discomfort, to visit in person an outpost of his Empire which had stood firm when all seemed lost and to do honour to a people who had displayed courage, fortitude and faith.

That night, after an arduous day ashore, the King re-embarked in the *Aurora*, which sailed at 10 p.m. for Tripoli. There the King disembarked, and the *Aurora* went back to Algiers. For this service the King made Agnew a Commander of the Royal Victorian Order.

Agnew's next task was concerned with the invasion of Sicily. In this operation his first responsibility was to take a slow convoy from French North Africa to the assembly point well to the south of Malta. After clearing Bone, Agnew told his ship's company that they had embarked upon one of the greatest operations so far carried out, and read out to them Admiral Sir Andrew Cunningham's stirring message to all ships.

The task of taking a slow convoy through those well-known waters should have proved easy. It would have been, had not the visibility been bad from the navigational point of view and had not the very slowness of the convoy invited errors which could never have occurred in the fast sweeps of the cruisers and destroyers. As it was, the Commodore of the convoy asked Agnew for his position when still to the north-west of Cape Bon. Agnew gave it, although he was far from satisfied, since all he had to reckon on was a somewhat unreliable position which had been obtained by wireless bearings a considerable time before. Moreover, the convoy had been ahead of time and had adopted a very wide zigzag in order to waste time—a perfectly sound manœuvre for that purpose, but one which would automatically increase any navigational errors. Agnew was far from happy. He knew that the convoy was in a comparatively narrow channel between two minefields and he was far from confident about his position. At last he obtained further wireless bearings. His suspicions were confirmed. They were well to the southward of the estimated positions. One wing of the convoy was already on the edge of the minefield. He signalled to the Commodore of the convoy to make an emergency turn to port. But signals take time to reach every ship in a convoy, and while he waited Agnew had agonising recollections of the tragedy of that minefield off Tripoli. As it was, the convoy turned and no ship hit a mine, but as if to underline the danger, one of its starboard wing ships exploded a mine in its paravane as it turned.

Having taken the convoy to the assembly point, Agnew hurried to Malta to refuel and then joined "Force H," whose duty it was to support the landings by naval bombardment and to guard against interference by units of the Italian Fleet coming either from Taranto or southwards through the Straits of Messina.

As a preliminary to the landings the *Aurora* and *Penelope*—together again after a long parting—carried out spirited and accurate bombardments of Taormina and Catania, both of which were strongly defended by the enemy. In the next few days there was little excitement but much patrolling, interspersed with occasional bombardments to give support to our ground forces, now firmly established in Sicily. Then Agnew took the *Aurora* and *Penelope* to Malta to refuel, and followed this by a series of bombardments of the enemy's communications in southern Italy. It was upon the roads and railways of Calabria that the enemy relied for the reinforcement and supply of his hard-pressed troops in Sicily, and it was against these, running along the south coast of Calabria, that the two cruisers concentrated with devastating effect, meeting only sporadic and ineffective resistance from shore batteries and aircraft.

This went on until Sicily was finally conquered and the Allies had secured a firm footing on the mainland of Italy. Then on August 9th, Agnew led a force of three other cruisers and four destroyers into the Tyrrhenian Sea and right up to the southern bastion of the Bay of Naples. The object was to bombard the ship-yards at Castellamare, at the southern side of the Bay of Naples. It would have been foolhardy to attempt this from the Bay of Naples side, guarded on the south as it is by the fortified peninsula upon which Castellamare stands and by the off-lying island of Capri which was also heavily fortified. Agnew therefore determined to carry out the bombardment from the southern side of the peninsula, lobbing the shells over the hills into Castellamare. Those hills are 3000 feet high, so the ships had to fire at extreme range in order that the shells should clear the hilltops and fall into Castellamare dockyard. Even then the shells only cleared the tops of the hills by a few feet. It was daring, impudent and unorthodox, but it was certainly effective, and it is very doubtful if the Italians had any idea where the shells were coming from.

Agnew carried out other bombardments of the Italian main-land, and then he was detailed to take an airborne division to Taranto to capture that port. The force set out from Bizerta on September 8th laden with troops and steamed east at high speed. Fortunately the weather was good, for the ships were crowded almost past endurance with troops and equipment. There was considerable risk, for the waters near Taranto had not, of course, been swept clear of mines, and there was no knowing whether heavy Italian ships might not engage the force, despite the fact that the official armistice with Italy had been signed on the night the force left Bizerta.

As it turned out, the Italian fleet steamed out to surrender as Agnew's force approached the harbour, and the landing was entirely successful.

Agnew did another trip from Bizerta to Taranto in order to reinforce our troops there, and then went north to the Salerno beachhead. Off that hotly contested beachhead the *Aurora* and her consorts bombarded day and night in support of our troops through-out the critical ten days. The ships engaged batteries, troops, tanks —anything and everything that provided a reasonable target the destruction of which would be likely to ease the pressure on the Allied troops. On one occasion the *Aurora* knocked out seven German armoured fighting vehicles with nine rounds—and earned a signal of appreciation from General Mark Clark. Then, on September 23rd, Agnew's Squadron—the *Aurora, Penelope, Sirius*—were detailed to lay the barrage preparatory to the army's big push. Each ship fired for forty minutes as fast as she could, smashed the German positions, and set woods and everything inflammable on fire. Throughout that day the ships fired on German troops and transports retreating along the Naples road. By evening the battle was won and the ships had played a big part in support of the army.

From Salerno, Agnew returned to Malta, only to sail east on October 4th for further action. It was on this voyage that he had his third experience of collision. It was due to another ship "cutting a corner" in anxiety to save time, and it did not have serious consequences, although it delayed the *Aurora* in Alexandria for a few days.

The Twelfth Cruiser Squadron had been sent to the Eastern Mediterranean to ease the strain on the cruisers there, who, with destroyers, had to make a dash into the Aegean each night to supply and reinforce the troops which we were striving to maintain on the Dodecanese island of Leros.

Originally we had landed on Cos and Leros—the former having an airfield—and had hoped that the Italians would immure the numerically inferior German garrison of Rhodes and so provide us also with that important air base. Things had gone wrong. The Italians on Rhodes had proved unreliable and the Germans had re-invaded and captured Cos. Moreover, large forces of the Luftwaffe had obviously been sent to the Aegean to deal with the situation.

Robbed of air support by the lack of the airfields on Cos and Rhodes, the succouring of our luckless garrison on Leros proved very expensive, and was in the end proved to be all to no purpose. The R.A.F. Beaufighters did their best at long range, but it was far from being enough to deter the Luftwaffe. Early in the proceedings the cruisers *Penelope* and *Carlisle* were hit and damaged, and several destroyers were either sunk or damaged. Then the *Sirius* was hit. The *Aurora* was near-missed in the same attack but escaped damage. Then, on October 27th, the *Aurora* was attacked by a formation of thirteen Stukas accompanied by Messerschmitt fighters, which held off our Beaufighters. The *Aurora* was soaked in spray from near misses as she zigzagged at high speed. Then a bomb hit. It landed on the anti-aircraft gun-deck and killed or wounded all the 4-inch gun crews and put the guns out of action, but mercifully it did not penetrate, so the ship could still steam fast. As they were tending the wounded another wave of aircraft came in, but they apparently thought that the *Aurora* was already done for, since they left her alone and attacked the destroyers. It was fortunate that they did so, for the *Aurora* had practically no anti-aircraft armament left in action.

Agnew took his damaged ship to Alexandria, and there he left her. During the phenomenally eventful commission with him in command, the *Aurora* had steamed over 110,000 miles and fired nearly 4500 6-inch shells in action. She had played her part in sinking at least forty enemy ships and carried out some forty bombardments of enemy territory.

Bill Agnew came home. He was a tired man. He says himself that when he joined the *Aurora* he was mad keen to get to grips with the enemy, but by the time he left her he felt himself tempted to hang back a little. "When that happens," he says, "it is time to go on the beach for a bit." After some richly earned leave Agnew took over command of the Navy's gunnery school at Whale Island, where he had learnt much that he had put to such excellent effect, and where he is now teaching others that "hair-trigger readiness" and cool attention to detail are the twin passports to victory at sea.

SIR BRUCE AUSTIN FRASER

G.C.B., K.B.E.

Admiral in His Majesty's Fleet

MOST MEN who have been intimately concerned with the development or production of weapons of war have little to do with the finished articles beyond perhaps witnessing "set-piece" demonstrations and receiving subsequent complaints from those called upon to use them. Few indeed are those who, having given years of their lives to the production of a weapon, are fortunate enough to be in high command when that weapon proves itself in actual combat against the enemy.

Admiral Sir Bruce Fraser is one of those fortunate few.

Bruce Fraser is a gunnery expert. He qualified in gunnery at the gunnery school at Whale Island, Portsmouth, as a lieutenant in 1911-12, and showed such promise in the science of naval gunnery, which was then growing and expanding very rapidly, that he was chosen to go from Whale Island to the Royal Naval College at Greenwich for an advanced course in gunnery. Then he was appointed to the Junior Staff at Whale Island, and later, after two years at sea, he returned again to Whale Island as an officer of the Senior Staff of that establishment. Six years later, after the last war, he was appointed as Gunnery Commander of the Royal Navy's premier gunnery school and experimental station.

Guns, gun-mountings, and gunfire control were his passions, and through most of his career he alternated periods of shore service in which he was engaged in developing material for the improvement of naval gunnery with periods at sea in appointments which enabled him to see the gear in operation during battle practices and form ideas for further improvements.

Perhaps his greatest work in the development of the material side of naval gunnery was done in the years 1933 to 1935, when he was serving as Director of Naval Ordnance at the Admiralty.

The new battleships of the *King George V* class had not then been laid down. It was not until March 4th, 1935, that the British Government produced its first White Paper on Defence. Up to that

Admiral Sir Bruce Fraser

Crown Copyright Reserved

time the people of Great Britain had been lulled into an entirely fictitious sense of security—a fool's paradise which was actively encouraged by the political leaders of the day. Hard, incontrovertible facts about Germany's secret rearmament were treated in the House of Commons as figments of Mr. Winston Churchill's vivid imagination. No Minister of the Crown had then declared that British disarmament had been carried "to the edge of risk." It was before the General Election after which Mr. Stanley Baldwin the Prime Minister made the astonishing admission that he could think of nothing "which would have made the loss of the election from my point of view more certain" than suggesting before the Election that the time for setting the defences in order was already long overdue.

Fortunately for Britain, and for the whole free world, however, there were in the Admiralty officers whose eyes were wide open to the future, who saw that replacements for our obsolete capital ships could not be much longer delayed, even by political procrastination, and who worked on undismayed by the apparently endless postponements of their hopes.

Among these officers was Bruce Fraser, then a captain. The tentative designs of the replacement battleships had already been drawn up, and as D.N.O., Fraser had a great deal to do with developing the design of their armament. The main armament of these ships was to combine weight of metal with high rate of fire, while the weight given to the armament was strictly limited by the other indispensable qualifications of the ships such as protection, speed, sea-keeping endurance, and all the latest developments in every realm of naval warfare, for the British Government still considered itself bound not to exceed the tonnage limit of 35,000 tons laid down by the Washington Naval Treaty twelve years before.

The outcome of inevitable compromise was the decision to adopt the new 14-inch gun, and to mount ten of these, eight in two quadruple turrets fore and aft and the other two in a twin turret superimposed just abaft the forward quadruple turret. Here was revolutionary design on two counts. The Royal Navy had never had 14-inch guns, although the old 13.5-inch mounted in the battleships which were new at the beginning of the last war and had since been scrapped had been considered one of the most successful big naval guns ever made. Nor had the British Navy ever before had a ship with four-gun turrets. These quadruple turrets, the mounting of the guns, and their methods of loading and of control, produced all manner of complications and problems. Fraser grappled with them, bringing to them long and wide experience, a very keen technical brain, and a single-minded determination to overcome them.

Overcome them he did. Guns and mountings proved satisfactory under test, as they did when H.M.S. *King George V*, the first and name ship of the class, underwent her trials. The first time one of these ships came into action against the enemy, however, there was tragedy. That was early on the morning of May 24th, 1941, when H.M.S. *Hood* and H.M.S. *Prince of Wales* intercepted the *Bismarck* south-west of Iceland. H.M.S. *Hood*, a 15-inch gun battle cruiser of last-war design, was hit and blew up with the loss of all but three of her company. The *Prince of Wales*, one of the new 14-inch gun battleships, was hit and damaged. The *Prince of Wales* was a new ship, barely out of dockyard hands and certainly not "worked up" to the Home Fleet standard of efficiency, so that the crew were to a great extent handling weapons with which they were not yet fully familiar. Under such conditions failures and breakdowns are to be expected, and the *Prince of Wales* certainly experienced trouble with her armament apart from the fact that one of her main turrets was jammed by a shell splinter.

On Boxing Day, 1943, however, the 14-inch guns and mountings of a ship of this class put up a very different performance. They were the guns and mountings of H.M.S. *Duke of York*, flagship of the Home Fleet and wearing the flag of Admiral Sir Bruce Fraser. The Commander-in-Chief watched with considerable satisfaction the excellent shooting of the *Duke of York* while battering the German battle-cruiser *Scharnhorst* with the guns and mountings on the design and development of which he had worked so hard six years before.

Every since June 28th, 1942, when Bruce Fraser had hoisted his flag in H.M.S. *Anson* as Vice-Admiral and Second-in-Command of the Home Fleet, he had been very conscious of the fact that all the movements of the Home Fleet, and even the strategy of the sea war in distant theatres of war, were circumscribed by the fact that the Germans kept a very powerful naval force in the fiords of northern Norway, well within the Arctic Circle. There was the 45,000-ton battleship *Tirpitz*, sister ship of the *Bismarck* and probably the most formidable warship afloat. There was the fast 26,000-ton battle-cruiser *Scharnhorst* with her nine 11-inch guns—a ship, which, theoretically at least, would be more than a match for any vessel which could catch her, and could show a clean pair of heels to any ship carrying heavier metal. There were, at one time or another, at least one of the "pocket battleships" and at least two of the heavy 8-inch gun cruisers of the *Hipper* class, and several destroyers of the powerful *Maas* class or *Narvik* classes. It was certainly a force to be reckoned with, and there were persistent rumours that it was to be joined by the new German aircraft-carrier *Graf Zeppelin* as soon as that ship had completed her trials in the Baltic.

Under any circumstances the presence of the strong German naval force in northern Norway would have had a profound effect upon the composition and disposition of the British Home Fleet, for a break out by one or more of the fast and powerful German ships into the Atlantic might well lead to such damage on the ocean trade routes before they could be rounded up that the war might be considerably lengthened.

That was the ordinary and continuous hazard, which demanded a naval strategy somewhat similar to that of the last war, but there was a more immediate danger, although it might not have so far-reaching an effect upon the course of the war. Enormous convoys of merchant ships carrying the products of the arms factories of Great Britain and the United States had to be escorted at frequent intervals to the North Russian ports of Murmansk and Archangel. It was no unusual thing for these convoys to consist of fifty or sixty ships—half a million tons of shipping was at stake each time, to say nothing of the valuable cargoes carried and the lives of the men who manned the ships.

Up to the end of 1942 the Germans had relied chiefly upon massed U-boats and strong forces of dive-bombers and torpedo-carrying aircraft based in northern Norway to inflict loss upon this traffic. But towards the end of that year the German aircraft disappeared from the Arctic, apart from a few reconnaissance aircraft. Perhaps this was because of the decisive defeat which they suffered when Rear-Admiral Burnett took through the convoy of September 1942, to North Russia and returned almost unmolested with a homeward-bound convoy—that was the first time escort aircraft-carriers with Sea-Hurricane fighters were used on a North Russian convoy. Perhaps it was because the Luftwaffe urgently required strong reinforcements in the Mediterranean following the Allied landings in French North Africa on November 8th of that year. Probably it was a combination of both courses.

In any event, the German High Command apparently decided to leave the task of interference with the North Russian convoys to a combination of surface ships and U-boats, backed by some long-range reconnaissance aircraft.

The geographical factors were heavily in favour of a fast surface force based in the northern Norwegian fiords and intent upon raiding the convoys destined for Murmansk or the White Sea. In the normal course of events the edge of the Arctic ice pack runs almost due south from Spitzbergen to Bear Island and thence south-eastward almost parallel to the coast between the North Cape and the entrance to the White Sea. Bear Island is only about 220 miles from the North Cape, so that the Russian convoys, however, widely dispersed their routes in the open ocean, had to converge into a channel 220 miles wide and about 500 miles long, with the enemy bases along its southern shore. When one considers that the speed of even a fast convoy would be less than half that of any surface raiders likely to be employed ; the fact of the approach of an east-bound convoy was more than likely to be reported either by a U-boat or by long-range reconnaissance aircraft; and the almost perpetual darkness of the winter months in those latitudes, the full strategical advantage to the enemy can be realised. An enemy raiding force would also have certain very important tactical advantages. Its margin of speed over the convoy would enable it to manœuvre in order to make its attack or attacks from any direction which might seem to offer the best prospects of success; the escorting forces and covering forces must needs be embarrassed by the convoy, have to conserve fuel, and face the fact that a badly damaged ship would have little chance of making the long voyage home to a dockyard port for repair.

That was the degree of the threat exerted by the presence in the northern Norwegian fiords of the fast and powerful German ships —a threat with which Bruce Fraser was to be preoccupied during the whole of his time as Second-in-Command of the Home Fleet and during several months of his time as Commander-in-Chief.

It seems that the seriousness of the threat produced by this German "fleet in being" was very clear to the German naval command, for, with the reluctance to risk the loss of ships which is so characteristic of a predominantly military nation, the Germans only

twice brought their surface ships within striking distance of a
North Russian convoy. The first occasion was on New Year's Day,
1942, when they were fought off by the escort under the command
of Captain Sherbrooke in H.M.S. *Onslow*, who was badly wounded,
and awarded the Victoria Cross for his conduct of the action. The
second time was on Boxing Day, 1943.

Time after time the Home Fleet put out to sea and remained to
the south-westward of North Russian convoys as they entered the
Bear Island-North Cape channel in the hope of being able to steam
in between the German ships and their bases if they should make
for the convoy, and thus try to bring them to decisive action. It
would be impossible to compute the weary man-hours expended on
all those fruitless sweeps. Small wonder that plans were laid for
the destruction of the German ships in their lairs. The plans for
attacking the German ships in the Norwegian fiords with midget
submarines were already well advanced by the time Bruce Fraser
hoisted his flag in H.M.S. *Duke of York* as Commander-in-Chief of
the Home Fleet on May 8th, 1943, but as Second-in-Command of
that fleet he had much to do with their inception.

It is interesting to note that the British midget submarines used
in North Norway—"*X* craft," they were called—were evolved by a
British submarine officer who, in the last war, was in disgrace for a
time because he left his ordered patrol position and penetrated the
enemy's defences in his small but ordinary *H* class submarine in
much the same way as the midget submarines of twenty-seven years
later.

The officer was Captain C. H. Varley, D.S.C., R.N. As a lieutenant
in command of submarine *H5*, Varley had been patrolling in his
allotted billet off Terschelling for days when, on July 11th, 1916, he
decided that his patrol position was futile and that he might as well
try his luck elsewhere. It was, of course, direct disobedience of
orders but, after all, Nelson had won a victory by disobeying futile
orders. At 2 a.m. next morning *H5* was off Borkum, where Varley
had some trouble with his periscope and a German destroyer, but
he continued to the eastward. By 11 a.m. on July 13th he was in
sight of the Wangeroog and Rote Island lights, where he dived and
went on submerged towards the Aussen Jade Lightship. These were
the three "lamp posts" at the very entrance to the principal harbour
of the German fleet in the Jade River. Next night a whole flotilla
of German destroyers appeared, but he was robbed of a successful

attack by his defective periscope. Nevertheless, he stayed there, in shallow water in the very entrance to the German main base. He was rewarded. At 10 a.m. he sighted a U-boat, attacked, and sank her. That was the end of *U51*. Varley was in a very tight place, but after some hair-raising experiences he brought *H5* safely back to Harwich. He was "scrubbed" for disobeying orders and leaving his patrol position, and it was not until a year later that the Admiralty relented and he was awarded the D.S.C. which he had so richly earned.

On September 22nd, 1943, the midget submarine attack took place. There was, of course, a strong force of the Home Fleet under Admiral Fraser in the offing in case the ferrets should bolt the rabbits from their holes.

The Home Fleet ships got no fun out of it, but the attack was brilliantly carried out by the midget submarines, which had to negotiate over thirty miles of heavily defended fiord before reaching their quarry. As a result of this attack the great German battleship *Tirpitz* suffered serious underwater damage and was effectively put out of action for several months.

The Commander-in-Chief, Home Fleet, heaved a sigh of relief. The most dangerous of the German ships had been disposed of, for the time being at least, but there still remained the *Scharnhorst*. It had been hoped that the midget submarine attack would deal with the *Scharnhorst* as well as the *Tirpitz*, but when the "X craft" got to the head of the Alten Fiord they found only the *Tirpitz*. As luck would have it the *Scharnhorst* had been at sea doing gunnery exercises the day before, and on completion of these exercises she had put into another fiord. It was rumoured at the time that the German Admiral had found it expedient to separate the two ships in order to prevent the spread of disaffection among their crews at their long inaction in the bleak Arctic. This has never been confirmed.

Be that as it may, the *Scharnhorst* remained the major threat to our North Russian convoys, and, in somewhat lesser degree, to our vital North Atlantic trade routes. In no circumstances could this latter threat be ignored. Again and again Admiral Fraser took his fleet in support of North Russian convoys in the hope of catching the *Scharnhorst*, but the German battle-cruiser preferred to exercise her threat rather than her strength—until the last week of December, 1943.

Having been so shy for so long, it seems curious that the *Scharn-*

horst should have chosen that particular convoy to attempt to raid. It may well be that the decision of the German Admiral Bey to sally forth was influenced by intelligence of another movement of Admiral Sir Bruce Fraser in his flagship H.M.S. *Duke of York*. On December 17th, 1943, the *Duke of York*, wearing the flag of Admiral Sir Bruce Fraser, steamed, in the grey half-light of an Arctic morning, between snow-clad hills to an anchorage in the Kola Inlet, the Soviet Navy's Arctic base. It was the first time that a British battleship, let alone the fleet flagship with the Commander-in-Chief on board, had visited a Soviet Russian harbour.

It was a good-will visit, and soon after the *Duke of York's* anchor had thundered down, Vice-Admiral Golovko, Commander-in-Chief of the Soviet Northern Fleet, accompanied by his liaison officer Captain Rigerman, was welcomed at the head of the *Duke of York's* gangway by Sir Bruce Fraser while the Royal Marine guard of honour stood at the "present" and the band played the Soviet National Anthem.

That day the Russian Admiral was shown all over the British flagship, and in the evening a Russian concert party, went on board and played balalaikas and accordions and sang national songs in the *Duke of York's* wardroom. Next morning Admiral Fraser was taken by General Andneyev to visit a Russian airfield and see some of the Russian dive-bombers and torpedo-bombers and their air crews. Afterwards he was taken back to the naval base in a Soviet submarine hunting craft and inspected a Soviet destroyer, on board which he was met by a guard of honour while the Russian naval band played "God Save the King." A tour of the naval establishments was followed by luncheon at the Soviet naval headquarters, at which toasts were drunk to King George VI, President Kalinin, Marshal Stalin and "the people of Great Britain and the British Navy coupled with the name of Admiral Fraser"—the latter toasts were proposed by Admiral Golovko.

After lunch Admiral Golovko took Admiral Fraser to a concert party in the Red Club, which was crowded with Russian and British officers and ratings. Meanwhile, other Russian naval officers were entertained on board the *Duke of York*.

The next morning, after an exchange of appreciative signals of goodwill, the British flagship sailed from Kola Inlet.

That is to say, the *Duke of York*, with the Commander-in-Chief Home Fleet on board, left Kola Inlet on the morning of December

19th. It is reasonable to suppose that Admiral Bey received the first reconnaissance report of the approach of a North Russian convoy on December 24th. Had he, from air reconnaissance or any other source, learnt of the visit of the British Commander-in-Chief in his flagship to Kola Inlet and the *Duke of York's* departure from there on the morning of December 19th, he would have calculated that, if she had proceeded, as was likely, at economical speed on a zigzag course, keeping well to the northward, as seemed probable, she would at that time be beginning to fuel in some British base. Had he been in possession of the knowledge of the visit to Kola Inlet and calculated thus, Bey would have concluded that he could raid the convoy without fear of interference from heavy ships, for the German air reconnaissance over the northern bases, at frequent intervals over the proceeding weeks, would have led him to believe that no other British capital ship could be at sea in support of the convoy.

Be that as it may, Admiral Bey knew on Christmas morning of the approach of the North Russian convoy to the Bear Island-North Cape channel, and that afternoon he put to sea in the *Scharnhorst*. From that moment until he came under fire of the *Duke of York's* guns late the following afternoon, he acted as if he felt no uneasiness regarding the possible presence in the area of any British heavy ship.

On the morning of Boxing Day the North Russian convoy—a very big one—was about 150 miles north of the North Cape and ploughing steadily eastward. It had, of course, a close escort of destroyers and corvettes to guard against U-boat attack, and as protection against surface raiders it was provided with a covering force of cruisers. These were the *Norfolk*, mounting eight 8-inch guns and the *Belfast* and *Sheffield*, each mounting twelve 6-inch guns. These cruisers were under the command of Vice-Admiral R. L. Burnett, whose flag flew in the *Belfast*. He probably knew more about Russian convoy work and conditions in the Arctic than any other British admiral. It had been he who had fought through to Russia the famous convoy of September, 1942, and it had been he who had come to the timely rescue of Sherbrooke's hard-pressed destroyers in December of that year.

Burnett had stationed his cruisers on the starboard bow of the convoy—that is, between the convoy and the bases from which the enemy surface forces might emerge.

It was still dark, but for once fine and with a good visibility, when Burnett's cruisers sighted the *Scharnhorst* at 9.30 on the morning of Boxing Day. The sighting was, in fact, virtually mutual. The *Scharnhorst* was coming up at high speed from the south-east so that the British cruisers were between her and the convoy.

By all the rules, the *Scharnhorst*, with her heavily armoured hull, her nine 11-inch guns, twelve 5.9-inch guns, and fourteen 4.1-inch guns, should have been able to drive her way through the cruiser screen, sinking one or more of them as she went, and then played havoc with the convoy and its close escorts. But from the very instant of sighting Burnett seized the initiative. While the convoy turned away to the northward under the orders of the Commodore, taking with it the close escort, Burnett swung his cruisers straight towards the enemy, illuminating the *Scharnhorst* with star shell and opening fire as he did so.

By adopting these tactics Vice-Admiral Burnett not only seized the initiative. Knowing that long periods of inaction in harbour are apt to result in the slowing down of the mental processes when faced with the need to take a sudden decision at sea, he gave Admiral Bey no time to think. Once the British cruisers had swung on to their south-easterly course and increased speed, they and the *Scharnhorst* were approaching each other at about 60 knots, so that they would have been practically alongside each other in a very few minutes. Moreover, Burnett was exploiting what experience had shown to be a weakness among German naval commanders—a reluctance to expose their ships to torpedo attack. This weakness had been discovered and exploited so successfully by Captain Sherbrooke on New Year's Eve, 1942, that he, with four lightly armed destroyers, had repeatedly fought off a pocket battleship and a heavy *Hipper* class cruiser accompanied by destroyers. Burnett knew that Admiral Bey would have recognised his cruisers and appreciated the fact that they had considerable torpedo armament.

Admiral Bey was faithful to his code. The *Scharnhorst*'s helm went over and she swung away. As she did so she received at least one hit from the *Norfolk*'s 8-inch guns. In a moment the German battle-cruiser had disappeared into the darkness.

Burnett re-formed his cruisers on the convoy, which turned again to the eastward, but he had much to exercise his mind. He did not think for a moment that the big German battle-cruiser was finally driven off. He was willing to bet that the enemy would try again, probably during the two and a half hours period of twilight which passes for day in those latitudes in mid-winter. The question was, from what direction would the *Scharnhorst* next try to attack? The German battle-cruiser had sufficient margin of speed over the convoy to enable her to attack from almost any direction, and Burnett could not be everywhere at once with his cruisers, while to disperse them in order to cover a greater area would be to invite defeat in detail. Everything depended upon the British cruisers being in the right place to intercept the *Scharnhorst's* next attack. The high speed of the enemy ship and the comparatively low twilight visibility would leave no margin for error.

Burnett ruled out attack from the west. He knew that the essence of German ideas of commerce raiding lay in sinking ships quickly and getting away quickly. A U-boat might follow a convoy to pick off stragglers, but a powerful surface raider would want to sink the maximum number of ships in the minimum time, particularly in winter conditions in the Arctic where two and a half hours of twilight was the only day. To do so the raider would attack from ahead and not from astern, where the speed of her attack would only be the difference between her speed and that of the convoy, so that there would be time and warning for the head of the convoy adequately to scatter.

Burnett therefore considered that the *Scharnhorst* would make her next attack either from right ahead of the convoy or from its port or starboard bow. He did not think that the raider would attack from right ahead, for from this direction the merchant ships of the convoy would present bad targets to the German gunners, a factor which would mitigate against hits during the approach and therefore increase the time taken in sinking ships. There remained the choice of the port and starboard bows. On the face of it there seemed no reason why the Germans should choose one in preference to another. Burnett had to guess. Yet his guess was not like sticking a pin into a list of runners at a race meeting in the hope of finding the winner. It was guess supported by reasoned argument. He knew that the German mind is nothing if not methodical. The *Scharnhorst* had found cruisers on the starboard bow of the convoy, therefore he would be likely to try the other bow next. There was also the probability that the Germans would not expect to find a supporting force on the north side of the convoy

—towards the edge of the ice pack. Of course, the German commander *might* reason that the British Admiral would move over to
the port bow, and therefore attack again from the starboard bow, but
that would be the second degree of cunning. The German mind
was usually too methodical for such reasoning, or too much aware
of the fact that once one started to think that way there was no end
to it but confusion. Anyway Burnett did not propose to allow
himself to get lost in a tortuous maze of argument and counter-
argument. He weighed up the situation and the probabilities as he
saw them, and he took his decision. It was not an easy decision to
take—too much depended upon it for any man's comfort—but he
took it. He led his cruisers across the bow of the convoy and
stationed them on the convoy's port bow. That is, he placed his
ships in the best possible position to intercept an attempted attack
from the north-eastward.

Burnett was right. At half an hour past noon the *Scharnhorst*
was sighted coming in towards the convoy from the north-east—
and the British cruisers were again between her and her prey.

Burnett repeated the tactics which had been so successful in the
morning. He swung his cruisers round and steamed straight at the
German battle-cruiser, opening fire and increasing to full speed as
he did so. It was impossible to tell if the *Scharnhorst* was again hit
in this action, but Burnett's threat of torpedo attack again proved
too much for Admiral Bey ; he swung the *Scharnhorst* away to the
eastward. Even as the big ship turned, however, one of her 11-inch
shells landed on the quarterdeck of H.M.S. *Norfolk*. That shell caused
casualties and damage, but mercifully it affected neither the steaming nor the fighting qualities of the ship.

This time Admiral Burnett did not re-form his cruisers on the
convoy as soon as the *Scharnhorst* turned tail. He followed her with
his three cruisers as she made off to the eastward and then hauled
round almost immediately on to a south-south-easterly course—the
course back to her hide-out in the northern fiords of Norway.

There were two reasons why Burnett did this. He knew that,
away to the south-westward between 150 and 200 miles away,
Admiral Sir Bruce Fraser in the *Duke of York* was steering an easterly
course towards the North Cape, with the cruiser *Jamaica* and four
destroyers in company. He did not, of course, know the exact
position of the Commander-in-Chief, for he was necessarily keeping
strict wireless silence, but he knew roughly where he would be and

what course he would be steering. Admiral Fraser, of course, knew
that the *Scharnhorst* had tried to raid the convoy in the morning
and had been driven off by Burnett's cruisers. He also knew of the
Scharnhorst's second attack at 12.30 p.m. and of the success of the
cruisers in again forcing her away from the convoy, for Burnett had
reported by wireless each time he was in action. These reports were,
of course, not addressed to the Commander-in-Chief. They were
addressed to the Admiralty in London in the sure knowledge that
the *Duke of York* would pick them up and that the Commander-in-
Chief would act upon them.

But Burnett also knew that, in the darkness which would be
upon them again in less than an hour, Admiral Fraser would have
little chance of intercepting the *Scharnhorst* if he had nothing more
than the action reports on which to go.

If the *Scharnhorst* was to be brought to action by the Commander-
in-Chief by skill rather than luck, Burnett would have to lead
Admiral Fraser to his quarry by shadowing the *Scharnhorst* and
reporting her position, course and speed at frequent intervals—
ostensibly to the Admiralty, of course.

Moreover, Admiral Burnett did not think that the *Scharnhorst*
would be likely to try again to attack the convoy, as it was already
getting late in the Arctic day, and it had taken the fast German ship
three hours to get into the position she had selected for her second
attempt. This view was confirmed as soon as the *Scharnhorst* shaped
course for the fiords, which she did as soon as she had disengaged.

What may be termed the second phase of the action then began.
The convoy, with its close escort, ploughed steadily on towards the
North Russian ports which were its destination. The *Scharnhorst*,
twice foiled of her prey by the determined handling of ships greatly
inferior in size, gun-power and protection, was steaming fast for
home, with the British cruisers shadowing her and reporting her
movements, which were eagerly taken in and plotted in the *Duke
of York* away to the south-westward.

It is interesting to recall that two of the three cruisers with
Vice-Admiral Burnett had played a prominent part in the hunting
down and destruction of the *Bismarck*—the only other first-class
unit of the German Navy to have risked the open sea anywhere
near the British Navy since the Norwegian campaign. H.M.S.
Norfolk had then worn the flag of Rear-Admiral Wake-Walker. The
Norfolk and her consort the *Suffolk* had shadowed the *Bismarck* for

thirty-one and three-quarter hours over a distance of nearly 1000 miles from the northern end of the Denmark Strait between Iceland and the Greenland ice pack to mid-Atlantic on the latitude of the English Channel. The *Norfolk*, moreover, was present at the sinking of the *Bismarck*, and was the only ship to be in contact with the enemy at the beginning and the end of that prolonged and widespread operation. H.M.S. *Sheffield* had been the only cruiser with Admiral Sir James Somerville's "Force H," which came up from Gibraltar. She was detached to make contact and shadow the *Birmarck* as soon as she was reported by a Catalina flying boat at 10.40 a.m. on May 26th. The *Sheffield* had duly found the *Bismarck* and shadowed her, been nearly torpedoed by our own aircraft, and had helped in guiding the *Ark Royal's* aircraft in to the attack which disabled the German ship's rudders and proved the decisive blow which led to her destruction next morning.

When Vice-Admiral Burnett saw that the *Scharnhorst* was committed to withdrawal towards the fiords, he signalled for four destroyers to leave the close escort of the convoy and join him. He knew that Admiral Sir Bruce Fraser had only four destroyers with him, and the *Scharnhorst* was showing such a turn of speed that he thought that more destroyers might be needed to stop or slow her down, although the weather was by no means perfect for high speed work by destroyers under conditions in which all spray froze as it fell and added to the topweight of the ships. He argued, too, that the close escort of the convoy could well dispense with the destroyers at this stage. There was no longer threat of attack by major surface forces and no U-boats had been detected for some time. It was unlikely, in fact, that the Germans would have U-boats operating in the same area as both British and German surface ships for fear of a costly mistake in identity through the periscope.

The shadowing by the cruisers was superlatively skilful. They kept touch and continually reported the progress of their far more powerful adversary in the Arctic gloom, and at the same time avoided being brought to action by the *Scharnhorst's* heavier metal. In truth, the German Admiral Bey made no attempt to fight off or to shake off the British cruisers, although he must have known that they were dogging him. It seems that he felt quite confident that the Commander-in-Chief of the Home Fleet was not in the vicinity with heavy British units, and that his speed was quite sufficient to take him to the shelter of the fiords without danger of the British cruisers drawing ahead in order to deliver a torpedo attack. Certainly he acted at that time like a commander with no anxieties. No doubt he had already framed, for the benefit of the German High Command and the gullible of this world a stirring account of his devastating intervention in the flow of supplies to Russia.

It must have been a very rude awakening for Bey when the *Duke of York's* wireless suddenly leapt out of the silence at 4.30 that afternoon. In point of fact it is doubtful whether the intercepted signal would have reached the German Admiral on the bridge of the *Scharnhorst* before he found himself under fire from heavy guns.

Admiral Sir Bruce Fraser had made full use of the reports from the shadowing cruisers, and had steered a course which would intersect that of the *Scharnhorst* at a point on the tumbled dark waters some thirty miles north-north-west of the North Cape. At the speeds being made good by the *Duke of York* and the *Scharnhorst* the ships should collide at that point at about 4.45 p.m.

The calculations were as sound as the reports from the cruisers. The great turrets with the design of which Fraser had had so much to do swung silently on to the bearing indicated. In a few seconds all was ready for opening fire. Then the Commander-in-Chief gave the order to break wireless silence with a signal to Vice-Admiral Burnett ordering him to illuminate the target with star shell. In an astonishingly short time, which seemed like hours to those who lived through it, the star shell guns of the *Belfast*, then about eight miles astern of the *Scharnhorst*, spoke. Another wait of seconds which seemed like years, and high above the *Scharnhorst* the star shell burst, the brilliant white flare came sailing down very slowly, supported as it was by its parachute, and as it hung in the sky it cast a great circle of rather ghostly radiance on the sea. In the centre of that circle was the *Scharnhorst*.

"Open fire." The curt order from the bridge of the *Duke of York* cut through the babel of orders and reports which would have spelt confusion to the lay mind but which told the gunnery officer of the battleship that all was well with his armament and the training of the men who manned it.

The bridge decks leapt as the big guns fired and their hot acrid blast whipped across the faces of those in exposed positions. From the funnels came a gout of smoke and scale shaken loose by the concussion—the phenomenon which has led so many Luftwaffe pilots to claim direct hits on our warships when all they have achieved has been the concussion of a near miss. But nobody on board the *Duke of York* heeded any of that, and least of all Bruce Fraser, standing on the Admiral's bridge. One of his staff officers said afterwards that he seemed quite the most detached man on board. He scarcely moved. He never spoke except to give a crisp order. He had got to grips with his enemy, and he was watching those guns and turrets he had developed in deadly action against the enemy.

He had good reason to be satisfied. At least one shell of the *Duke of York's* first salvo hit the *Scharnhorst*. But it did not do so in any vital place, and the German battle-cruiser at once sheered away to port. Suddenly confronted by heavy metal which prevented him from continuing his course direct for the Norwegian fiords, Admiral Bey at once took uncompromisingly to flight. He steered east, and called upon his engineers for every knot of speed which they could squeeze out of boilers and engines. Bey may have had some dim hope that by using his speed he might be able to out-distance his pursuers, shake them off in the Arctic darkness, and eventually double back to the shelter of the fiords, but his first reaction was simply to get away from the *Duke of York's* salvoes of 14-inch shells.

There followed a stern chase, with the *Duke of York* firing with her forward turrets in the hope of so damaging the fleeing *Scharnhorst* that her speed would be reduced and it would be possible to bring her to close action. Meanwhile, the *Scharnhorst* replied with her after guns, hoping to slow down the *Duke of York* and so make sure of escape.

This went on for nearly an hour and a half. It was gunnery at its most difficult, and although the *Scharnhorst* was seen to be again hit on several occasions, and fires broke out on board the German ship, her speed was not affected and it was very soon painfully clear that she was gaining on the British flagship, for the range was steadily increasing. The *Duke of York* was not hit, but a splinter from one of the *Scharnhorst's* 11-inch shells cut her wireless aerial. This, however, was soon made good, Lieutenant H. R. J. Bates, R.N.V.R., climbing the mast with great gallantry to effect temporary repairs. It would be difficult to overestimate the importance of Lieutenant Bates's initiative, skill and courage at that stage of the action, for it enabled Admiral Sir Bruce Fraser to continue to keep in communication with his other forces and to marshal them for the final destruction of the enemy.

Soon after 6 p.m. the *Duke of York* ceased fire. The *Scharnhorst* had succeeded in drawing ahead so far that she was out of range. When the signal reporting the fact was received in the Admiralty the deepest gloom reigned. It seemed that the *Scharnhorst* was going to get away after all. The Admiralty, of course, could not take in the Commander-in-Chief's orders to his ships, as these were given by wireless with a very limited range.

Bruce Fraser, however, remained calm and confident. Fond as he was of his guns, he was not the man to put all his eggs into one basket when other baskets were available to him. His job was to defeat and sink the enemy, and to that end he would use every weapon at his disposal.

As soon as the *Scharnhorst* had turned away to the eastward and began to show that she had a margin of speed over the *Duke of York*, Admiral Fraser had ordered his four destroyers—the British *Savage*, *Saumarez* and *Scorpion* and the Norwegian *Stord*—to proceed at their utmost speed in the weather conditions prevailing in order to gain bearing on the *Scharnhorst* and reach a position on her bow from which to deliver a torpedo attack.

The conditions were far from suitable for high-speed destroyer work. There was a swell and a fairly heavy sea running from the north-west, with a strong wind from the same direction. Wind and sea were therefore on the quarter of the destroyers as they tried to make their best possible speed to the eastward. Such conditions make destroyers yaw badly and this yawing had the inevitable effect of reducing their speed made good along their chosen course. The commanding officers of the destroyers, moreover, had to keep a close watch on the sea and do their utmost to prevent sea and spray coming on board, for this froze at once and, apart from its liability to interfere with the efficiency of weapons, it added to the top-weight of the ships, made them sluggish and unhandy, and reduced the chances of survival for any ship badly damaged. These, however, were the normal hazards of destroyer work in the Arctic in winter, and the commanding officers were familiar with them. They took every care they could, consistent with the overriding aim of drawing ahead of the fleeing *Scharnhorst*, and this they succeeded in doing.

Thus it was that very soon after the *Duke of York* had been forced to cease fire as the *Scharnhorst* was out of range of her 14-inch guns, firing broke out ahead. It was the *Scharnhorst's* reaction to the attack by the four destroyers.

Led by Commander M. D. C. Meyrick in H.M.S. *Savage*, the destroyers pressed home their attack with the utmost gallantry, oblivious at that stage to the weather as well as to the withering fire from the *Scharnhorst's* exceptionally powerful secondary armament. To be sure, the *Scharnhorst's* fire, as has happened more often than not in the case of German ships attacked at close range by smaller craft, went high, but it was none the less unpleasant for that. Beneath a veritable canopy of tracers the destroyers dashed in to a range of 2000 yards before turning with their helms hard over, firing their torpedoes as they did so, and then zigzagging away out of range.

The attack had been pressed home with such determination and to such a range that there was little chance of the German battle-cruiser being able to avoid the torpedoes. In pressing home the attack to such decisive range, Commander Meyrick was acting in accordance with training as well as instinct. Moreover, he did not know that Vice-Admiral Burnett had detached four destroyers from the convoy escort, which were coming down to the south-east as fast as they possibly could. He thought his four ships were the only destroyers in the neighbourhood, and that the whole responsibility of stopping the *Scharnhorst* therefore rested upon them.

Hit by several torpedoes—it is impossible to say how many—the *Scharnhorst* lost speed. Judging from the volume of the fire which she directed at the destroyers as they retired from the attack, her armament was not impaired, but her speed fell off abruptly and considerably. That was the most important thing, and by far the most desirable result for which the destroyers had hoped.

With the *Scharnhorst* no longer able to make her full speed, Admiral Fraser's flagship came up rapidly, and before long the *Duke of York's* guns were again in action—this time at a rapidly closing range. Almost at once hits were scored and very soon almost every salvo was hitting, battering the German battle-cruiser into impotence as the *Bismarck* had been battered into impotence by the guns of the *King George V* and the *Rodney* almost exactly two years and seven months before. Very soon it was obvious that the Germans could no longer keep the fires on board their ship under control. Flames swept most of her length, and through the shell holes in her sides could be seen the angry glare of internal fires, but even so the Germans kept up a return fire for some time with such guns as remained in action, although the sting and accuracy had gone out of the German gunfire, and no British ship was hit.

Admiral Burnett's cruisers *Belfast*, *Norfolk* and *Sheffield*, the cruiser *Jamaica* which had been with the Commander-in-Chief, the four destroyers *Musketeer*, *Matchless*, *Opportune* and *Virago* from the convoy escort—all closed in like hounds to the kill.

On the bridge of the *Duke of York* Admiral Sir Bruce Fraser, still standing silent and almost motionless and watching everything that happened, saw the danger. " Overs " from ships on one side of the German battle-cruiser might hit a British ship on the other side of the German. Worse, a torpedo might miss or run under the *Scharnhorst* and find a British bottom. It was time the hounds were called off.

" Clear the area of the target, except for those ships with torpedoes and one destroyer with searchlight." The terse order was obeyed immediately. The hounds drew off, realising that their Commander-in-Chief was about to order the final act. Then, as a destroyer's searchlight illuminated the outline of the *Scharnhorst*, which had become difficult to distinguish because of the glare of the fires in the night, H.M.S. *Jamaica* closed in and fired torpedoes. They hit and exploded with a terrific roar, sending flames and debris from the burning ship high into the smoke which billowed over her. Then the smoke dispersed for a moment and the *Scharnhorst* could be seen lying on her port beam, with the plates of the ship which were above water glowing redly from the heat of the fires. Then, with a great rush of steam and smoke, she sank. The British ships closed in at once to look for survivors. They were able to rescue only thirty-four men from the *Scharnhorst's* company of nearly one thousand. Admiral Bey went down with the ship he had so mishandled.

Admiral Sir Bruce Fraser turned his force homewards. He had good reason to be satisfied, as had all those whose business it was to concern themselves with the strength and dispositions of our naval forces. The *Tirpitz* lay in Altenfiord still seriously damaged as the result of the attack by British midget submarines on September 22nd. True, there were reports and signs that the Germans were trying to repair her, but such repairs could only be of a temporary nature, designed to make the ship sufficiently seaworthy to undertake the voyage south to a German dockyard port. These repairs were allowed to proceed for six months, until they were completed, for they absorbed quite a considerable amount of German war effort. Then, just as the great ship was about to leave Altenfiord for a dockyard port, Sir Bruce Fraser struck again, this time with the Fleet Air Arm, using the new Barracuda dive-bomber and torpedo-bomber. All the Germans' work went for nothing, and the *Tirpitz* remained at Altenfiord, more seriously damaged than ever.

That Fleet Air Arm attack, however, did not take place for several months after the sinking of the *Scharnhorst*. It was not necessary. Bruce Fraser knew that he had the *Tirpitz* "where he wanted her"—that is, he knew where she was and that she could not put to sea for operations—and, as he steamed away from the Arctic on the night of December 26th, he at last had the *Scharnhorst* "where he wanted her" too—at the bottom of the sea. No longer was there any considerable threat of a break out into the Atlantic by powerful surface forces of the enemy. No longer was there need to keep always ready at our northern bases a fleet strong enough to be able to intercept or hunt down, and in any event, sink, ships as big and powerful as the *Tirpitz* and the *Scharnhorst*. That meant nothing less than the freeing of our naval strategy from a requirement which had circumscribed it throughout the last war and through four and a quarter years of this war. Freed of that responsibility we could reinforce to strike elsewhere. It would not be long before far away Japan felt the impact of the destruction of the *Scharnhorst*. Bruce Fraser had deserved well of his country and of the cause of the United Nations in both hemispheres, and as the *Duke of York* steamed south-west he received a personal message of congratulation from the King, and many other congratulatory signals.

The fact that the *Tirpitz* and the *Scharnhorst* no longer had to be reckoned with also had its effect upon the naval strategy of the United States, apart altogether from the promise of stronger British naval forces in the Far East. Twice during the time that Bruce Fraser was Second-in-Command and Commander-in-Chief of the Home Fleet, strategy had made it necessary for ships of the Home Fleet to be detached to the Mediterranean. One was at the time of the Allied landings in French North Africa in November, 1942, and the other was during the invasion of Sicily eight months later. On each occasion the weakening of the Home Fleet could not be accepted because of the threat of the powerful German ships in northern

Norway, so the gaps in the Home Fleet caused by the necessity for sending ships to the Mediterranean had to be filled by a Task Force of the United States Navy, which crossed the Atlantic to reinforce the depleted Home Fleet.

As Second-in-Command of the Home Fleet, Bruce Fraser did not have a great deal to do with the first of these two American Task Forces, which was commanded by Rear-Admiral Robert C. Giffen, who became almost a legendary figure among the sailors of the Home Fleet as the man who wore the biggest boots in two navies —he is a man of enormous proportions—and who used to walk untold miles whenever he went ashore, and dash up the Grampians or any other available mountains.

When the second United States naval Task Force came over, however, at the time of the invasion of Sicily, Bruce Fraser was Commander-in-Chief. As such he came into close and intimate contact with the Americans, and he "went over big"with them— chiefly because he so obviously knew his job, but was quiet and unassuming. No man ever heard Bruce Fraser parade his knowledge or experience—it is, in fact, the most difficult thing in the world to make him talk about himself even for a minute or two. Nor has Bruce Fraser ever been known to stand on ceremony or dignity as regards his rank. He is completely and genuinely "unspoilt"—it seems strange to apply the word to one of our greatest Admirals, but there is no other term which quite describes his whole attitude to life and to those with whom he comes in contact.

There is a true story which illustrates this, and his love for a gentle "leg-pull."

It happened one day that Fraser was taking the dog-watch air on the quarterdeck of the *Duke of York* when an oiler which had been alongside wanted to cast off. Without looking up to see who was on the flagship's quarterdeck, a deck hand of the oiler, with the outspoken independence of his kind, shouted: "Ain't there any bloody bastard what'll cast off this bloody hawser."

Without a moment's hesitation the Commander-in-Chief answered: "All right—just coming—but why the bloody hurry?" And Fraser cast off the hawser himself.

Bruce Fraser is a man with a great liking for people—a trait which may seem strange in one who has devoted so much of his life to the development of material. He loves a party and his completely natural manner banishes all self-consciousness, and he makes a point of asking to dinner in his flagship the young officers of the fleet and all those who do not normally see much of the limelight; such men as those who run local signal stations, look after the boom defences and protective minefields of harbours.

During his time in the Home Fleet he gave much time and thought to improving such amenities as existed for officers and men at the far northern base. He was always accessible to all and was a frequent visitor to all the ships under his command. There was not a young ordinary seaman in a destroyer who did not know the Commander-in-Chief. To give himself some exercise he started his own allotment on one of the islands, and dug out all the heather and peat himself.

He is an easy man to serve with but a difficult man to serve "up to" because the standard he sets is so high. There is no room in his philosophy of life for inefficiency, and less than none for laziness.

With his tremendous aptitude for shrewd, far-sighted, and reasoned thought over a problem, he is intensely independent. He never accepts precedent for precedent's sake and will never accede to anything being done "just because it was done before." He must be convinced that there is no better solution. To this end he is always most willing to listen to an expert, however junior in rank, and he gives great weight to human capabilities in weighing a problem.

It sounds a slow method, but with Fraser it is not slow. He makes his decisions quickly and then acts upon them extremely fast and will not be diverted from his purpose except by the most cogent arguments, and these must convince him personally of their value.

Fraser's temperament makes him a most considerate master, for all the high standard which he sets and demands. He will never set a subordinate any task which he would not or could not himself undertake, and, above all, he never fusses. If a man does his best and his best is good enough, he will satisfy Bruce Fraser. If he does not do his best he will have short shrift. If he does his best, but his best is not good enough, it will be a matter for Fraser's sincere regret that the man has failed. It will not be considered his fault, but just his nature. Praise from Bruce Fraser is rare, but it is always ungrudgingly given when it is really deserved.

Fraser's consideration for subordinates from whom he expects so much was shown when the King visited the Home Fleet in August, 1943. On the first evening there was the usual dinner party to all the Admirals and Captains of the fleet. On the next evening the Commander-in-Chief arranged a dinner party to the King to which were asked twenty-six officers of the fleet, all of the rank of Commander or below and representative of every different branch of the Service. He insisted that two midshipmen should attend and that the Warrant Officers should also be represented. After the dinner a gunner from one of the destroyers told the Commander-in-Chief's secretary that he was glad to have lived to see the day when a Warrant Officer could be so honoured.

Although it was August, Christmas pudding was served—in the dark, with flaming rum. In the pudding were twenty-six sixpences. The King got two. These Fraser had mounted on ebonite powder boxes made in the *Duke of York* and presented them as "The King's Sixpence" to each of the two Princesses.

It was during the time that the second American naval Task Force was reinforcing the Home Fleet that Fraser did something that was quite typical of him, but which had never been done by any other British Admiral—he took the wheel in an American aircraft-carrier operating at sea in war-time.

The aircraft-carrier was the *Ranger*, wearing the flag of Rear-Admiral Olaf M. Hustvedt, U.S.N. The Commander-in-Chief had asked permission to go to sea in her "unofficially" in order to see how they and how the American Navy worked, and Admiral Hustvedt had most willingly given his permission.

American naval discipline, like American army discipline, is somewhat different to the British. In the British Navy officers and men are apt to be very much on their dignity and conscious of their ranks and ratings in harbour, but will relax the standard of discipline at sea, particularly at action stations and under actual action conditions. In the American Navy it is the reverse, and it is an almost unheard of departure from tradition for a senior American officer to visit the crews' quarters or any part of the ship other than his own living quarters and action station while a ship is at sea. That there are merits in both systems goes without saying, and it would be quite impossible to say which is the best. Probably it is a question of temperament. The American sailor certainly would not like the British way, and there is no doubt that much of the American conviction of British "stiffness," so far as the navy is concerned, comes from seeing only how the British idea of discipline works in harbour or ashore off duty.

Be that as it may, Bruce Fraser broke through ideas and tradition in the U.S.S. *Ranger* that day, and he did so with a spontaneity and genuine goodwill that left enthusiasm instead of resentment in its trail.

There grew up between Fraser and his men and Huftvedt and his men a friendly co-operation which, although its first acknowledged duty was the tireless pursuit of efficiency in war, had its light-hearted side. On Independence Day, 1943, Admiral Sir Bruce Fraser's Secretary brought a parcel into his cabin in H.M.S. *Duke of York*. When it was opened it was found to contain a magnificent cake, which had been made on board the United States flagship and sent over to the British Commander-in-Chief. Bruce Fraser mentioned this one day in conversation with Admiral Harold Stark, the admiral commanding the U.S. Naval Forces in the European Theatre of War, whose headquarters are in London. On Independence Day, 1944, Admiral Fraser was in London, having relinquished his command of the Home Fleet, and he received a beautiful cake embellished with all sorts of naval emblems from Admiral Stark.

When the United States Task Force was about to leave the Home Fleet and return to American waters Bruce Fraser received an invitation to pay an informal visit to the wardroom of the American aircraft carrier *Ranger*. He went, and found himself surrounded by laughing American naval officers while he played the central part in an extempory ceremony—the presentation to him of a large bronze medal which had been made on board the American flagship to commemorate the happy and successful collaboration of the United States Task Force and the British Home Fleet. On the obverse were engraved the White Ensign and the Stars and Stripes, and on the reverse a representation in enamel of the ship. This was presented by Captain Rowe of the *Ranger*, with a verse in memory of "The Home from Home Fleet."

Although Admiral Sir Bruce Fraser was for many years closely associated with the technical and material development of the Royal Navy, he has seen a great deal of service afloat in various parts of the world and witnessed much history in the making.

He was born in London on February 5th, 1888, and was prepared for the Navy at Bradfield College before entering H.M.S. *Britannia* as a Naval Cadet in 1902. Two years later he went to sea as a midshipman in H.M.S. *Hannibal*, but was transferred to H.M.S. *Prince*

George, and in that ship he was at Brest at the time of the celebrations following the Entente Cordiale. As a young lieutenant, before he specialised in gunnery, he served in H.M.S. *Lancaster* in the Mediterranean when that ship was commanded by Captain Sydney Freemantle (now Admiral Sir Sydney Freemantle), and later in H.M.S. *Boadicea*, the flagship of Rear-Admiral Sir Robert Arbuthnot, who lost his life in H.M.S. *Defence* at the Battle of Jutland.

Fraser's first appointment as a fully-fledged gunnery officer came at the beginning of the last war. It was to H.M.S. *Minerva*, and he served in that ship for two years. The *Minerva* was an old cruiser which was employed chiefly on convoy escort duty in the Red Sea and Eastern Mediterranean, but she was present during the Gallipoli campaign. In the *Minerva* Fraser, as gunnery officer, took part in several landing operations. These were of a minor character but they proved valuable experience. It was the first introduction to amphibious operations of the man who was destined to command the British naval forces in the Far East in war—a theatre of war where amphibious operations were to play an all-important part in the defeat of Japan.

H.M.S. *Minerva* was for a time guard-ship at Akaba, at the head of the Red Sea. While the *Minerva* was on this duty she embarked a seaplane. This was Fraser's first experience of using aircraft as a naval weapon—a science which he did much to develop in later years.

Bruce Fraser would be the last man in the world to claim the possession of psychic powers. Nevertheless, there occurred when he was serving in H.M.S. *Minerva* an incident which showed that he was capable of having what his American friends would call a "hunch" and, what is more rare, the moral courage to act on a "hunch."

The *Minerva* had been told to go to a rendezvous on a desolate stretch of the Arabian coast to pick up Colonel W. F. Stirling, an officer on the staff of Colonel T. E. Lawrence (Lawrence of Arabia), who had been on a secret mission and would arrive at the rendezvous by air.

The *Minerva* duly arrived and anchored off the rendezvous, but there was no sign of Colonel Stirling. Fraser was sent ashore but could find no trace of him. The *Minerva* waited, growing anxiety permeating those on board who were "in the know." At length the captain of the *Minerva* reluctantly decided that it was no good waiting longer. The hinterland was waterless desert and the victims of an air crash would assuredly have died in the desert if they had not been killed outright in the crash.

So H.M.S. *Minerva* weighed anchor and left. Several hours later Bruce Fraser went to his captain and asked him to put the ship about and return to the rendezvous as he was quite certain that Colonel Stirling had just arrived there. Fraser could give no reason for his conviction, but he persuaded the captain. The *Minerva* returned to the rendezvous and there they found Colonel Stirling. The aircraft had made a forced landing in the desert and he had just succeeded in reaching the coast after a journey of great hardship. Fraser's "hunch" had been right and a valuable life and much important information had been saved.

After leaving the *Minerva* Bruce Fraser spent a year on the staff of the gunnery school at Whale Island, Portsmouth, and was then appointed gunnery officer of the new 15-inch-gun battleship *Resolution*, which was then completing for service. After the Armistice H.M.S. *Resolution* went to the Black Sea, where there existed one of the most confused and complicated international situations of all time.

Russia was in the throes of the Bolshevik revolution, which had led to civil war between the Bolsheviks and all sorts of counter revolutionary forces. During the first stages of the revolution the Western Powers had been preoccupied with the defeat of the Central Powers, and their interests therefore lay with any and every force in Russia which would oppose the Germans and Austrians and thereby prevent the transfer of German divisions to the western front. The anti-revolutionary forces seemed to offer the best prospect of resistance to Germany, so they naturally received the initial support of the Western Powers. Moreover, it seemed for a time that the Bolsheviks were doomed to defeat at the hands of the coalition of White Russians and others against them, while Persia was very nervous of an extension of Bolshevik influence to the Caspian Sea and beyond. This, of course, would involve the oilfields, in which Great Britain was very interested, particularly at a time when relations with the United States of America were strained over the Anglo-Japanese Alliance. The combination of these factors led the British Government to back the anti-Bolshevik elements—a resolution which was fortified by public indignation

at the massacres and atrocities committed by certain sections of the
revolutionary party—and active British assistance was given to the
Whites both in the far north and in the Black Sea.

Add to the confusion caused by the Russian scene the fact that
the Greeks and the Turks were at war; and that the major part of
the French fleet in the Black Sea had mutinied, and one begins to
appreciate the difficulties with which British naval officers were
faced in the Black Sea in 1919 and 1920.

Fraser was promoted to Commander while serving in H.M.S.
Resolution in the Black Sea, and then served for a time as Executive
Officer in the ship. This was no sinecure. British naval discipline
never broke down, but it was under considerable strain, both by
reason of the general atmosphere of mutiny and revolution and
because the men, not unnaturally, wanted to get home for some
well-earned post-war leave instead of being kept messing about with
an unofficial and incomprehensible war in a distant sea. Bruce
Fraser learnt a lot in those days about dealing with the British
sailor under difficult conditions, and he put what he learnt to excellent practice.

In 1920, however, Bruce Fraser left the *Resolution* and was given
another job—which was to land him behind prison bars.

The White Cossacks of the Kuban, the Georgians, and the inhabitants of Azerbaijan had formed an anti-Bolshevik alliance, which
was being supported by the Persians. The British Navy was already
represented by a few small craft in the Caspian Sea, but it was considered necessary to reinforce this in order to support the Persians
and the anti-Bolshevik alliance of the Caucasus, as well as to give
greater protection to the oil fields and refineries of Baku. To this
end Bruce Fraser was told to take command of a detachment of
fifty British naval ratings and take them to the Caspian. Fraser
had been specially selected for this task because a skilled gunnery
officer was badly needed in the Caspian.

Fraser and his men duly arrived one afternoon at Baku, the oil
port on the western shore of the Caspian which was in Azerbaijan
territory. During the night, however, Baku suddenly and without
warning declared itself for the Bolsheviks. The counter revolution
in that part of the world came to an abrupt conclusion, and Fraser
and his fifty sailors found themselves in a Russian prison. There
was nothing Fraser could do about it.

There followed eight long months before diplomacy succeeded

in obtaining the release of Fraser and his men. The prison at Baku was far from comfortable and some of its arrangements were primitive in the extreme, while the food was hardly that to which British sailors had been accustomed. In particular, there was a great lack of green vegetables, and Fraser feared an outbreak of scurvy among his men. On one occasion he succeeded in bartering, through the bars of the prison, for a supply of spring onions for his men. No scurvy, however, developed, and the men were still fairly healthy when they were at last released.

It is a queer commentary on the muddles of the years immediately following the last war, and upon the reconstitution of Russia as a great union of Soviet States and our powerful ally, that the first British admiral to visit a Soviet naval base in his flagship should have languished in a Russian prison during the growing pains of the U.S.S.R. Nor is that the only seeming contradiction. Bruce Fraser is the only British Admiral to wear the narrow green and orange ribbon of the Order of Suvarov, First Class, with which he was honoured by Marshal Stalin in February, 1944. The Order of Suvarov was founded by the Soviet government late in 1943, and is in itself a mark of the progress of the new Russia from the bigotry of revolution to the realism of a powerful member of the United Nations, for Alexander Suvarov, in whose memory the Order was founded, was the great Russian military genius of the eighteenth century. He served Catherine the Great and her successors. Essentially he, like all the soldiers of his time, was the servant of royalty. He remains, however, the foremost military hero of Soviet Russia as he was of Tsarist Russia. Did he not defeat the hitherto invincible armies of Frederick the Great and carry his victories to the actual invasion of Berlin?

And in considering the reaction of public opinion of the Western Powers to the mass killings and other excesses of the early years of struggle of the Bolshevik revolution it is as well to remember that Stalin the Georgian and Voroshilov the pit-boy from the Don basin, who virtually founded the Red Army, worked closely together and were usually in violent opposition to the atrocity-thirsty Trotsky. Voroshilov and Stalin, who first made the arms of the revolution immortal by their defence of Tsaritsyn—the modern Stalingrad, would have nothing to do with massacre, looting, rape and the rest, holding that it was bad for discipline among the troops and did the revolution untold harm in the eyes of the world.

When Bruce Fraser was finally released from Baku prison he returned to England and spent a year at the gunnery school at Whale Island. That appointment brought him up to date with the latest developments and thought in the realm of naval gunnery, while combining the less strenuous life of a shore appointment—which he sorely needed after his experiences—with plenty of interesting work.

Then, in 1922, Fraser went to the Admiralty for the first time. For the next two years he served there under the Director of Naval Ordnance and the Director of Torpedoes and Mining while engaged in developing the new gunnery fire control table which embodied all the lessons learnt during the war.

A fire-control table is, in effect, a combination of a number of automatic calculators, all of them arranged to work in collusion and so that their individual results will appear on a central plot or picture representing the second-to-second progress of the gunnery problem in a naval action. The speed and course of one's own ship and of the enemy, the ranges taken by all the range-finders, the spotting corrections and reports of the spotting officer or observer in an aircraft, the direction and strength of the wind—even the allowances to be made for the temperature of the ammunition and the degree of wear of the guns and the amount the earth will turn during the time of flight of the shells. All these and other factors go into the various components of the modern fire control table; and on the table itself, upon a sheet of paper kept moving at the scaled-down speed of the action, there appears a complete "picture" of what is going on. This will give the hitting gun range (the range to be put on the sights in order to hit the enemy) at any moment; it will detect any errors made by the control officer aloft in estimating the enemy's course or speed; and will enable the gun action to be continued "blind" if the view of the control officer is blanketed by smoke.

Mechanism of this sort is, of course, extremely complicated, delicate and costly, and the fire control tables are therefore mounted deep in the ship behind armour in a highly secret compartment known as the Transmitting Station, which is really the gunnery nerve-centre of the ship.

It may be wondered why, in developing the new fire control table, Bruce Fraser worked under the Director of Torpedoes and Mining as well as under the Director of Naval Ordnance. The reason is twofold. The fire control table, although primarily a gunnery instrument, is also of assistance to the torpedo control organisation in action. Moreover, electricity and electric machinery are the responsibilities in a British warship of the torpedo department, and therefore the design and supply of the many electric motors, relays, and switch gear involved in the fire control table is the responsibility of the Director of Torpedoes and Mining.

After two years of this scientific and highly technical work at the Admiralty, Commander Bruce Fraser was appointed Fleet Gunnery Officer of the Mediterranean Fleet. In this capacity he was responsible for the gunnery training and performance of the fleet. He was accommodated in the fleet flagship and was on the staff of the Commander-in-Chief as his adviser on all matters pertaining to gunnery. In this capacity Bruce Fraser served two Commanders-in-Chief during his two years in the Mediterranean. The first was Admiral Sir Osmond Brook, whose flagship was H.M.S. *Queen Elizabeth*. The second was Admiral Sir Roger Keyes, who flew his flag in H.M.S. *Warspite*. During the latter period Bruce Fraser came into close contact with Admiral Sir Dudley Pound, who was then serving as Chief of Staff to Admiral Keyes. It was an association which was to be continued in more dangerous times.

The midsummer promotions of 1926 raised Bruce Fraser to the rank of Captain, and he was then appointed head of the Tactical Section of the Naval Staff at the Admiralty. Here again he was studying the lessons of the last war as well as those of many peace-time exercises and was framing the future, but this time he was framing tactics to make the fullest use of weapons rather than developing the weapons themselves. And again he was in close contact with Dudley Pound, who was then serving at the Admiralty as Assistant Chief of the Naval Staff.

After rather more than two years as head of the Tactical Section at the Admiralty, Bruce Fraser got his first command at sea. This was a cruiser, which is usual for junior captains, but Fraser's appointment was in command of H.M.S. *Effingham*, flagship of the East Indies Squadron. This appointment showed that Fraser had already been singled out as one of the "coming men" destined for high command. He remained on the East Indies Station from 1929 to 1933, during which time he served as flag captain to three Commanders-in-Chief—Sir Bertram Thesiger, Sir Eric Fullerton, and

Sir Martin Dunbar-Nasmith, V.C. On the latter's staff he was Chief of Staff as well as flag captain in command of the flagship.

It was in 1933 that Fraser returned from the East Indies Station and went to the Admiralty as Director of Naval Ordnance. His work in that capacity in developing the main armament of the projected battleships of the King George V class has already been mentioned, but this was by no means all his work. He was also concerned with the design, development, and testing of the 5.25-inch gun with its dual-purpose mountings, allowing it to be used as an anti-aircraft as well as a low-angle weapon. These guns have been so successful that they have become the secondary armament of battleships and the main armament of aircraft-carriers and light cruisers. In addition to the development of guns and mountings, Fraser as D.N.O. did a great deal of immensely valuable work on the problem of controlling the anti-aircraft fire of destroyers.

In all this work Bruce Fraser showed himself, not before his time but in the nick of time, and conversant with all the latest problems, tactical as well as technical. It would be impossible to compute the number of lives and ships which might have succumbed to the Luftwaffe if it had not been for the work which Fraser did on these subjects, and for the fact that he brought to these problems a mind which was for ever ranging ahead into the realms of possible future developments.

In his next appointment, too, Bruce Fraser laid foundations for which the Royal Navy and the whole cause of the United Nations had to be thankful when war came. This appointment was to command the aircraft carrier *Glorious* in the Mediterranean Fleet, of which Admiral Sir William Fisher was then Commander-in-Chief.

There is a popular belief in many quarters that a gunnery specialist, whose faith and training has been with big ships and big guns, is incapable of adjusting himself to the air weapon and is therefore the implacable enemy of progress so far as air power is concerned. Like so many sweeping statements, this is a fallacy, and it may truly be said that, in proportion to the time he spent with the naval air arm, he did as much as for the progress and development of Fleet Air Arm technique as he did for naval gunnery.

Fraser took over command of H.M.S. *Glorious* in 1935—that fateful and anxious year in the Mediterranean, when Mussolini defied the League of Nations and invaded Abyssinia, and it seemed as if the "collective action" urged by the League would degenerate into a war between a highly prepared Italy and a totally unprepared Britain, who had had the temerity to take the lead in proposing the sanctions demanded by the League against the aggressor.

Admiral Sir William Wordsworth Fisher realised that in the fight against tremendous odds which threatened to develop in the Middle Sea it would be necessary to discount the material superiority of the enemy by the sea sense, high degree of training, and morale of the British sailor. Moreover, he realised that in the sort of war which threatened, the British training and imperturbability under action conditions could best be exploited at night, when it might be expected that the latin temperament of the potential enemy might lead to excitement and confusion.

It was this reasoning which led Admiral Fisher to practice his fleet whenever possible in night attack and encounters—a policy which paid such handsome dividends at the Battle of Cape Matapan six years later. Meanwhile Bruce Fraser, with the help and encouragement of his Commander-in-Chief, was busily engaged in developing the technique of night operations of aircraft carriers and night flying by the carrier-borne aircraft—a science which up to that time was virtually in its infancy.

The progress made in night flying from aircraft carriers by the *Glorious*, and the development in technique and training which took place under Fraser's command made possible the germination of the idea of attack by carrier-borne aircraft on an enemy fleet in harbour—an idea which was later to be developed into a plan by Captain Lyster, who relieved Fraser in command of the *Glorious*, and under Lyster's direction to yield the amazing victory of Taranto on November 11th, 1940. Fraser's work laid the foundation of that victory just as surely as Fisher's work laid the foundation for the victory off Cape Matapan.

Bruce Fraser's task in developing night flying and training his air crews in its technique was difficult in the extreme, for there were scant opportunities for taking an aircraft carrier to secluded waters for intensive trials and training. War was threatening and the aircraft carriers had to remain fully operational and at short notice for fleet work with the Commander-in-Chief. Nor could the damaging of aircraft be lightly accepted, for such aircraft as the Fleet Air Arm possessed in those days were priceless, there being virtually no reserves. Moreover, during the eastern Mediterranean crisis the Fleet Air Arm aircraft had to perform a double duty.

Whenever the fleet put to sea they had to operate from the carrier, and provide the Commander-in-Chief with such air cover as lay in their power, but whenever the fleet returned to harbour the Fleet Air Arm aircraft had to fly off their carriers, land at a shore airfield, and constitute what was virtually the air defence of Egypt and the Suez Canal, the Royal Air Force in that part of the world being in those days little more than a skeleton transport organisation. Vision and keenness, however, surmounted all obstacles.

During the first year of Fraser's period in command of H.M.S. *Glorious* Admiral Sir Dudley Pound was serving as Chief of Staff to Admiral Sir William Fisher. Dudley Pound had been nominated to relieve William Fisher as Commander-in-Chief, but he had felt that the year of crisis was no time for him to take over the Mediterranean command from the man who had served there so long and knew it so well. At the same time he felt that it would be advisable for him to study at first hand the manifold problems of the Mediterranean before taking over as Commander-in-Chief when the international situation clarified. He therefore volunteered to serve as Chief of Staff to Sir William Fisher although in the ordinary course of events he was far too senior for such an appointment. And as Chief of Staff and later as Commander-in-Chief, Dudley Pound gave great assistance to the go-ahead gunnery expert who had turned his hand to the problem of the Fleet Air Arm.

Bruce Fraser's time in command of H.M.S. *Glorious* came to an end in 1937 and he returned home. A little more than six years later he was able, by sinking the German battle-cruiser *Scharnhorst*, to avenge his old ship, for the *Glorious* had been sunk, together with her two attendant destroyers, by the *Scharnhorst* at the end of the Norwegian campaign of 1940.

Fraser was promoted to the rank of Rear-Admiral on January 11th, 1938, and his old friend and collaborator Admiral Sir Dudley Pound, who was still Commander-in-Chief in the Mediterranean, promptly asked him to be his Chief of Staff. Fraser accepted the appointment and returned to the Mediterranean ; and to a further period of anxiety, alarms, excursions, and international complications.

The Spanish Civil War was raging and threatening to spread to the countries which were using Spain to try out new material and new methods of warfare, and beyond them to the whole of Europe. Germany and Italy were openly assisting General Franco, Russia was assisting the Spanish republicans; France was, more clandestinely, implicated. A cordon of "observers," many of them retired British naval officers, had been cast round Spain's land frontiers in the hope of "keeping the ring." Then there had appeared, in waters round Spain, submarines of no known nationality, which sank several ships. International action was called for against the "pirate" submarines. A conference had been held at Nyon, just far enough from Geneva to make it clear that it was not under the auspices of the League of Nations, where the General Assembly was in troubled session at the time. The conference had decided upon a system of international naval patrols, each nation being responsible for a certain sector. This was a counsel of collective perfection which could never have been efficiently carried out, even if some of the nations to whom sectors had been allotted possessed the ships or the desire to institute the patrols. The Spanish Mediterranean coasts were the most dangerous, and the patrol sector in this area had not been fixed by the Nyon Conference. They had been left to be arranged by the British Commander-in-Chief in the Mediterranean, having due regard to the need for achieving a compromise between the need for effective patrols and the *amour propre* of the nations concerned. There had followed the bombing of the German "pocket battleship" *Deutschland* and its effects upon an already truculent Germany.

Such were the ingredients of the situation with which Bruce Fraser, as Chief of Staff to Sir Dudley Pound, had to deal. But these international affairs were far from being the sum total of his work. War was looming large on the horizon, and Dudley Pound was determined that, despite the needs of the international situation and the humanitarian work of the Royal Navy, his fleet should be worked up to, and remain keyed to, the very highest state of training. In this he was ably abetted and assisted by his Chief of Staff, and a tremendous programme of exercises and manœuvres was worked out, each one being closely dovetailed into the others so that not a moment of time nor a gallon of fuel should be wasted. A member of Pound's staff once remarked to him that his captains would be tired out and would have no time to study the lessons of one exercise before taking part in another. He retorted that captains would have to spend long hours on the bridge in war-time, and that war could not be relied upon to wait for officers to digest one action at their leisure before being again at sea in the face of the enemy.

S.S.   K

The training of a fleet is, of course, the responsibility of the Commander-in-Chief, but the preparation of a series of exercises, manœuvres, and drills, and their subsequent analysis, is the task of the Chief of Staff. Bruce Fraser was worked harder than any man in that hard-worked fleet, but everybody from the Commander-in-Chief down was repaid by the realisation that the highest efficiency was attained and that nothing that could have been done in training for war had been left undone.

After the Munich Agreement in 1938 Bruce Fraser decided that he wished to see the Western Desert and the Libyan frontier for himself. He accordingly took forty-eight hours' leave from Alexandria and drove out alone in a hired car to the Italian border, where he put up at a hotel at Sidi Barrani. He was, of course, *incognito*, and in the evening while he was wandering in the foothills of the great frontier escarpment he was arrested as a suspicious character by a private of the Egyptian army. The soldier had no bayonet on his rifle and said that he would have to go to the guard-house to get it, in order to be able to escort his prisoner in the proper manner. Fraser, who is always amicable and reasonable, offered to hold the soldier's rifle while the bayonet was fetched. The soldier agreed and left Fraser with the rifle. Then he returned, fixed the bayonet, and marched Fraser to the guard-house in the regulation manner and turned him over to the sergeant in charge of the post. The distinguished prisoner was duly released when the local authority had been called in and Fraser revealed his identity and gave a satisfactory explanation of his movements.

Bruce Fraser is always anxious to see things for himself. When he had relinquished command of H.M.S. *Glorious* he had toured Spain in his car during the Spanish Civil War in order to observe conditions at first hand. Later, when he gave up his appointment as Chief of Staff in the Mediterranean, he drove his car home to England through Italy.

The international situation grew even more menacing. In October it reached first-class crisis dimensions and what amounted to war stations had to be taken up by the ships of the Royal Navy, which had been hastily mobilised. Here was additional strain on the Chief of Staff, involving much work and clear thinking, not of the parochial type dealing with only the Mediterranean as one component of impending naval war, but with the problems of mobilisation for war on a world-wide scale, for it was obvious that the manifold needs at sea could only be met by taking ships and men from one fleet to reinforce elsewhere.

Finally, however, crisis abated. Mr. Neville Chamberlain, the then Prime Minister, flew to Munich and "plucked from this nettle danger" a respite of eleven months in which to put in order the defences of an Empire which had been sacrificed over a period of twenty-one years on the altar of political expediency to the accompaniment of the reiterated shibboleths of blind idealists.

Both Sir Dudley Pound and Bruce Fraser were to work near-miracles during the respite, but neither of them were to do so in the Mediterranean. Fate called them both to higher work, and in each case it did so through tragedy. Dudley Pound became First Sea Lord and Chief of the Naval Staff in succession to Admiral Sir Roger Backhouse, who died in office. Bruce Fraser became Third Sea Lord and Controller of the Navy in succession to Vice-Admiral Sir Reginald Henderson, who also died in harness.

Before the war high naval officers and Admiralty officials in a position to judge were unanimous in averring that the Navy had never before had a Controller to equal "Reggie" Henderson. He had had the handling of all the initial stages of the naval rearmament programme, having to start virtually from scratch, with a navy so reduced in strength that Sir John Simon's "beyond the edge of risk" was but a half-truth, with shipyards and armament works stultified and almost paralysed by long years of slump, and with politicians who persisted in seeing the red light as a nice safe green.

It would be impossible, as well as invidious, to try to cast a comparison between Henderson and Fraser as Controller of the Navy. For the most part they grappled with somewhat different problems, and the successes of the former inevitably contributed to the results obtained by the latter. Suffice to say that the Navy, and the cause of the war at sea, was superbly served by both; Fraser providing for Henderson a successor with the brain, energy and experience for one of the biggest jobs in the world.

Rear-Admiral Fraser became Controller of the Navy on March 1st, 1939. During the initial, pre-war, months of his office he was dealing with the existing rearmament programme, urging it onward in every detail, for he was under no illusion as regards Hitler's patience or intentions, and he saw that the Berlin-Rome-Tokio triangle might well involve a naval war on a world-wide scale.

During this stage of his office Bruce Fraser had much to do with the new battleships of the *King George V* class, the armament of which he had done so much to develop, but he was far from being concerned only with heavy ships. His experiences in H.M.S. *Glorious* had convinced him of the absolute necessity of numbers of aircraft carriers in modern war, and he continually urged an acceleration of the aircraft carrier construction programme—which was just as well, since Britain entered the war with only one modern carrier, the *Ark Royal.* He also accelerated the cruiser programme, for our cruiser force was manifestly too small to deal even with trade defence problems on a world-wide scale. Nor was he slow to realise that the key to survival, if not to ultimate victory, lay in more destroyers and escort vessels. He had not been blind to Germany's U-boat building, both before and after its legalisation by the exchange of notes between Sir Samuel Hoare and Herr Ribbentrop which passed into the archives as the "Anglo-German Naval Agreement."

In all his work as Controller Bruce Fraser was enormously assisted by certain personal qualities. Shipbuilders, contractors, and the rest were quick to realise that they were dealing with a man who was completely and transparently sincere, who did not even know the meaning of intrigue or political *quid pro quo*, but who, for all his simplicity of outlook, had a brain capable of realising and even solving their technical problems almost before they themselves were aware of them.

Then came the war, and with it the immediate recourse by Germany to unrestricted submarine warfare. The cry was at once for more and yet more escorts for our convoys. Yet the building of other ships had to continue and our shipbuilding and engineering resources were not yet expanded or keyed to war-time levels of production. Escorts had to be produced quickly, and without interfering with other essential shipbuilding. Fraser met the emergency with the production of the corvettes, which held the U-boats at bay in the Atlantic and kept the sinkings of Allied merchant ships from reaching dangerous figures. So successful were the production of the first emergency anti-submarine measures that Mr. Winston Churchill, the then First Lord of the Admiralty, was able to tell an anxious House of Commons that our patrol and escort forces had been trebled in the first six months of the war.

Fraser had been quick to see that purely British production could not keep pace with the demand for small ships of the destroyer, escort vessel, and corvette types. He therefore carried out a comprehensive survey of all the shipbuilding resources of the Empire, and very soon Canada, Australia, New Zealand, South Africa, India and a great many colonies were producing the smaller types of warships required to combat the U-boat threat.

He also saw that the proportion of ships suffering damage was so high that they could not all be repaired in British dockyards without serious dislocation of the shipbuilding and production programmes. The seriousness of this problem may be judged from the fact that in the early summer of 1940 no less than sixty-two British destroyers were in dockyard hands, either being repaired or waiting to be repaired. Bruce Fraser was one of the prime movers in the negotiations which led to the arrangements for British ships to be repaired in the dockyards of the United States of America, and in the naval side of the more comprehensive Lease-Lend agreements.

In May, 1940, Bruce Fraser was promoted to Vice-Admiral, and was made a K.B.E. in the Birthday Honours of the following year. It would be difficult to find an honour more richly deserved.

Bruce Fraser's time as Controller of the Navy was a period of very hard work, yet he got through the work and, unless faced with some unexpected and very urgent matter, he did not indulge in midnight sessions at the Admiralty. These were a habit of many officers in the Admiralty, but Fraser never agreed with them, contending that they made for slow thinking and faulty decisions reached by tired brains. If he did not, as he often did, obey a summons to spend the week-end at Chequers with the Prime Minister, Fraser, a bachelor, always went to his mother at Moseley and spent Sundays there.

Every Thursday the Controller used to lunch with Sir James Lithgow, Controller of Merchant Shipbuilding; Sir Harold Brown, Controller-General of Munitions Production at the Ministry of Supply, and Sir Charles Craven of the Ministry of Aircraft Production. These formed a sort of luncheon club and called themselves "The Boilermakers."

Bruce Fraser left the Admiralty in the early summer of 1942, and on June 28th of that year he hoisted his flag in H.M.S. *Anson*—one of the new battleships of the *King George V* class—as Second-in-Command of the Home Fleet, of which Admiral Sir John Tovey was Commander-in-Chief.

As soon as he felt that he was "on top of his job" as Second-in-

Command, Fraser did something quite typical of him. He felt that he ought to see some action at first hand and learn the latest developments under action conditions. Three days after joining H.M.S. *Anson* he asked Admiral Tovey's permission to go in the aircraft carrier H.M.S. *Victorious* on a North Russian convoy operation "to gain experience." Tovey acceded. Later, some Home Fleet ships were required to go to the Mediterranean to assist in covering the passage to Malta of the all-important relief convoy of August, 1942, the close escort of which was commanded by Rear-Admiral Harold Burrough. Fraser asked Tovey if he could go to the Mediterranean for the operation. Tovey agreed, and Fraser went in H.M.S. *Rodney*. His presence in the Mediterranean was purely "unofficial" and in no way affected the commands of the escorts or the covering force. Bruce Fraser merely did what he set out to do—see things for himself when they were "at their stickiest" so that he would be better fitted to deal with situations of the sort with which he might be confronted when in command.

For the rest, Bruce Fraser's time in the Home Fleet was concerned with covering the passage of the convoys to North Russia, and with endless sweeps in the hope of luring the *Tirpitz*, *Scharnhorst*, and other German ships out of their fiords in northern Norway and bringing them to action.

On May 8th, 1943, Fraser, who had been made a K.C.B. in the Birthday Honours of 1942, hoisted his flag in H.M.S. *Duke of York* as Commander-in-Chief of the Home Fleet in succession to Sir John Tovey. The high light of his time as Commander-in-Chief was, of course, the sinking of the *Scharnhorst* on Boxing Day, 1943. In recognition of his services in that action Fraser was made a G.C.B. on January 3rd, 1944, and was promoted to the rank of Admiral (he was already acting in that rank) on February 7th, 1944.

It was obvious that, with the *Tirpitz* and the *Scharnhorst* disposed of, there would come a regrouping of the fleets; and, since the surrender of the Italian fleet, heavy ships were not required in the Mediterranean except for bombardment purposes. It followed that the centre of gravity of British naval power, so far as the battle fleet was concerned, would shift eastwards. Mr. Curtin, the Australian Prime Minister, hinted as much when he reported to the Federal Parliament in July, 1944, on the results of his recent talks in London and Washington. When Mr. Curtin said: "Large and powerful British forces will become available in the Pacific theatre this year," it was clear that he was speaking chiefly of naval forces, for the British Army and Air Force were fully committed in Europe and on the India-Burma frontier.

There could be no better man to command a greatly reinforced Eastern Fleet on the offensive than Bruce Fraser. Admiral Sir James Somerville had done great work out there in the lean years, but he had been constantly at sea since 1940 and needed the comparative rest of a shore appointment. When Bruce Fraser turned over the command of the Home Fleet to Vice-Admiral Sir Henry Moore in June, 1944, the fact that he was destined to command the Eastern Fleet was kept secret by the Admiralty. Among the uninformed this led to rumours that Fraser was in disgrace or out of favour for a variety of highly improbable reasons. That embarrassment was also caused at the other side of the world was evidenced by the following typical signal from Sir James Somerville to Sir Andrew Cunningham, the First Sea Lord. "When may I divulge my movements," Somerville signalled. "I am finding it increasingly difficult to conceal my interesting condition?"

The Admiralty duly announced Sir Bruce Fraser's appointment as Commander-in-Chief of the Eastern Fleet on the 1st August, 1944, and in December 1944 when the British Pacific Fleet was formed, his appointment as Commander-in-Chief of that fleet. In the words of Mr. Winston Churchill in his personal message of congratulation to Fraser after the sinking of the *Scharnhorst*, "All comes to him who knows how to wait."

LEONARD WARREN MURRAY

C.B., C.B.E.

Rear-Admiral, Royal Canadian Navy

LEONARD MURRAY, now Commander-in-Chief of the Canadian North-West Atlantic, is the first Canadian officer ever to hold the full responsibilities and operational powers of a Commander-in-Chief in a vital area in time of war. He is the only officer of the Royal Canadian Navy to have held an appointment as deputy to the commander of a Task Force in the United States Navy. He has had the queer experience of commanding a belligerent force which was operating under the strategic control of an admiral whose country was not even at war. And he is probably the only flag officer serving to-day in one of the major navies of the United Nations who has ever stood trial for his life on a charge of being a bandit.

Murray's excursion into alleged banditry arose out of a love of sport and a small matter of five dozen bottles of beer.

It happened this way. Murray, as a lieutenant, was serving as navigating officer of the light cruiser *Aurora*, which had been presented to the Royal Canadian Navy by the British Government, when that ship visited the Pacific coast of Mexico soon after the last war. During the visit it was decided to make a shooting expedition inland. The party was to consist of the Captain of the *Aurora*, the British Consul, the United States Consul, three Mexican gentlemen who could, of course, speak Spanish, and Lieutenant Murray; and the scheme was to ride to a place twenty-eight miles inland, spend the night in hammocks slung under trees, and go in search of game early next morning before the sun got too hot. The commissariat for the expedition was to go by ox-cart and was to consist of the camping equipment, guns and cartridges, food, and five dozen bottles of beer. The members of the expedition did not expect to consume all five dozen themselves, but took an ample supply as it was intended to have a party and regale the "city fathers" of the village of San Martel, which was their destination. The whole expedition was amply organised, particularly the commissariat, and the ox-cart duly left in the early afternoon.

Apparently the strain of ensuring the departure of the ox-cart in the heat of the day was too much for southern lethargy. In any event, the Mexican members of the party were not ready to leave at the scheduled time of 5 p.m. One delay led to another, and it was not until after 9 o'clock in the evening that they finally mounted and rode off after the ox-cart.

They had been riding for about two hours when somebody noticed that the tracks of the ox-cart took a wrong turning. To carry on without any commissariat was unthinkable, so the whole cavalcade went off on a hue and cry after the ox-cart. They rode several miles before they came up with the ox-cart, which was meandering along in complete indifference to time or direction. For ten miles the horsemen escorted the commissariat—at ox-cart pace—and saw it safely across a river and back on to the so-called road to San Martel. Then impatience got the better of them. If they did not go ahead they would not arrive before it was time to go out after such game as they expected to find—chiefly rabbits—and they would get no sleep at all. They accordingly removed from the ox-cart their guns and cartridges and hammocks and rode on, bidding the driver follow at his beasts' best speed and not to wander off the route under pain of the most dire penalties.

They arrived at the village of San Martel at about half-past two in the morning. Their greeting was anything but friendly. The appearance, at that time of night, of seven armed and mounted men was altogether too much for the local authorities, and the would-be shooting party was promptly surrounded by truculent gendarmes armed to the teeth. After some parleying it transpired that there had lately been a number of robberies in the district and that villagers and police were fully convinced that nobody but bandits would ride in armed at such an hour.

The local authorities wanted the party to ride on under guard to a place sixteen miles away where there was a jail where they could be securely locked up, but this the naval officers of the party stead-fastly refused to do. The seafaring life had not accustomed them to the saddle, and they had already ridden nearly forty miles that night. After further parleying it was agreed that they should sleep in the hammocks under the trees in a group surrounded with a guard of men with loaded rifles. So they turned in—but not to sleep. The commotion had roused the whole village, the devout population of which had repaired in a body to the parish church to sing Te Deums in thankfulness for their deliverance from robbery and rape.

At eight o'clock in the morning Murray and his companions were put on trial for their lives before the Mayor, the Magistrate, and the Chief of Police. The proceedings were complicated by language difficulties, and it was only after an hour and a half of argument and complete inspection of all the party's equipment, firearms and ammunition, that an acquittal was obtained. They were, however, far from free of their embarrassing predicament. If, the village authorities said, the party had really ridden all that way in order to shoot rabbits, they certainly should shoot rabbits. What was more, they should return to the village on completion of the shoot, when they would pay to the local taxes a contribution which would be assessed in accordance with the size of the bag. The authorities were, of course, careful not to indicate whether a large bag would mean a small or a large assessment, but they made it very clear that the sportsmen were to be accompanied while shooting by armed guards to ensure that they did not escape their obligations.

While all this parleying was going on, however, another complication had set in. The ox-cart had duly arrived and promptly been looted by the villagers, some of whom were showing signs of being troublesome as a result of the beer. The "city fathers" had missed the beer because of the trial, and were inclined to be even more troublesome on that account. And anyway, the sun was already high and any rabbits would have gone to ground long since.

In the general confusion the shooting party was able, by dint of much jockeying for position, to make good its escape on horseback, secure in the knowledge that they would not be pursued very far because horses were not kept in the village owing to the lack of water. Once away, they made a wide detour and returned eventually to the port where the *Aurora* was lying. They reached there about four o'clock in the afternoon, having ridden through the heat of the day and, incidentally, covered about seventy-five miles on horseback in nineteen hours—but shot no rabbits!

The story of Murray's career is one full of varied experiences, nearly all of which have stood him in very good stead in the positions of responsibility which he has subsequently had to assume. It is also a story of continued uncertainty as to the future of his

career, which was frequently overshadowed by national policies and
political influences. That was inevitable, for Murray's story is, in
many respects, the history of the Royal Canadian Navy.

Leonard Warren Murray was born at Granton, Nova Scotia, in
1896, and entered the Royal Naval College of Canada in January,
1911. The college had then just been opened and Murray was one
of the cadets of the first term to pass through that establishment. In
January, 1913, Murray went to sea in H.M.S. *Berwick*, a cruiser of
the Fourth Cruiser Squadron in the Home Fleet. Thus Murray's
first sea-going appointment was in a ship of the Royal Navy and
not of the Royal Canadian Navy.

At that time the Royal Canadian Navy was already in difficulties,
as it was a bone of contention in the conflict of policies between the
two political parties in Canada. The Liberal Party, under the
leadership of Sir Wilfred Laurier, had embarked upon the creation
of the Royal Canadian Navy in 1910, and the Service was therefore
stoutly supported by the Liberal Party. One of the first measures
following the creation of the Canadian Navy was the establishment
of the Royal Naval College of Canada at Halifax, where Murray
had been one of the first cadets.

In the elections of 1911, however, the Liberals were defeated at
the polls and the Conservatives were returned to power, a new
government being formed under the leadership of Sir Robert
Borden as Prime Minister, although the Senate remained predominantly Liberal.

Sir Robert Borden was impressed by the insistence of the British
authorities on the growing imminence of war in Europe; he was
convinced by the argument of the British Admiralty that the newly-
formed Royal Canadian Navy would be too late to play any valuable
part in the forthcoming war, and that what was really needed was
a system whereby Canada would provide a contribution for the
manning of the British Fleet.

Such a system Sir Robert Borden loyally tried to put into effect,
but he was opposed and prevented from doing so by the predominantly Liberal Senate, which would authorise no action that
would not continue the newly-formed Canadian Navy sponsored
and founded by their party.

While the political deadlock retarded development and reduced
confidence among Canadian naval officers and men, Murray was
training with the Fourth Cruiser Squadron of the Royal Navy. The

Fourth Cruiser Squadron was then commanded by Rear-Admiral Sir Christopher Cradock, who subsequently lost his life at the Battle of Coronel. In October, 1913, the squadron reopened the North America and West Indies Station, which has been in peace time one of the Royal Navy's foreign stations ever since. Within two months Admiral Cradock's ships were spread among the ports of the Gulf of Mexico, protecting British lives and British interests in the revolution which had broken out. The presence of the ships proved sufficient, and the necessity for landing personnel did not arise until some months later. By the time the United States forces landed and occupied Vera Cruz in April, 1914, Murray, then a midshipman, was back in the Naval College at Halifax, taking a course of instruction under the rather depressing circumstances of awaiting the final dissolution of the Royal Canadian Navy, which he had entered so hopefully on its foundation only just over three years before.

Meanwhile, the seemingly interminable negotiations, hampered as they were by political bias, were at last nearing agreement. One of the terms of the agreement finally reached was that the Canadian Naval College would continue to supply a number of officers to the Royal Navy each year. Those officers who had already graduated from the college were accordingly offered appointments in the Royal Navy, and Murray was appointed to H.M.S. *Lancaster* as a Midshipman R.N., with orders to join that ship at Bermuda on August 14th, 1914. Just before he sailed to take up the appointment, however, war broke out.

The outbreak of war at once changed the fate of the Royal Canadian Navy, which was at that time dying, with its two ships long laid up and the officers and men who had been borrowed from the Royal Navy returned to that Service. The Royal Canadian Navy was at once mobilised as such. Among many others, Murray's appointment for service in the Royal Navy was abruptly cancelled, and he was appointed instead to H.M.C.S. *Niobe*, which was hastily being made ready for sea.

Some weeks, however, elapsed before the *Niobe* could be commissioned for sea, and in the interim Midshipman Murray was employed as a cipher officer at the Naval Service Headquarters at Ottawa. For an intelligent and receptive young officer there can be few jobs more interesting than that of cipher officer at a great administrative naval headquarters in the weeks immediately following the outbreak of war. Murray was both, and he found the experience most enlightening. Handling signal traffic dealing with matters which would not normally come within the scope of an officer of his seniority, he gained a deep insight into the problems of mobilisation, administration and disposition of naval forces, and the defence of maritime trade. It was experience upon which he was to draw gratefully twenty-five years later, when he had to grapple with these problems as Deputy Chief of the Naval Staff in Ottawa.

After three weeks as cipher officer, Murray joined the *Niobe*, which was then ready for sea. She was commissioned under the command of Captain R. G. Corbett, R.N., with the officers and men of the two R.N. sloops, *Algerine* and *Shearwater*, lately paid off at the Pacific coast base of Esquimalt, backed up by 120 Newfoundland naval reservists and a large number of ex-naval ratings of the Royal Navy then living in Canada. Many of the latter were "King's Pardon" men who flocked to the colours with the Canadian volunteers. Throughout the winter of 1914 and the early spring of 1915 he served in the *Niobe*, to which ship was allotted the arduous task of patrolling and controlling the trade off the port of New York, but, of course, outside the limit of territorial waters, for the United States was neutral. Throughout that arduous winter of long nights, bitter cold, and fierce gales, Murray was midshipman in charge of small boats boarding and examining merchant ships stopped by the *Niobe*, and was more than once midshipman of a prize crew detailed to take a suspicious ship into a Canadian harbour for more thorough examination and search. It was a hard school, but Murray learnt in those months more practical seamanship than many another naval officer will learn in the whole of a long career. He also learnt to be self-reliant and to act on his own judgment and initiative, and he learnt to appreciate the complexities of the enforcement of a blockade, and more than a smattering of the principles of International Law involved.

In 1915 he was to be given even greater scope to exercise his own judgment and initiative. The Canadian Navy was short of experienced officers, as was hardly to be wondered at after the vicissitudes to which the Service had been subjected in the pre-war years, and Murray, although still a midshipman, was appointed as junior watch-keeper of a small patrol vessel. In June, 1915, his ship was detailed to organise a group of patrol vessels to work around the coasts of the Gulf of St. Lawrence and Newfoundland, and Midshipman Murray found himself in the position of gunnery officer of a whole group of ships manned by crews in which few men had ever seen a gun fired. It was his job not only to train them in the use of their weapons, but to handle the whole of the administrative side of the gunnery organisation of all the ships, demanding the ammunition, accounting for its expenditure and the necessary armament stores, and arranging for their handling and storage on board the ships. It was very much a case of "learning as you go along" for the gunnery officer as well as for his pupils, but somehow they got through, although Murray says to-day: "Thank God it was all before the days of the present stringent magazine and explosive regulations."

At the end of the Gulf of St. Lawrence season Murray had a brief period of service in H.M.C.S. *Rainbow*, operating in the Pacific as far south as Acapulco, in Mexico. Then, on December 1st, 1915, he received his commission as a Sub-Lieutenant. There can have been few officers who have crowded so much experience and so much responsibility into their careers before receiving their first commissions.

March, 1916, saw Murray once again serving with the Royal Navy. In that month he joined H.M.S. *Leviathan*, flagship of the North America and West Indies Station. The *Leviathan* then flew the flag of Vice-Admiral Sir L. E. Patey, but he was later relieved by Vice-Admiral Sir Montagu Browning—universally known as "Hooky" Browning because of the steel hook which did duty for the left hand which he had lost in an accident.

The *Leviathan's* chief duty at that time was escorting the big troop convoys across the Atlantic. It was a dull job, but it gave Murray valuable experience in the handling of large and valuable convoys, particularly as he was employed as assistant to the Fleet Navigating Officer during the time when the medium and slow speed trans-Atlantic trade convoys were organised and the system of their control and communications was worked out. This experience was to be of inestimable value to Murray in September, 1939, when he was Deputy Chief of the Naval Staff at Ottawa. In that post Murray had the lion's share in organising the Canadian end of the trans-Atlantic convoy system. When the *Athenia* was sunk by a U-boat north-west of Ireland within a few hours of the outbreak of war and it became obvious that Germany was embarking upon unrestricted submarine warfare, for the waging of which her U-boats were already on their stations on the Atlantic trade routes, immediate steps were taken to institute the convoy system. Murray saw to it that there was no delay other than the time required to allow sufficient shipping to accumulate to form a reasonable-sized convoy, and the first convoy sailed from Halifax on September 16th, 1939—six days after Canada had formally acknowledged a state of war with Germany.

Murray was serving in the *Leviathan* when, on April 10th, 1917, "Hooky" Browning visited the United States Fleet at Hampton Roads immediately after the United States had entered the war. At Hampton Roads at that time Murray made many friends among officers of the American Navy, and formed an admiration for that service. Both friendship and admiration have since been consolidated and broadened.

Promoted to Acting-Lieutenant in January, 1917, Murray was still a very junior officer when, in March, 1918, he was appointed to the battleship H.M.S. *Agincourt* in the Grand Fleet. In this ship he took part in the excitements of April, 1918, when for a few hours it seemed that the Grand Fleet would at last be able to bring the German High Seas Fleet to action, only to have its hopes dashed as a result of an accident to a German ship's engine-room and the subsequent successful attack of a British submarine.

The British Admiralty, and Admiral Beatty, had been nervous about our Scandinavian convoys ever since the tragedy of October 17th, 1917, when one of the convoys and its weak escorts had been virtually wiped out by a German cruiser force. It was in the hope of repeating this success that Von Scheer took the German High Seas Fleet to sea on its last sortie on April 23rd, 1918. It was some time before it was realised that the German Fleet was, in fact, at sea. Then the Grand Fleet sailed from Rosyth for the Long Forties. The *Agincourt*, which had been at Scapa Flow, and the *Hercules*, which had been at Invergordon, put to sea to support and strengthen the covering force of one of our Scandinavian convoys which was at sea at the time.

With the Grand Fleet steaming eastwards and the High Seas Fleet steaming northwards from the Heligoland Bight, it seemed that the stage was set for action, but fate intervened. The German battle-cruiser *Moltke*, which was leading the van of Von Hipper's scouting group ahead of the High Seas Fleet, had a cracked "A" bracket—the bracket which supports the propeller-shaft just before the propeller—which had been inefficiently repaired. On April

25th, when Von Hipper's force was west of Stavanger, the "A" bracket fractured, and the propeller shaft "whipped" so much that great damage was done to the engine-room and some boiler-rooms were flooded.

Von Hipper, however, was reluctant to abandon the operation, and ordered the *Moltke*, which was able to steam on one engine, to retire on Von Scheer, escorted by three torpedo boats. The *Moltke* was doing so when she was torpedoed by the British submarine *E42*, and so damaged that it was with difficulty that she was towed back to harbour by the battleship *Oldenburg*. This double misfortune was too much for Von Scheer. He turned the whole High Seas Fleet back to its bases, whence it was only emerged in order to surrender.

Acting-Lieutenant Murray was present at that historic surrender. Although only an acting-lieutenant, he was at that time performing the duties of First Lieutenant and Navigating Officer of the *Agincourt*, one of the largest ships in the Grand Fleet, owing to the illness of these two officers.

Murray did not return at once to the Royal Canadian Navy after the Armistice. He was confirmed in the rank of Lieutenant and appointed to the light cruiser H.M.S. *Calcutta*, flagship of Sir Alan Everett, commanding the Eighth Cruiser Squadron. The captain of the *Calcutta* was Percy Noble, now Admiral Sir Percy Noble, until lately head of the British Admiralty Delegation in Washington. Percy Noble had a great flair for dealing with men, and from him Murray learnt a great deal of the art of looking after the interests of his men and obtaining the combination of a happy and efficient ship.

Sir Alan Everett in the *Calcutta* was destined to reopen the North America and West Indies Station, which had been in abeyance during the latter years of the war, and Murray was greatly looking forward to returning to the western side of the Atlantic, but he was doomed to disappointment. The departure of the *Calcutta* for the West Indies was delayed, and in the interval Murray, who had shown great aptitude in H.M.S. *Leviathan* and H.M.S. *Agincourt*, was selected to specialise in navigation, so instead of crossing the Atlantic he had with great regret to leave the *Calcutta* and go instead to the Navigation School in the dockyard at Portsmouth. His return to the Western Atlantic was, however, only postponed, and when he did go it was in the proud and responsible position of fully qualified Navigation Officer of the light cruiser *Aurora*, presented to Canada by the United Kingdom, and the most important ship of the Royal Canadian Navy.

The years following the Great War of 1914-1918 were years of retrenchment in all navies and of uncertainty and anxiety for all naval officers. In no navy was this so marked as in the Royal Canadian Navy, where not only careers were at stake, but the existence of the whole Service was often in doubt. The Canadian people felt that they were very far removed from any threat of future wars, and that in any case they could not afford to maintain a navy which would be capable of guarding Canada's long coast lines or her interests overseas. In the circumstances the maintenance of a small navy was inevitably regarded as an expensive sentimentalism rather than as an essential nucleus around which to build a strong force if the need should ever again arise.

Such was the uncertainty as to the future that, when Murray had the unpleasant experience in the smoking-room of the Navigation School at Portsmouth of reading in an evening paper a report that the Royal Canadian Navy had been disbanded, he had no reason completely to discredit it. He spent several anxious days before it became apparent that it was merely a book-keeping transaction coupled with the disbandment of the temporary and "hostilities only" officers and men. The permanent members of the Royal Canadian Navy were, in fact, disbanded on paper, but were put back on the strength of a new Royal Canadian Navy on the following day.

Uncertainty and anxiety persisted, however, for there was no denying that the people of Canada were not greatly interested in naval affairs. The British Government regarded the circumstances and prospects of the Royal Canadian Navy with some concern, as well as the naval forces of the other Dominions and of India. In March, 1917, the Imperial War Conference had requested the Admiralty to consider what would be the most effective post-war scheme of naval defence for the Empire. The result had been an Admiralty Memorandum of May, 1918, which recommended the creation of a single Imperial Navy under central authority both in peace and war, to which the countries of the Empire should contribute contingents. This scheme was rejected by the Dominion Ministers. The result was two-fold. The British Government, at the instigation of the Admiralty, invited Admiral of the Fleet Lord

Jellicoe of Scapa to head a naval mission to visit India and all the
Dominions to discuss naval needs and advise the Dominion Governments. Meanwhile the Admiralty settled down to reconsider the
question and in October, 1919, produced a further Memorandum on
the subject, the opening sentence of which was: "In view of their
decision on the Admiralty Memorandum of May, 1918, the
Dominions can now best contribute to the naval defence of the
Empire by building up their own Navies."

Lord Jellicoe and his mission had left Portsmouth on February
21st, 1919, and had already visited India, Ceylon, Australia, New
Zealand and various Pacific islands and was nearing Canada before
the second Admiralty Memorandum, which framed the policy for
the whole work of his mission, was issued at home, and it was not
received by Lord Jellicoe until December 5th. The Jellicoe Mission
had arrived at Esquimalt on November 8th, where it was met by
Admiral Sir Charles Kingsmill, the Director of the Naval Service of
Canada. Lord Jellicoe had already visited Ottawa before he received
the text of the new Admiralty Memorandum, but he went back to
Ottawa for a second visit before leaving Canada.

There had been considerable discussion regarding the disposal
of various ships which, with the coming of peace, were redundant
to the Royal Navy, and it had been suggested that these should be
allotted to the Dominions to assist them in building up their own
navies. The suggestion had been accepted in principle, and this news
had reached Lord Jellicoe when he was in New Zealand. The
important thing for Lord Jellicoe to know was whether the British
Government proposed to make gifts of these ships or whether they
expected the Dominion Governments to buy them. As late as
December 1st, when he was halfway through his Canadian tour,
Lord Jellicoe cabled to the Admiralty: "Matters would be greatly
facilitated if position regarding gift of ships were clear," but the
only reply he received was to the effect that ships would be ear-
marked for the Dominions after January 31st, 1920, but whether for
gift or purchase could not be guaranteed.

By the nature of his mission and by reason of his naval rank
Lord Jellicoe had to deal with the Admiralty, which has no power
to give away or sell ships without the authority of the Treasury.
The Treasury is the guardian of the taxpayers' money, and the ships
in question had been built with the taxpayers' money, so that the
Treasury could hardly be blamed for not wishing to give them

away when it was felt that they might well have been purchased. The resulting delay in taking a decision was unfortunate, but it was inherent in the British system of government.

The extent to which this uncertainty embarrassed the work of the Jellicoe Mission, and the state of affairs in Canada as regards the future of the Royal Canadian Navy, are well expressed in the following extract from a personal letter written by Lord Jellicoe to Mr. Walter Long, the First Lord of the Admiralty, and quoted in full in Sir Reginald Bacon's biography of Lord Jellicoe:

"3.12.19.

"My Dear First Lord,

"I have sent two or three telegrams since arrival here on the subject of the attitude of the Canadian Government towards a Naval policy for Canada. I felt it necessary to do this because the situation is critical.

"Sir Robert Borden, pressed hard by Mr. Ballantyne, is in favour of an immediate start being made. On the other hand, some Ministers wish to postpone matters either for political or for financial reasons.

"Mr. Ballantyne, who is very much in earnest, is concerned that unless the matter is settled now, before I leave Canada, nothing will be done for several years. He tells me distinctly that unless a serious start is made now, he intends to wipe out completely the present Canadian Naval Service, as being a pure waste of money. He is right.

"For this reason a very sympathetic attitude towards Canada is most desirable now. If possible, modern ships should be offered as a gift. Light cruisers and submarines are the principal requirements. I trust that the Admiralty will be able to do this, so that the opportunity of starting Canada on the right lines may not be lost."

The following extract from Lord Jellicoe's report on his tour in Canada is also of interest as showing the Canadian people's attitude to their navy at that time, as well as the way in which ill-considered statements in the British House of Commons may be used for political purposes abroad. The report was dated January 1st, 1920.

"While there is a very considerable section of the population which is fully alive to the vital importance of Sea Power, there is another section which does not consider it necessary for Canada to take any part in Naval defence, and yet a third section which looks with the greatest suspicion upon any such steps being taken in the direction of Canada's participation in Naval defence, as it might draw the Dominion into war.

"A recent statement in the House of Commons to the effect that the Home Government has not yet been able to decide upon a future Naval policy, has been seized upon in Canada by those who are opposed to taking a share in Naval defence as a good argument for delaying matters."

It all seemed very depressing, yet Lord Jellicoe's visit to Canada certainly did help those in the Dominion who wanted to revive the Royal Canadian Navy, and was largely instrumental in preparing the ground for Canada's acceptance of ships from the Royal Navy when it was finally decided that these should be gifts to the Dominions from the Home Government.

Thus the Canadian Government accepted the gift of one light cruiser, two destroyers, and two submarines. The light cruiser was H.M.C.S. *Aurora*, in which ship Murray crossed the Atlantic, serving as her Navigating Officer.

The ships of the reconstituted Royal Canadian Navy trained and exercised with the Royal Navy of the North America and West Indies Station, so Murray was able to see more of his former shipmates in H.M.S. *Calcutta*, the flagship of that station. The Canadian ships attained a high standard of efficiency, and all seemed to be going well with the Royal Canadian Navy.

But not for long. Two years later, in the middle of 1922, it was again dragged into the arena of Canadian party politics. There was a change of Government at that time, and the new Government, looking round for ways and means to economise, promptly made an arbitrary reduction of 40 per cent in the Navy Estimates. The Royal Canadian Navy was once again reduced to a condition of virtual impotence. The politicians responsible could not, or would not, see that a cut of this magnitude in naval expenditure would reduce a virile and useful force to the level of virtual uselessness, so that by saving 40 per cent of the expenditure they were throwing away the remaining 60 per cent in addition to all the money which had been invested in the Service in the past two years ; but it is one of the inherent weaknesses of the democratic system of Government that the short-term view of those momentarily in power so often prevails.

Murray felt the new set-back to the Royal Canadian Navy very deeply. He was now the senior surviving officer who had graduated from the Royal Naval College at Halifax, and he already felt a heavy responsibility for achieving success with the Canadian Navy. This was no easy matter, with the fortunes of the whole Service fluctuating with every change of Government, but he felt, even at that time, the importance of giving careful consideration to every action taken, since in a young Service these actions and decisions would be likely to become precedents for future usage.

Murray was whole-heartedly enthusiastic about the Royal Canadian Navy, and held firm in his belief in it whatever the politicians and public opinion of Canada might think, but he was in a very difficult position. The *Aurora* had been paid off. The Canadian Navy, reduced as it was to a complement of 483 officers and men, had no appointment suitable for a fully qualified navigating officer of his seniority and experience. In other words, he was out of a job in the Service which he loved. Moreover, it seemed very doubtful whether the Royal Navy would give him employment, for that Service was busily engaged in "axing" hundreds of officers of about his seniority. To these Service worries was added that of his personal position. The fact that he had married gave him an added responsibility during that difficult year of 1922 which marked a major crisis in the life of a young and eager naval officer.

At this time Murray was made a most tempting offer to leave the Naval Service and try his hand in the organisation and operation of a large manufacturing business. Many men would have accepted the offer as a heaven-sent solution to his problems, but Murray did not. He rejected the offer of lucrative employment ashore, sent a request to Naval Headquarters, Ottawa, to be appointed for service in the Royal Navy in order to gain experience, obtained a Master Mariner's certificate as an insurance in order to secure some sort of sea-going employment if both the Admiralty and the Naval Headquarters at Ottawa refused him an appointment. Then he retired into the wilderness on unemployment pay to await the decision of the Admiralty.

Murray's decision to stake everything on the continuance of his chosen career as a naval officer was, after three months of suspense, rewarded with the good fortune which courage deserves. He was appointed Second Navigating Officer to the battleship H.M.S. *Revenge*, the flagship of Admiral Sir Arthur A. M. Duff in the eastern Mediterranean. Here was experience and to spare. The *Revenge* had been sent out from the Grand Fleet—which after the war became known as the Atlantic Fleet—to reinforce the British in the Bosphorus. The confusion of the immediate post-war years had produced a most difficult situation in that area. Mr. Lloyd George's Government had decided to back the Greeks against the Turks, in a dispute in which practically every European country had a finger. The Turks, however, had experienced a great national resurgence under Mustapha Kemal—afterwards Ataturk, first President of the Turkish Republic and staunch friend of Britain. Under his leadership the Turks had driven the Greeks out of Anatolia in ignominy both to the Greeks and to those nations who had encouraged the Greek excursion into Asia Minor with words but were not prepared to go further in the cause of their erstwhile allies. It was fortunate that they were not, for strength and sympathy were both on the side of the new Turkish Nationalists under Kemal. They, having won a great and spectacular campaign, not unnaturally wished to see it consolidated by international treaty. Moreover, they wished to take over control of Constantinople—Istanbul as it is now called—which was then still under a serio-comic regime known as "Inter-national Control."

The situation was tense and a renewal of war with Turkey was expected almost hourly by those on the spot. Naval officers and sailors dyed their white duck suits in strong coffee, and dug trenches on the Asiatic shores of the Bosphorus and the Dardanelles. The diplomacy of General Sir Charles Harington averted hostilities and eased the situation by the treaty which he signed at Mudonia, on the shores of the Sea of Marmora. Nevertheless, a British army of 4000 men faced 40,000 well-equipped Nationalist Turks across an agreed line at Gebse, while the British naval force under Admiral Duff stood by to give, from the ships, such artillery support as would be possible in that hilly country. Meanwhile the chancelleries of Europe buzzed, and the peoples showed less than no interest.

Preparing for bombardment by indirect fire gave the navigating staffs of the ships plenty to do, while the strong currents of the Bosphorus and the sudden gales of the Sea of Marmora and the

Black Sea saw to it that they did not forget their ordinary navigation or seamanship.

In May, 1923, by which time the Treaty of Lausanne had put
an abrupt end to the tension in the eastern Mediterranean, H.M.S.
Revenge returned to England, and Murray was then transferred to
H.M.S. *Queen Elizabeth*, flagship of the Atlantic Fleet. His appointment was as Assistant to the Master of the Fleet. The title is a
survival from the old days of sail. To-day the Master of the Fleet
is the Fleet Navigating Officer on the staff of the Commander-in-
Chief.

As Assistant to the Master of the Fleet in the *Queen Elizabeth*
Murray learnt a lot. As a result of the experiences of the war, which
staffs had now had time to analyse in detail, all sorts of new developments in material and new tactics had been worked out. The Atlantic Fleet was the "proving ground" for all these new weapons and
theories of how best to handle them and defend against them.
Everything, whether gun, torpedo or aircraft, resolved itself into
tactics, and it was the business of the Master of the Fleet and his
Assistant to analyse these after every exercise and make recommendations for their alteration or improvement. In this forcing house
Murray grew rapidly in experience and mental stature, gaining
insight into all manner of complicated manœuvres and developing
a quick critical faculty enabling him to see quickly what was wrong
and make constructive suggestions for improvement. Moreover, in
the *Queen Elizabeth* Murray came into contact with a number of
naval officers whose names were to be written large in naval history
—such men as William Wordsworth Fisher, who was to be Commander-in-Chief in the Mediterranean during the critical days of
1935 and to whose development of the night-fighting technique the
Navy owes a big share of the victory of Cape Matapan; Charles
Forbes, who was to be Commander-in-Chief of the Home Fleet in
the first fifteen months of this war; John Cunningham, who is
now Commander-in-Chief in the Mediterranean; and many others.

After a year in the *Queen Elizabeth*, however, it was time for
Murray to go back to the Navigation School at Portsmouth for
what is known as the "big ship course," in which navigating officers
have to qualify before being entrusted with the sole charge of the
navigation of a "first-class ship"—meaning a battleship, battle-
cruiser, or aircraft carrier. Murray qualified with ease, and because
of his showing was retained at the Navigation School on the staff

of the establishment as an instructor in navigation and in fleet
tactics and manœuvres.

That appointment was of short duration, for the Royal Canadian
naval authorities found that they now had a suitable appointment
in Canada for Murray, and recalled him to Halifax, where he served
as executive officer of the naval barracks for the next two years.
After that he was again released by the Canadian authorities for sea-
service with the Royal Navy, the Canadian Navy having no ships
in which a navigating officer of his seniority and experience could
undergo the sea service which was necessary in order that Murray
should qualify for promotion.

Murray spent the next six months as navigating officer of the
battle-cruiser *Tiger*, the second heaviest ship in the Royal Navy
at that time. Then he was selected for a course of study at the Royal
Naval Staff College.

While at the Staff College there occurred an amusing incident
which, incidentally, showed the way in which Murray's restless
mind was for ever looking ahead. An amphibious operation was
being planned by the Staff College, and Murray was acting as Chief
of Staff to the officer detailed to act as naval Commander-in-Chief
of the operation being planned—only as an exercise, of course. It
therefore fell to Murray to organise the convoys and their escorts
for the expedition. When the plans of the three Services were complete and had been examined by the directorates of the Staff Colleges,
a meeting of all concerned in the Staff Colleges of all three Services
was called to discuss the plans. At this meeting Murray was severely
criticised by the then Deputy Director of the Naval Staff College
for having put as many as thirty-six ships in a single convoy. To
group as many ships in one convoy was considered, by contemporary
thought at that time, to be almost suicidal. Yet in 1940, when
Murray was Deputy Chief of the Naval Staff in Ottawa, he found it
necessary to group as many as seventy ships in a convoy—and the
officer commanding the escorting forces of the Royal Navy, and
who successfully escorted these immense convoys, was the officer
who had been Deputy Director of the Naval Staff College and had
objected so strongly to Murray thinking in terms of thirty-six-ship
convoys!

In 1929 Murray was promoted to the rank of Commander and
was appointed to command the Canadian Naval Station on the
Pacific coast, with headquarters at Esquimalt. His duties were to

plan the requirements in case of war, and lay the foundations for naval expansion in that event. It was a pretty comprehensive assignment and there was little enough with which to go to work, for the naval expenditure was rigidly limited, and even such expansion as could be visualised in the event of war had to be planned within the narrow limits of such budgetary provisions as could be considered probable.

It was small enough in all conscience. Murray had at his disposal only one destroyer and two minesweeping trawlers, and with these he had to stage strategical and tactical exercises which had sufficient realism to interest officers and men.

For two and a half years Murray laboured on the Canadian Pacific coast. He must often have thought that he was being called upon to make bricks without straw, but his eagerness to see that the Royal Canadian Navy should, for all its diminutive size, yield nothing in efficiency to other larger navies surmounted all obstacles, and his long experience in the Royal Navy, particularly in dealing with tactical problems, proved invaluable.

From Esquimalt Murray went to Ottawa, where he served as Naval Staff Officer at the Naval Service Headquarters for a year before again being appointed to sea. This sea appointment was in command of the Canadian destroyer *Saguenay* and as senior Royal Canadian officer afloat. Here was an appointment after his own heart. At last he was in command of Canadian ships at sea, with the task of organising and training their crews under realistic conditions at sea. He worked them hard, but his keenness was infectious and officers and men repaid him for the trouble he took in working out all sorts of exercise and drills to promote their efficiency. As a result the destroyers of the Royal Canadian Navy, now raised to four in number, acquitted themselves well when Murray led them to take part, for the first time, in large-scale manœuvres with the British Home Fleet in West Indian waters.

In 1934, however, Murray had to leave the sea-going ships and take over command of the Atlantic coast of Canada. This command was based on Halifax and involved a great deal of administrative work, including the direct command of a dockyard. Here again, he had an eye to the future, and many of the steps which he took were consciously designed to facilitate rapid expansion in the event of war. And even in the days when Murray was in command at Halifax the threat of war was coming nearer owing to the failure of the collective security ideal to stop Mussolini's invasion of Abyssinia and the growing pace of German rearmament.

Murray stayed at Halifax for the normal period of two years. Then he was again released for service with the Royal Navy, and crossed the Atlantic to take up an appointment as one of the "Duty Commanders" in the Operations Division of the Naval Staff of the Admiralty. Then he served for a time as executive officer of H.M.S. *Iron Duke*—the grand old ship which had worn Admiral Jellicoe's flag at the Battle of Jutland, but was then in a sad, semi-demilitarised state—acting as experimental and gunnery training firing ship at Portsmouth. From the *Iron Duke* Murray went to the Imperial Defence College for a course of study lasting a year. In August, 1938, he was promoted to the rank of Captain and at the end of that year returned to Canada as Director of Naval Operations and Training at the Canadian Naval Headquarters in Ottawa.

By that time war was imminent. Munich provided a breathing space, but Murray was under no illusions of it being more than a breathing space, an hour of which must not be lost in preparing for the struggle which had by now become inevitable. All Murray's experience, and particularly his recent experiences at the Admiralty and at the Imperial Defence College, had fitted him for the post he held, and he threw himself into his new tasks with tremendous energy and enthusiasm. He began making a routine of working for a fourteen-hour day, and since then he has often worked longer hours, but never shorter.

On the outbreak of war Murray became Deputy Chief of the Naval Staff in Ottawa.

His two greatest tasks as Deputy Chief of the Naval Staff were the organising of the Canadian end of the Atlantic convoy system, and organising and controlling the rapid expansion of the Royal Canadian Navy. Looking back over his pre-war career one is struck with the way in which experiences which seemed of little account at the time proved of immense value to him in the testing time of war. Those three weeks as cipher officer at Naval Headquarters at the beginning of the last war had shown him what to expect on the outbreak of war. His time in the *Niobe* and in the *Leviathan* had taught him the problems to be faced in the control and protection of shipping. His long preoccupation with the training of the small peace-time Royal Canadian Navy and his passionate keenness that it should be an efficient nucleus around which to build expansion was bearing fruit.

The peace-time strength of the Royal Canadian Navy was 1683 officers and men, with 500 naval reserves, and 1000 volunteer reserves. The first problem of expansion with which Murray had to deal was to absorb the flow of man-power which rapidly became available, for recruits came in by thousands from people who had shown scant interest in naval affairs in the forgetful years of peace. Admiral Murray has himself said: "This expansion was only made possible by the presence in Canada and the United States of a large number of officers on the retired list of the Royal Navy. By arrangement between the two navies, these officers were made available to the Royal Canadian Navy on mobilisation, and their experience and enthusiastic application to the problems of their adopted Service cannot be over-emphasised. These officers were available for service even before the Royal Canadian Navy was empowered to call up its own reserves, and their knowledge enabled the growing Service to carry on for the first two or three years of the war, until the various Naval Reserve and Naval Volunteer Reserve officers were sufficiently trained to allow responsibility to be placed on their shoulders."

The next problem was to provide ships of a simple type which could be manned efficiently by crews consisting largely of partially trained amateurs while these were gaining the necessary experience and becoming professionals.

Both problems were to a great extent resolved by Germany's immediate recourse to unrestricted submarine warfare and the consequent introduction of a widespread convoy system. Hard pressed for escort vessels, and for almost every other type of ship, Admiral Fraser, the Controller of the Navy at the Admiralty, evolved the corvette, a type of escort vessel which could be built quickly and without interfering unduly with other shipbuilding. Moreover, the corvette was simple as to machinery and armament.

Here was a type of ship peculiarly suited to the needs of Canadian naval expansion, for corvettes could be built in many of the shipyards of Canada and could be manned by semi-experienced seamen with little previous knowledge of naval matters. Murray stood squarely behind his Chief of the Naval Staff, Admiral Nelles, in forming and carrying out a policy which involved the building of corvettes at every available building site in the country and in manning them by Canadians as they left the building yards. Thus

the Royal Canadian Navy expanded as fast as these little ships could
be built. Since then other more powerful warships have been
built in Canada, notably frigates, and destroyers of the Tribal
class, and the expansion of the Royal Canadian Navy had, by May,
1944, already reached a stage when from a peace-time establishment
of just over 3000 officers and men, including reserves, it had reached
a strength of 77,000 officers and men.

When France collapsed and Britain stood alone against Germany
and Italy, Canada and the United States of America agreed upon a
policy of common action for home defence of the North American
Continent. A permanent body, known as the Canada-United States
Joint Defence Board—was set up to co-ordinate plans for common
defence in case of need. Murray was one of the original members of
this Board.

In October, 1940, Murray again went to sea—this time commanding the Halifax Force with his broad pendant as Commodore
First Class flying in H.M.C.S. *Assiniboine*. No submarine threat
having then developed in Canadian waters, the Royal Canadian Navy
placed this force at the disposal of the British Admiralty, to be used
where the U-boats were operating. They were employed on the vital
task of protecting our North Atlantic trade routes, and were therefore placed under the command of the Commander-in-Chief,
Western Approaches, who was then Admiral Sir Percy Noble, who
had been Murray's captain in the *Calcutta*. In order to administer
the Canadian ships working with the Royal Navy, Murray was
appointed to command H.M. Canadian Ships and Establishments in
European Waters. As such he had his headquarters in London.

Having been a member of the Canada-United States Joint
Defence Board, and being available in the United Kingdom during
the early part of 1941, Murray was selected to assist the High
Commissioner for Canada in the negotiations which led to the
signature of the Protocol to the Leased Bases Agreement between
Great Britain and the United States of America, and he was privi-
leged to sign that Protocol on behalf of his country. This Protocol
concerns Canada's interest in Newfoundland as a base for defence,
and confirms that both Great Britain and the United States recognise
this interest and will consult Canada before making any change in
the main agreement which would affect Newfoundland.

By May, 1941, the Canadian naval building and training programme was beginning to bear fruit. At the same time the German

U-boats had begun to attack our convoys farther west than they could be escorted from the United Kingdom. It was obviously necessary therefore to give the convoys adequate anti-submarine escorts for the whole of their voyage. The decision to do so could not be implemented from one side of the Atlantic alone owing to the comparatively low fuel endurance of the anti-submarine escorts available. It followed therefore that a great convoy escort base would have to be established on the west side of the Atlantic, to work almost as an "opposite number" to Liverpool.

The late Admiral of the Fleet Sir Dudley Pound was First Sea Lord at the time. He was very sensible of the great and growing contribution to the Battle of the Atlantic being provided by Canada, and he had formed a high opinion of Commodore Murray's experience and ability during the latter's few months in London. He therefore requested the Royal Canadian Naval authorities to allow Murray to command the new base in Newfoundland and the ships that were to operate from it. The Canadian naval authorities agreed, and Murray accepted with alacrity. Here was a really big job. He had to organise both a big new base and the operation of the escort forces on the western end of the North Atlantic trade routes, amounting to upwards of seventy ships—destroyers and corvettes.

There was a tremendous amount to do and, as usual, very little time in which to do it. The harbour was ridiculously small to be used as a base for more than seventy ships, but fortunately only a proportion of them were in port at one time. There were no wharves or jetties capable of holding even a destroyer during the frequent gales. Murray had to start almost single-handed and build up his staff as officers became available. His normal working day of fourteen hours was extended to eighteen hours, and that proved barely enough in the early days of the Newfoundland base. His secretary did not arrive until nearly two months had passed, but his Chief of Staff, Captain R. E. S. Bidwell, R.C.N., arrived two weeks after operations commenced. Murray received most valuable help from Captain C. M. R. Schwerdt, C.V.O., C.B.E., R.N., who had been Naval Officer in Charge of the port up to that time.

In an astonishingly short time, however, the new base was fully operative and it, and the ships based on it, were playing a very important part in the ceaseless Battle of the Atlantic.

Then there happened one of the most peculiar incidents in the history of international relations. The Prime Minister of Britain and the President of the United States met at what is known as the "Atlantic Meeting." At that meeting it was decided that the United States would help to deliver the goods as well as to produce them. A delivery service was to be added to the "arsenal of democracy." To facilitate the administrative control of this new service the Atlantic Ocean was divided into two zones of strategic influence. Thus, from September 15th, 1941, the date of the establishment of the two Atlantic zones, until the day of the Japanese attack on Pearl Harbour, Murray and his forces were waging war under the strategic control of an Admiral whose country was still neutral.

Murray's many friendships in the United States Navy, which had begun when he visited Hampton Roads in H.M.S. *Leviathan* when the United States entered the last war, and which had been extended by associations consequent upon his membership of the Canada-United States Permanent Joint Defence Board, proved invaluable at a time when many complicated problems arose out of the completely different status of the two forces involved in the Western Atlantic.

In September, 1942, Murray was moved from Newfoundland to take command of the Atlantic coast of Canada. Early in the following year he enjoyed, for a period of six weeks, an appointment in the United States Fleet as Deputy to the Commander of the United States Naval Task Force No. 24. This American Task Force had been giving great assistance in the war against the U-boats in the north Atlantic, but it had been decided that trade defence in the north-western Atlantic should be taken over completely by the still growing Royal Canadian Navy, with such assistance as was necessary from the Royal Navy and other Allied Navies, so that the United States Navy should be entirely free for service elsewhere. It was during the transition period, while Murray was taking over the responsibilities which had been shouldered by the American Task Force No. 24 that he was appointed as Deputy to the Commander of that force.

The Newfoundland Command had been absorbed in the Canadian Atlantic Coast Command in the previous month, and on April 1st, 1943, Murray, now a Rear-Admiral, took over control of all the shipping and escorts operating from Canada or Newfoundland. He was given the title and status of Commander-in-Chief, Canadian North-west Atlantic and thus became the first Canadian officer ever to hold the full status of a Naval Commander-in-Chief in war.

One of Murray's great assets is that he is a good "mixer," an asset which has been exploited by circumstances throughout his career. Apart from his friendships among officers of the United States Navy, he has a host of friends in the Royal Navy. As a result of his long periods of service with the Royal Navy he knows as much about its tradition and its work and about the outlook and aspirations of its officers and men as most British naval officers. When he was in London on an official visit in June, 1943, he daily attended the Staff Meeting at the Admiralty at which the heads of all the divisions of the Naval Staff and many Admiralty departments bring up urgent day-to-day matters for discussion under the chairmanship of the Vice-Chief of the Naval Staff. At one of these meetings Murray took a count and he found that out of the thirty-five officers present he had been shipmates with, or had served on close intimate terms with twenty-two.

In Newfoundland, and in his present appointment as Commander-in-Chief, Canadian North-west Atlantic, he has had many dealings with our Allies, having had serving under his command ships of the Polish, Netherlands, Norwegian and Fighting French Navies, the crews of all of which looked to him for advice, help and some of the comfort which their own countries were unable to provide. Murray deals with them faithfully and sympathetically, and in so doing he is greatly helped by his wife, who has lived much abroad and is an excellent linguist with a personal and intimate knowledge of many of the peoples of Europe, particularly the French.

Much of Murray's flair for friendship and dealing with others lies in his essentially straightforward approach to anybody or anything with which he may be confronted. It would never occur to him to be tortuous or ironic. Moreover, he is a firm believer in the creed that the sole object of the shore staff at the base is to serve the ships at sea and make the lives of their crews easier. When a ship arrives at a base under Murray's command, fresh provisions, mail, and the rest are waiting on the jetty and placed on board within twenty minutes—or else . . .

As Commander-in-Chief of a great and vital area of sea and sea coast, Murray is a very busy man, but, because he is really interested in every move and every experience of his ships, he is never too busy or too tired to receive the commanding officers of his ships on their return to harbour. This has been a considerable factor in the success

of the comparatively inexperienced commanding officers of many
of the ships in the rapidly expanding Royal Canadian Navy. They
always feel that they can approach their Commander-in-Chief and
get a sympathetic hearing and some well-chosen advice—sometimes
forcefully administered but always direct and very much to the
point.

Although Rear-Admiral Murray is so closely concerned with the
war in the Atlantic, his great hope is that the war with Germany
and the U-boats will be finished while he is still sufficiently junior
as a flag officer to obtain command of a Cruiser Squadron or Task
Force in the war against Japan.

Crown Copyright Reserved

Rear-Admiral Leonard W. Murray

ROBERT ST. VINCENT SHERBROOKE

V.C., D.S.O.

Captain Royal Navy

THE Nottinghamshire village of Oxton, in the Sherwood Forest, has a highly prized possession. It is a White Ensign—the battle ensign under which men gave their lives in one of the most gallant naval actions of this century, and under which Robert St. Vincent Sherbrooke of Oxton Hall earned the Victoria Cross.

R. St. V. Sherbrooke was christened "Robert," but he has never been known by that name. From the day of his christening he has been called Rupert, this departure from the name given him by his godfathers and godmothers having been adopted by common consent to avoid confusion with his uncle Robert Sherbrooke.

There have been Sherbrookes at Oxton Hall since the fifteenth century, and Robert Sherbrooke seems to be surrounded by naval tradition. His very name—St. Vincent—proclaims it. This he got from his grandmother, who was a Jervis, and a descendant of Admiral John Jervis, who became the first Lord St. Vincent after the victory off Cape St. Vincent on February 14th, 1797. That victory—"Old Jarvie's Valentine," as the sailors called it—was won against odds of 2 to 1, and Admiral Sir John Jervis led into action muttering: "A victory is very essential to England at this moment." Robert St. Vincent Sherbrooke's victory of December 31st, 1942, was against far heavier odds, and it was very essential to both England and Russia.

Robert Sherbrooke's grandfather served in the Royal Navy. So did his father, who earned a D.S.O. in the last war. Ships' names as well as family names seem to play their part. Robert Sherbrooke won his D.S.O. in H.M.S. *Cossack*, one of the most famous ships of this war, and his V.C. in H.M.S. *Onslow*, a successor to the ship of the same name in which Admiral Sir John Tovey won his D.S.O. at the Battle of Jutland.

The action in which Sherbrooke earned his Victoria Cross seems curiously unreal even to-day. It has come to be known as the Battle of the Barents Sea. It was fought on the last day of 1942 right up "on the roof of the world," five hundred miles within the Arctic Circle, where at that time of year the sun never rises, and so-called day is limited to rather less than three hours of murky twilight around noon. Even now it is not certain exactly what enemy forces took part, or exactly how they operated.

What is certain is that Sherbrooke fought off, with his destroyers, a greatly superior German force and thereby saved from annihilation merchant ships and merchant seamen carrying important supplies to Russia in the time of her need. As Sherbrooke himself said afterwards: "Had the roles been reversed, the convoy would not have arrived at its destination complete and practically undamaged." The truth of the matter seems to be that the British destroyers bluffed the enemy, "ran rings round him" and sent him off smarting and damaged from an action in which, according to all the rules, he should have had things all his own way. This Sherbrooke did by seizing the initiative and exploiting the spirit of the offensive. As has happened so often at sea, the Germans showed themselves quite unable to cope with what their text-book sailors would undoubtedly have characterised as sheer madness.

The conditions in those high northern latitudes in mid-winter are difficult to appreciate.

The convoy which was to be guarded by Sherbrooke's destroyers had assembled in an Icelandic fiord just before Christmas. Then it blew a full gale from the westward. Two of the destroyers which were to form part of the escort were hove to south of Iceland for twenty-four hours. One of them—the *Achates*, which was to meet a very gallant end a few days later—sprang her foremast, but was able to make good the damage and join the convoy escort. Another destroyer, H.M.S. *Bulldog*, sustained such damage through the weather that she had to return to the United Kingdom for repair, and took no further part in the operation. Even in the shelter of a fiord destroyers were dragging their anchors, and there was no rest for officers or men.

It was early on the afternoon of Christmas Day, 1942, that the close escort of destroyers under the command of "Rupert" Sherbrooke in the *Onslow*, met the convoy, and course was shaped to the Barents Sea.

On December 27th another storm set in. For the next three days the wind was of gale force; there were heavy seas, and frequent squalls of snow and hail. In that weather and with no real daylight, it was not to be wondered at that some ships got separated from the main body of the convoy.

There had been no attack by the enemy, but the weather seemed to be serving the Germans well. Eight merchant ships and one destroyer became separated from the convoy. All these ships eventually arrived safely at their destination, but their disappearance at this early stage added considerably to Sherbrooke's anxiety.

The separation of this destroyer from the close escort of the main body of the convoy was to have a considerable effect upon the subsequent action with the enemy.

Conditions on board the destroyers remaining with the main body of the convoy were terrible. The temperature was well below zero. Spray, swept almost continuously over the ships and in that weather, froze where it fell. The wire guard rails round the ship's sides became solid bulwarks of thick ice It was only with the utmost difficulty and hardship that the guns could be kept sufficiently free to be fought. Inter-ship communication was slow and unreliable because the cold made the hands of the signalmen on the bridges almost incapable of working their signalling lamps, and even numbed their minds.

For Sherbrooke, anxiety was added to almost incredible discomfort. A minesweeper had been sent to search for the missing ships, but no word had been heard of them. The main body of the convoy was approaching the area in which attack was to be expected. The edge of the Arctic ice pack was well south of Bear Island, so that the possibilities of evasive action were strictly limited. The convoy had to pass through a channel less than 200 miles wide between the north of Norway and the southern edge of the ice.

Moreover, ice from the freezing spray was adding so much top-weight to the ships that it would seriously threaten their stability in the event of them sustaining damage in action. And all the time there was the unending but heartbreaking work of keeping the guns sufficiently free from ice to enable them to be brought into action at short notice if the enemy should suddenly appear.

Fortunately, however, the weather moderated. December 30th was a fine day, and it was possible to chip away the worst of the ice from the ships, reduce the topweight of the ice and ensure some foothold round the guns. It was also possible to collect some of the stragglers from the convoy and to get the convoy and its close escort into order.

Late that evening the destroyer *Obdurate* reported sighting the conning-tower of a U-boat, which dived immediately, on the starboard side of the convoy. Whether this was in fact a U-boat has never been established. A two-hour search by two destroyers proved fruitless. The alarm, however, was an earnest that interference by the enemy was to be expected.

On the morning of Thursday, December 31st, Sherbrooke had with him, apart from his own ship H.M.S. *Onslow*, the destroyers *Obedient*, *Obdurate*, *Orwell* and *Achates*; the corvettes *Rhododendron* and *Hyderabad*; and the armed trawler *Northern Gem*. This force formed the close escort for the twelve merchant ships.

The *Achates* was an old destroyer, but armed with 4.7-inch guns. The destroyers of the "O" class were all new ships, but they were by no means equal in fighting qualities. So great and urgent had been the Royal Navy's need for destroyers that the ships had been completed in haste although the guns and mountings designed for them were not ready. So it happened that the only two ships of this class which were armed with modern 4.7-inch guns and could be characterised as "fleet" destroyers were the *Onslow* and the *Oribi*— and the *Oribi* was not with the force. The other "O" class ships— *Obedient*, *Obdurate* and *Orwell*, had been armed with old 4-inch guns as a temporary measure in order that their commissioning should not be delayed. The commanding officer of one of these ships remarked naïvely in his report of the action that: "The ships' companies conducted themselves in an exemplary manner, and it should be recorded that none of these ships had been in commission for more than three months. Also that the breeches of their 4-inch guns were stamped with the date 1915."

Sherbrooke knew that his escort force was terribly undergunned for its task of ensuring delivery to Russia of the products of the British and American war factories, but he and his men did not flinch.

At 8.20 a.m. on New Year's Eve, H.M.S. *Hyderabad* sighted two destroyers to the southward. These were at first thought to be Russian destroyers which had come out from Kola Inlet to meet the convoy and help to escort it on the final stage of its voyage. These two destroyers were soon afterwards sighted by H.M.S. *Obdurate*, and Sherbrooke ordered the *Obdurate* to close them and investigate their identity. This was established beyond doubt when, at 9.30 a.m., the two unknown destroyers opened fire on the *Obdurate* at a range of four miles. They were ships of the powerful German *Maas* class, mounting 5-inch guns, but retired before the 4-inch gunned *Obdurate*.

The German ships had been "ridden off," and there was no reason to suppose that they had actually sighted the convoy. The *Obdurate* reported the enemy to Sherbrooke in the *Onslow* and fell back towards the convoy, being careful to remain between the convoy and the bearing on which the German ships had been last sighted. Even as the *Obdurate* disengaged and withdrew, it was established that there were three—and not two—of these big German destroyers.

Sherbrooke acted instantaneously on hearing that the enemy was in the vicinity. He turned the *Onslow* towards the stern of the convoy—its most vulnerable point—increased speed, and ordered the *Orwell*, *Obedient* and *Obdurate* to join him. Thus he was concentrating his small force and leading it to the best position to defend the convoy from attack. At the same time H.M.S. *Achates* began to lay a smoke screen across the stern of the convoy, which was ordered to make an emergency turn to the south-eastward.

At this time the visibility was fairly good for the Barents Sea on the last day of the year. Between the south-east and south-west there was three-quarters light and it was possible to see nearly ten miles; between north-east and north-west there was half-light with a visibility of about seven miles. Even so, for most of the ships the position and course of the action had to be judged solely from the gun flashes seen through the murky twilight.

While the destroyers were concentrating, and Sherbrooke was leading them towards where the gun flashes of the enemy destroyers had shown them to be engaging the *Obdurate*, another strange ship was sighted. This appeared as a large but ill-defined shape, almost indiscernible against the dark horizon to the north-west and in the intermittent snow-squalls.

Sherbrooke altered course and steamed straight for this strange ship in order to establish her identity. Suddenly, when the range was down to $4\frac{1}{2}$ miles, the ship altered course and opened fire on the *Achates*. Her first broadside revealed her identity of class. The eight flashes from four symmetrically placed twin turrets showed that she was a 10,000-ton cruiser of the *Hipper* class, armed with 8-inch guns.

The British destroyers were in an exceedingly dangerous situation. They were not yet concentrated, and they had a valuable and vulnerable convoy in their charge. Already there had appeared three German destroyers, each one of them far more powerful than Sherbrooke's ships, and now a heavy cruiser with great hitting power and an armoured hull had come on the scene. The odds were fearful. By all the laws of probability the Germans should be able to wipe out the British escorts and then annihilate the convoy. Sherbrooke, however, was undaunted and, as has so often happened in the war at sea, the inferior British force seized and exploited the initiative.

Only the *Orwell* was then in close company with the *Onslow*. Sherbrooke led round to starboard, thus keeping between the enemy and the convoy. Moreover, he steered so that the British destroyers continued to close in on the big German cruiser. The *Onslow* and *Orwell* fought back at the cruiser, which had by this time tried without success to shell the rear ships of the convoy.

In a very few minutes the German cruiser showed that she did not like the opposition from the two British destroyers. She broke off the action and altered course away under cover of smoke.

This move by the enemy confirmed Sherbrooke's suspicion that the Germans were afraid of a torpedo attack by his destroyers. That knowledge dictated the British tactics for the remainder of the action. To exploit the German fear, however, was a matter of difficulty. It meant that a convincing feint had to be made at every possible opportunity. Yet the bluff must never be called. If the British destroyers actually attacked and fired their torpedoes the Germans would know that there remained between them and their prey of the convoy nothing but a few ridiculously small guns.

Having driven off the enemy in this initial engagement, Sherbrooke turned his destroyers at speed to rejoin the convoy. He knew that there were other powerful enemy ships in the vicinity, and one German force might well be trying to draw him off so that another could play havoc with the convoy virtually without opposition, for only the *Achates*, the two corvettes and one trawler remained with the merchant ships.

A few minutes later the enemy cruiser again tried to close in on the convoy, but again Sherbrooke led his destroyers towards his big adversary, steaming as if to deliver a torpedo attack. Again the enemy was unable to face this threat, and altered course away under cover of smoke.

Just after ten o'clock the German cruiser tried again to approach the convoy, and actually fired a few spasmodic and ineffective salvoes at the rear ships of the convoy. The *Onslow* at once led round towards the enemy and opened fire with her 4.7-inch guns at a range of just over seven miles—a range at which the 4-inch guns of the other "O" class destroyers were ineffective. The *Achates* was not with the *Onslow*, but continued to carry out the invaluable task of laying smoke screens across the stern of the convoy.

Within three minutes of the enemy's turn towards the convoy she was being hit by the *Onslow*. Three shell hits were seen and there may have been more. This treatment was evidently not to the liking of the 8-inch gun cruiser, for she at once put her helm over and again broke off the action and retired under cover of smoke.

By these tactics Sherbrooke succeeded in forcing the enemy away from the convoy as well as "fending him off" and by ten minutes past ten the German cruiser was outside effective gun range of the merchant ships.

Sherbrooke then took the *Onslow* and the *Orwell* to a position where they would be between the convoy and the enemy if he should again attack, and detached the *Obedient* and *Obdurate* to lay more smoke to conceal the convoy.

The manœuvring of the destroyers at high speed during these actions presented their commanding officers with problems other than tactical. They had to watch the wind, sea, and swell, as well as the enemy, and regulate their helm and speed orders so as to reduce to the minimum the spray which came inboard, for this froze solid at once and threatened to put guns and other equipment out of action. So cold was it that even after firing twenty rapid salvoes the guns felt cold to the touch.

A few minutes later the *Hipper* class cruiser again altered course to starboard—towards the convoy—and began firing 8-inch gun broadsides at the *Onslow*.

Within a minute or two a German broadside fell close over the *Onslow's* forecastle, followed by another. The enemy had found the range. Sherbrooke at once began to zigzag to dodge the enemy's shells, but the German opened a rapid fire and very soon a salvo of 8-inch shells straddled the *Onslow* amidships. One shell of this salvo burst very close on the port side and splinters holed the *Onslow's* hull in several places.

The happenings of the next few minutes are best described in the words of Lieutenant Commander T. J. G. Marchand, R.N., who was on the bridge of the *Onslow* at the time.

"Soon after, an 8-inch shell exploded on the top of the *Onslow's* funnel, splitting it open almost to the level of the upper deck, making a pepper-dredge of the afterside of the bridge.

"At this stage a W/T operator appeared and reported to the gunnery officer in a most calm, unperturbed and apparently unconcerned voice, yet with a touch of annoyance and regret, that he was afraid that the set had 'blown up.' His colleague in the compartment had been killed outright alongside him.

"At the time I was standing facing forward, with the magnetic compass between me and Captain Sherbrooke. I had no knowledge of any casualties on the bridge until I looked round. Then I saw that Captain Sherbrooke had been hit in the face and was in a pretty bad way. Almost at the same moment, though I cannot recollect any shock, we were hit immediately in front of the bridge, under 'A' and 'B' guns. 'B' gun was put out of action and most of its crew either killed or wounded. The shell under 'A' gun had penetrated just below the upper deck and exploded on the mess desk, killing or wounding most of the forward damage control and repair party. Fire broke out at once in the vicinity of both hits, and the ready ammunition which caught alight made things very difficult. We then sustained a near miss which blew in the ship's side under 'A' gun on the waterline and led to considerable flooding. To ease the effect of the wind on the flames, the *Onslow* turned away and reduced speed to 15 knots.

"The hits were sustained at about 10.16 a.m., and at about 10.35 a.m. the Medical Officer insisted that Captain Sherbrooke should go below to his sea cabin for attention as he was bleeding badly and, so far as I could see, his left eye was hanging down his cheek.

"Before he would agree to go below, Captain Sherbrooke received reports of the damage and that the main engines and steering gear were still in efficient working order, and that the worst of the holes had been effectively plugged. He was temporarily blind and in great pain, but he retained all his other faculties and ordered that the ship be kept as far as possible between the enemy and the convoy and that everything was to be done to get the fires under control."

Sherbrooke ordered Lieutenant-Commander D. C. Kinloch, R.N., the commanding officer of H.M.S. *Obedient* and the next senior officer, to take command of the flotilla. The command of the *Onslow* devolved upon Lieutenant-Commander T. J. G. Marchand, R.N.

Kinloch at once ordered the destroyers to join him. He was in an unenviable position. He had at his disposal three fully effective destroyers mounting 4-inch guns. The *Onslow* had her armament out of action, was seriously on fire forward, and her speed was reduced owing to hull damage. It was obvious that the *Onslow* could no longer hope to lie in the line of battle against vastly superior forces, and she made her way to the head of the convoy.

Marchand's description of the condition of the *Onslow* at this time is vivid: "The whole of the forward guns had been put out of action by hits, and the after guns by failure of power and the formation of ice on the breech blocks. The remaining hands available forward were employed in fighting the fires, and also those who could be spared from aft. We had also sustained various splinter holes in the engine-room and boiler-rooms, and at one stage the appearance of things produced a very alarming picture. We were, of course, making thick black smoke. The safety valves had lifted, and smoke and steam made a beautiful study of black and white. The ship was gradually taking up a list to port due to the near miss. The bridge was almost uninhabitable due to the choking smoke from the fires forward. The noise rendered speech practically impossible. Then came a message to say that there was a fire in one of the boiler-rooms and that water was making its way into the engine-room. Most of the electrics and practically all the wireless had been wrecked."

At this stage various other ships were sighted and reported, and two German destroyers were seen to have joined the *Hipper* class cruiser. These destroyers, however, were content to play a purely passive role, and followed the cruiser about without taking any part in the actions.

At 10.45 a.m. the *Hipper* class cruiser, now followed by the two destroyers, again approached the convoy. Lieutenant-Commander Kinloch in H.M.S. *Obedient* followed the tactics which Sherbrooke had demonstrated with such success. He turned the destroyers towards the enemy and made smoke to shield the convoy. He could not, however, at this stage engage the enemy owing to the extremely short range of his old guns.

The German cruiser opened fire on the *Achates*, which was still laying smoke in the rear of the convoy. The *Achates* was soon hit and holed forward. This reduced her speed to 15 knots. Then she was hit on the bridge, this shell killing her commanding officer, Lieutenant-Commander A. H. T. Johns, R.N. A minute or two later she was hit in the hull on the port side, and one of her boiler-rooms received considerable damage from splinters from a shell which burst close alongside.

Although so severely damaged, and with her commanding officer killed, the *Achates* continued to struggle on and add to the smoke screens between the enemy and the convoy. The official report of the action states that "this considerably hampered the accuracy of the enemy's gunfire and prevented him from appreciating the convoy's movements." It was not until one o'clock in the afternoon that the *Achates* asked the trawler *Northern Gem* to stand by her. The *Northern Gem* picked up the survivors and the *Achates* sank at 1.30 p.m.

Meanwhile the German cruiser had shifted her fire to the three "*O*" class destroyers, which were now within range and engaging the enemy—their 4-inch guns fighting the German 8-inch guns. At least four hits were seen on the enemy during this engagement, but it is unlikely that the small British shells caused more than superficial damage to the armoured German cruiser. During this phase of the action the *Obedient* was straddled by a salvo and her wireless aerials were shot away. The destroyers, however, achieved their object. The range began to lengthen, showing that the Germans had hauled away. They had again been "ridden off" the convoy by the destroyers.

Kinloch led his destroyers back to rejoin the convoy, all the time keeping between the convoy and the bearing of the *Hipper* class cruiser and her two inexplicably inactive destroyers.

While the destroyers were rejoining the convoy another heavy ship opened fire on the rear ships of the convoy. The splashes of the shells from this ship were much bigger than those from the *Hipper* class cruiser, and it was evident that a "pocket battleship," armed with 11-inch guns, had arrived on the scene.

Kinloch led his destroyers to lay a smoke screen between the convoy and this new assailant. One ship in the convoy was hit on the stern by a shell, but was able to continue with the convoy, and the "pocket battleship" ceased firing when the destroyers reached a position between her and the convoy.

Almost immediately afterwards, the *Hipper* class cruiser and her two destroyers were sighted at a range of only four miles and steaming in towards the convoy.

Once again Kinloch adopted the tactics used by Sherbrooke and swung his destroyers towards the enemy. Fire was opened simultaneously by both sides, but the enemy altered course away. Again the British had exploited the German fear of torpedo attack. During the engagement H.M.S. *Obdurate* was straddled and suffered casualties and damage from splinters of a shell which burst just short.

The destroyers were now in an exceedingly awkward position. The *Achates* was sinking. The *Onslow* was so damaged as to be virtually out of action. Both the *Obedient* and *Obdurate* had received some damage. The *Orwell* was the only ship which had sustained no damage. And these destroyers, with their tactics limited by the necessity of guarding the convoy at all costs, had against them a "pocket battleship," a heavy cruiser, and at least two powerful *Maas* class destroyers.

Help, however, was now close at hand. A force of British cruisers which had been covering the convoy operation were nearer than had been expected, and at this moment they appeared out of the murk at full speed and opened fire on the enemy. The first that the Germans knew of the presence of the British cruisers was that they were being straddled and hit by salvoes of twenty-four 6-inch guns. Both the "pocket battleship" and the *Hipper* class cruiser were hit. One of the German destroyers was sunk. The other German ships retired with considerable haste to the shelter of the Norwegian fiords, and the convoy sailed on to Russia without one merchant ship having been lost. The Royal Navy had, by bold tactics and by seizing the initiative, performed another of those miracles in defence of the Merchant Navy of which this war has been so prolific.

Sherbrooke said afterwards: "Able to choose his time and place of attack, and possessing a superior force, it is difficult to understand the enemy's general lack of initiative, and particularly the failure to use his destroyers . . . various vivid memories of the battle remain, and one conviction: that, had the rôles been reversed, the convoy would not have arrived at its destination complete and practically undamaged. The lesson to be learnt, I think, is that warships which remain in harbour cannot fight and win battles."

In the sorely damaged *Onslow* the news of the appearance of Rear-Admiral Burnett's Tenth Cruiser Squadron was passed round the ship at once. Particular care was taken to see that it reached the engine-room and boiler-room personnel and the repair parties who were still giving such sterling service. As Marchand said afterwards: "Knowledge that the enemy were now having to compete with something their own size removed the sense of worry which each had felt since the action began, and the efforts to get the fires under control and some part of the gun armament back into operation continued unflaggingly."

The news was, of course, also reported to "Rupert" Sherbrooke, who had given orders that he was to be kept informed throughout of the course of events. All the afternoon the survivors on the *Onslow* fought the fires and damage, and it was not until 6.30 that night that Marchand got a chance of visiting Sherbrooke. The former's description of this incident is memorable. "The scene," he wrote, "on going to see Captain Sherbrooke at 6.30 p.m. in his sea cabin, amid the strong pungent smells of burning cordite, wood, rubber, and so on, in the light of a solitary oil lamp, took me back instantly to the day I had seen the spot in the old wooden *Victory* where the surgeon had plied his trade."

That evening the *Onslow* left the convoy and went on at 20 knots, although she had a list of 14 degrees to starboard and was down by the bows. The ship arrived at Murmansk during the forenoon of the next day—January 1st—in foggy weather. Sherbrooke and twenty other seriously wounded men were put ashore—the dead had been buried at sea the previous night—and then it occurred for the first time to officers and men that it was New Year's Day.

It was while in hospital in Russia that "Rupert" Sherbrooke learnt that the King had awarded him the Victoria Cross. In reply to the congratulations of the officers and men of his destroyer flotilla Sherbrooke made the following signal:

"This award is a tribute to the force in general and I hope will be taken by the next of kin of those who lost their lives as some measure of their country's appreciation."

A few days later the following announcement appeared in the *London Gazette*:

"The King has been graciously pleased to approve the award of the VICTORIA CROSS, for valour in the defence of a convoy, to: Captain Robert St. Vincent Sherbrooke, D.S.O., Royal Navy.

"Captain Sherbrooke, in H.M.S. *Onslow*, was the Senior Officer in command of the destroyers escorting an important convoy bound for North Russia. On the morning of the 31st December, off the North Cape, he made contact with a greatly superior enemy force which was attempting to destroy the convoy. Captain Sherbrooke led his destroyers into the attack and closed with the enemy. Four times the enemy tried to attack the convoy, but was forced each time to withdraw behind a smoke screen to avoid the threat of torpedoes, and each time Captain Sherbrooke pursued him and drove him outside gun range of the convoy and towards our covering forces. These engagements lasted about two hours, but after the first forty minutes H.M.S. *Onslow* was hit, and Captain Sherbrooke was seriously wounded in the face and lost the use of one eye. Nevertheless, he continued to direct the ships under his command until further hits on his own ship compelled him to disengage, but not until he was satisfied that the next Senior Officer had assumed control. It was only then that he agreed to leave the bridge for medical attention, and until the convoy was out of danger he insisted on receiving all reports of the action.

"His courage, his fortitude and cool and prompt decisions inspired all around him. By his leadership and example the convoy was saved from damage and was brought safely to its destination."

Murmansk is a good port for disembarking supplies for the Soviet, but climatic and other conditions militate against first-class hospital treatment for a man as grievously wounded as was Sherbrooke. This was soon realised, and a decision had to be taken whether to risk his life on passage in a destroyer to the United Kingdom. The doctors despaired of saving his life if he remained in Murmansk, so the other risk was taken. He was embarked in a destroyer for passage to the United Kingdom. Few who appreciated the extent of his wounds believed that he would live to be landed on this side of the North Sea. Courage and fate, however, prevailed; and although Sherbrooke lost his left eye, he preserved not only his life, but his spirit. His experiences have aged him beyond his years, but his personality seems to have grown. It would be difficult to find a man who commands greater respect among those whom he leads and whom he now trains.

Long before the Battle of the Barents Sea, "Rupert" Sherbrooke had earned the D.S.O. in action against the enemy in waters within the Arctic Circle. This was during the Second Battle of Narvik, which not only burnt out the German wasp's nest in the Narvik area, but avenged Captain Warburton-Lee (who was posthumously awarded the first naval V.C. of the war) and his gallant men, who had faced fearful odds in those fiords a few days previously.

Sherbrooke was at that time Commanding Officer of the famous H.M.S. *Cossack*. He had joined that ship on New Year's Eve, 1940, and, after having exchanged ships with Captain Vian at the time the *Cossack* made her epic rescue of British merchant seamen from the prison ship *Altmark*, rejoined the *Cossack* before the German invasion of Norway in April, 1940.

Germany invaded Norway on April 9th, 1940. It was an invasion planned and carried out by stealth and treachery. In the northern Norwegian ports hordes of armed Nazis swarmed from ostensibly peaceful merchant vessels and fishing boats to take defenceless ports by surprise.

The most important of the northern Norwegian ports is Narvik. Not only has it a magnificent harbour, but it is the North Sea terminus of the railway from the iron mines of Northern Sweden— mines producing the highest grade iron ore, which is of incalculable value in the production of armour plate and tool steel. The only other outlet for this ore is the port of Lulea, in Sweden, near the head of the Gulf of Bothnia, and this is closed by ice for more than half of the year.

Germany was well aware of the importance of Narvik. So was Great Britain—and on April 10th a small British destroyer force entered the fiords despite the enemy's preponderance of strength and inflicted serious damage on a superior and well prepared enemy. It was in this very gallant action that Captain Warburton-Lee sacrificed his life and won the Victoria Cross.

Captain Warburton-Lee's force, however, did not entirely dispose of the German hornet's nest in Narvik harbour and its surrounding fiords. A larger and more powerful force was therefore organised and sent to the northern Norwegian port. This force was under the command of Vice-Admiral W. J. Whitworth, whose flag flew in the battleship *Warspite*. This was the only heavy ship present, and it is worth remembering that the insistence of the German propaganda organisation that the *Warspite* had been sunk by a single bomb played no inconsiderable part in persuading Mussolini and his henchmen that it was safe to enter the war.

Among the force employed in the Second Battle of Narvik was H.M.S. *Cossack*, with Sherbrooke in command.

The approach to Narvik is up the long Ofot Fiord. For fifteen miles of its length Ofot Fiord is narrow—not more than two miles wide, and running between steep mountains. Then it opens out into a sheet of open water twelve miles long and, on the average, about five miles wide. Narvik town and harbour lies on the south side at the inner end of this wide water, which divides east of Narvik into the long and very narrow Rombaks Fiord and the bay known as Harjangs Fiord.

The approaches to Narvik were, in fact, an ideal place to ambush an attacking force. It was known that the Germans had in the fiord several destroyers of the powerful *Maas* class armed with 5-inch guns and torpedo tubes, and it had been reported that batteries had been established on Baroy Island, guarding the entrance, and at at least two places on the long narrow neck of Ofot Fiord. Moreover, there was a mined area off the entrance.

There were nine destroyers, under the command of Commander J. A. McCoy in H.M.S. *Bedouin*. Sherbrooke was second in command of the flotilla, and led the port wing of the screen ahead of the *Warspite* as the force passed Baroy Island and entered the neck of Ofot Fiord. It was on the port hand that the establishment of shore batteries in the narrows had been reported, but no signs of these batteries were seen.

At 12.28 p.m., just after entering the narrows of Ofot Fiord, one enemy destroyer was sighted ahead. Fire was opened on this destroyer at extreme range two minutes later, but was checked as it was found impossible to see the fall of shot. The weather was calm, but a fine drizzle fogged the lenses of binoculars and rangefinders.

Five miles farther up the narrows the leading destroyers again engaged an enemy destroyer. Within the next ten minutes two more German destroyers were sighted, and these opened fire on the leading

British ships. Their shells straddled one of the destroyers, but scored no hits.

Soon afterwards one of our scouting aircraft signalled "Look out for enemy destroyer in bay one mile ahead on the starboard hand." This was the first of the ambushes, with the enemy destroyer hiding in one of the numerous inlets in the hope that the British force would pass within easy torpedo range before discovering the trap.

Before reaching this lurking destroyer, however, yet another enemy destroyer appeared out of Bogen Bay, on the port hand. This destroyer opened fire at once, and shells began to fall close round the *Cossack* two minutes later. The enemy ships were manœuvring so as to keep all their guns bearing on the British destroyers as the Germans fought a retreating action up the fiord. They were firing with considerable accuracy and the *Eskimo* was soon straddled, but not hit.

As the British destroyers came abreast the German destroyer, which had been reported by aircraft as lurking in one of the inlets on the starboard hand, she opened fire. She was at once engaged by the *Punjabi* with her 4.7-inch guns and pom-pom. Almost simultaneously the *Cossack* was straddled, and she also opened fire on the German at a range of only just over 3000 yards. The *Cossack's* third salvo hit the German amidships. She was soon heavily on fire but still had some guns in action. She was, however, left to be finished off by the rear ships, as the *Cossack* and her escorts were already engaged with three German destroyers ahead of them.

Just after this, aircraft reported torpedoes approaching, and Sherbrooke had to swing the *Cossack* under full helm to avoid one of them which was running on the surface.

In the next twenty-five minutes the *Cossack* was straddled by no less than sixteen of the enemy's salvoes, and Sherbrooke had his hands full dodging them. So well did he do this that the *Cossack* did not receive one direct hit, although she sustained some damage from the splinters of a shell which burst close alongside. These splinters perforated the hull plating and caused considerable flooding of the provision room and mess decks.

Two minutes after the last of these straddles the *Cossack* had another very narrow escape. Three torpedoes were suddenly seen coming straight for the ship. There was no time to take any

Captain R. St. V. Sherbrooke

avoiding action. Sherbrooke could only watch them coming. Were they going to hit, or weren't they? Miraculously they all missed. One passed just ahead, another just astern, and the third right under the ship below the bridge. It must have been a matter of inches only. Those few seconds of suspense are among Sherbrooke's most vivid memories of the Second Battle of Narvik.

After that there was a lull in the action for a few minutes. Then it broke out again, and the *Cossack* was again straddled but not hit. By this time, too, the enemy shore batteries at Narvik were also firing.

A moment or two later yet another German destroyer was sighted on the port bow in the entrance to Herjangs Fiord. This ship was at once engaged by the *Cossack* and badly hit. She was left to be finished off later by other ships while Sherbrooke pressed on towards Narvik.

Shortly after this the *Cossack* was again very nearly torpedoed. Three torpedoes were seen approaching from the direction of a German destroyer off Narvik point. This destroyer had been heavily hit by gunfire and was on fire. The torpedoes were avoided—just— but Sherbrooke had to put the *Cossack's* port engine full speed astern in order to dodge them.

By 2.15 p.m. it was clear that all the German destroyers in the Ofot Fiord had either been put out of action or were seeking refuge up the long narrow Rombaks Fiord beyond Narvik. In these circumstances Sherbrooke decided to investigate Narvik harbour and sink any enemy warships which might be lying there. The other British destroyers were ample force to deal with such Germans in the fiords as had not already been sunk or reduced to helpless and burning hulks.

Sherbrooke had been warned by the *Warspite's* aircraft that a large German destroyer was lying outside Narvik harbour, but as the *Cossack* approached the harbour no warship could be seen. As the *Cossack* rounded the point of land on which stands the light-house at the harbour entrance, however, Sherbrooke saw a powerful *Maas* class destroyer near the wharf on the eastern side of the harbour.

Both ships opened fire simultaneously at a range of less than 3000 yards. The German ship fired five salvoes from her main armament before her heavier guns were silenced by the British fire. The *Cossack*, however, had not come through unscathed. She had

been hit by four 5-inch shells. One of these wrecked the main
gunnery control installation. Another severed a main steam pipe
and the connections of the steering gear, so that the *Cossack* had
become out of control. At 2.22 p.m. she grounded forward due south
of the lighthouse. Nor was this the full extent of her troubles. Fire
was raging in a mess deck adjacent to the forward magazine, so
that this had to be flooded. The flooding of this compartment, of
course, made the ship even more firmly aground.

Meanwhile, her guns still engaged the German destroyer, the
range of which was now down to 2000 yards, until it became evident
that she had been abandoned by her crew. The *Cossack* then ceased
fire, and Sherbrooke ordered a whaler—the only boat which was
still serviceable—to be manned by an armed crew and lowered with
a view to taking the enemy destroyer by boarding.

The situation in Narvik harbour was then extremely confused.
The shore batteries had ceased fire, having apparently been pulverised
by the *Warspite's* 15-inch shells, but Sherbrooke had no idea where
the Germans were. Nine merchant ships in the harbour had been
sunk in the previous Wednesday's battle, but there were still thirteen
merchant ships afloat. Sherbrooke wanted to ensure the capture of
these ships, but his own ship was aground and immovable. He
accordingly ordered H.M.S. *Kimberley* to come into the harbour and
help.

The *Kimberley* very soon arrived, but Sherbrooke saw at once
that she had suffered damage which made her unhandy—a defect
which might have proved fatal when trying to manoeuvre in a
harbour crowded with ships and wrecks. He therefore told the
Kimberley to withdraw and ordered H.M.S. *Foxhound* into the
harbour.

The *Foxhound* entered the harbour soon after 3 p.m. As she
approached the apparently abandoned German destroyer she was
greeted by hot machine-gun and rifle fire from the shore. The
Foxhound then fired a few single rounds into the German destroyer,
which blew up and sank.

Meanwhile, the *Cossack* remained aground, with her crew working feverishly to effect temporary repairs to her damage. Most of
this work, of course, fell upon the shoulders of the engine-room
department, and it is noteworthy that Sherbrooke afterwards
reported: "Under the able direction of the Engineer Officer,
Lieutenant-Commander (E.) W. F. B. Lane, the difficult situation

which arose from damage, flooding, and grounding, was admirably and rapidly dealt with."

At five o'clock in the afternoon a howitzer opened fire on the *Cossack* from a position somewhere behind the town. Its fire was uncomfortably accurate. The shells fell in line with the ship and the first round was 150 yards over, the second 75 yards over, and the third 20 yards over. It was a very unpleasant situation for a ship aground and incapable of moving. The howitzer, however, never fired the fourth round which, by the rules, should have been a direct hit. Sherbrooke could not see the howitzer and could only judge the direction from which the shells came. Some men and a mast could, however, be seen on a small hill about $3\frac{1}{4}$ miles away, and the *Cossack* fired three salvoes at this target. Sherbrooke wrote afterwards: "I cannot think that we had the luck to hit a howitzer whose whereabouts were only vaguely known, but the howitzer did not fire again."

Soon after this the other ships of the British force were seen passing down Ofot Fiord to the westward, having finished off all the German destroyers. It was very trying for Sherbrooke and his crew to see other ships withdrawing while the *Cossack* remained aground and more or less helpless. There was no hope of refloating the ship for several hours as the tide was low. Sherbrooke wrote in his report: "I should like to pay tribute to the excellent behaviour of the ship's company throughout the action and the high morale sustained during a very trying interval when the remaining British warships had apparently left and the *Cossack* was aground in a particularly vulnerable situation."

Not long after this Sherbrooke received a report that twelve German bombers were approaching up the fiord. Since the ship seemed certain to be destroyed if attacked, and was only fifty yards from the shore, Sherbrooke gave orders for all the confidential books and papers to be destroyed. As Sherbrooke said afterwards: "This was considered by those concerned to be a glorious opportunity to burn store accounts, signal logs, and any document which might at any time prove troublesome. Even Lloyd's Register was cremated."

Much to Sherbrooke's relief, the German bombers did not arrive, but he still had plenty to cause him anxiety. First he discovered that there were about 2000 Germans in Narvik town and that there had been a German U-boat in the harbour the previous day.

By eight o'clock that night considerable progress had been made with the temporary repairs. Holes had been plugged and bulkheads shored; the steering gear was made to work; the steam pipe repaired, and steam raised in one boiler. The ship had also been lightened as much as possible forward. At that time H.M.S. *Kimberley* returned with orders to tow the *Cossack* off. The attempt failed, and Sherbrooke arranged to try again at four o'clock the following morning, when the tide would again be high.

Three-quarters of an hour before that time, however, the *Cossack* was able to get off under her own power. She had been hard and fast aground fifty yards from a hostile coast for nearly thirteen hours. She had fired nearly 850 4.7-inch shells and over 500 rounds of pom-pom in the action, and had had eleven men killed and nineteen wounded.

Robert St. Vincent Sherbrooke was born at Oxton Hall on January 8th, 1901. He was at sea as a midshipman during the last two years of the 1914-18 war, serving in H.M.S. *Canada*, which is still in the service of the Chilean Navy as the *Almiralte Latorre*. In that war Sherbrooke had no commitments, but he vividly remembers an occasion when he was in charge of a picket boat at Scapa Flow in bad weather. Trying to go alongside H.M.S. *Courageous* he hit the gangway halfway up, snapped it, and saw the lower half of the gangway drift away on the tide, together with a senior officer who was cordially disliked by the midshipman. "Any pleasure I might otherwise have had at this sight," says Sherbrooke, "was quickly dispelled when I looked up to see the Admiral—Sir William Goodenough—standing on the quarterdeck surveying myself and my handiwork with a horny eye."

Sherbrooke's first service in destroyers, apart from a few months as an Acting Sub-Lieutenant, was when he commanded H.M.S. *Vanoc*, which was working from Gibraltar during the Spanish Civil War. It was a busy and trying time, though one would hardly think so from "Rupert" Sherbrooke's brief description of this phase in his career. This is what he says: "I had many interesting missions to carry out—philanthropic and otherwise—such as exchange of civilian hostages, and taking periodical protests at interferences with British shipping to the rival Spanish authorities. I also headed an official delegation of one to look for German gun installations and barracks in Spanish Morocco."

In this war "Rupert" Sherbrooke served in command of destroyers

until he was so badly wounded in the Battle of the Barents Sea.
When he recovered sufficiently he was appointed to command a
Fleet Air Arm training station in Scotland. There he has been
instilling into adventurous youth his implicit belief in the ideals
of the Royal Navy.

SIR EDWARD NEVILLE SYFRET

K.C.B.

Vice-Admiral in His Majesty's Fleet

VICE-ADMIRAL SIR NEVILLE SYFRET, who commanded the forces which covered the passage of a vital convoy to Malta; the naval forces during the capture of Diego Suarez; and the fleet under whose protection the Allied landings were effected in North Africa, is South African born and bred.

He was born near Cape Town on June 20th, 1889, the son of Edward Ridge Syfret, and received his preliminary education at the Diocesan College, South Africa, before joining the Royal Navy as a cadet in May, 1904.

Sir Neville Syfret is now Vice-Chief of the Naval Staff at the Admiralty in London.

Syfret has been a good cricketer. As a midshipman he played for the Royal Navy against the M.C.C. at Lord's in 1908. That was before the institution of the annual Navy v. Army match. The first of these series of matches was played at Lord's in 1909, and Syfret played for the Royal Navy, this time as a sub-lieutenant.

It is most unusual for both the Chief Cadet Captains of a "term" of naval cadets at the Royal Naval College, Dartmouth, to climb the promotion ladder to flag rank. This has been the case with Syfret's "term." Edward Neville Syfret and Arthur John Power were made Chief Cadet Captains at Dartmouth on the same day. Both specialised in gunnery; both have reached flag rank, their names having been next to one another in the Navy List ever since they appeared in it as midshipmen; both have given to the Royal Navy and the Empire service of an order which cannot be purchased. Needless to say these two are great friends.

As a young lieutenant, Syfret specialised in gunnery, and he spent practically the whole of the last war in the North Sea as gunnery officer of the light cruisers *Aurora*, *Centaur* and *Curacoa*, of the Harwich Force.

He was promoted to the rank of Commander in June, 1922, at a period when so many naval officers were facing the prospect of having their naval careers ruthlessly terminated owing to disarmament and demands for economy.

As a commander, Syfret held the responsible appointment of Fleet Gunnery Officer in the Mediterranean Fleet. Later, as a captain, he commanded the naval gunnery school at Devonport, the light cruiser *Caradoc* on the China Station, and the battleship *Ramillies* in the Home Fleet. The latter was one of the ships in which he was to fly his flag in war.

Just before the outbreak of the present war Syfret was in command of the battleship *Rodney* in the Home Fleet. In November, 1939, he became Naval Secretary to the First Lord of the Admiralty —then Mr. Winston Churchill—and was promoted to the rank of Rear-Admiral on January 5th, 1940, while holding that appointment.

The post of Naval Secretary to the First Lord of the Admiralty is often regarded as something of a sinecure, holding promise of coveted appointments in the future. It has, however, one great disadvantage. One of the duties of a Naval Secretary is to submit the names of officers available and suitable for such high appointments as fall vacant. This means the acceptance of great responsibility, but it also entails a complete negation on the part of the Naval Secretary of any claims which he may himself have to an appointment, for a Naval Secretary can hardly recommend himself for a flag appointment at sea, however much he may desire it. For Syfret the post of Naval Secretary held another disadvantage. It tied him to the Admiralty just after the outbreak of war, when the one thing he desired above all else was to hold a command at sea in face of the enemy.

Syfret, however, was destined for high command at sea in time of war.

In June, 1941, Syfret was given a sea command—that of a cruiser squadron. He was overjoyed at going back to sea, but he little knew how much and varied fighting experience he was to gain in the next two years.

Within seven months the Admiralty allowed it to be known that Syfret was commanding "a force in the Mediterranean." There were very good reasons why the Admiralty could not be more specific at that time. There is no surer way to forearm the enemy than to let him know the strength and composition of the forces which are being ranged against him.

The first that the public knew of what Syfret had been doing was in the early days of August, 1941, when Mr. A. V. Alexander, the First Lord of the Admiralty, went to the microphone and broadcast "the thanks of the nation" to Vice-Admiral Sir James Somerville and Rear-Admiral Syfret and the officers and men of the Royal Navy and Merchant Navy for a successful accomplishment which he described as "an event which will stand out in the naval history of the war."

This feat was the running of a vital troop and supply convoy through to Malta despite great efforts by the enemy to destroy the ships.

That was the convoy to the escorts of which Sir James Somerville made his famous signal: "The convoy must go through." Somerville commanded the heavy forces covering the passage of the convoy, and Syfret the close escorts of the convoy.

Nothing less than the fate of Malta hung upon the safe arrival of the reinforcements and supply ships. This was a fact almost as well known to the enemy as to the British commanders, so that when Syfret sailed with the convoy from Gibraltar he appreciated that the Germans and Italians would do their utmost to destroy him and his charges. Moreover, for a large convoy and naval force to sail in secrecy from Gibraltar was quite impossible. One had only to glance at a newspaper of almost any day of that period of the war to see the work of the watchers at La Linea and Algeciras, overlooking Gibraltar Bay. Attempts were, of course, made to mislead the enemy by sailing the ships to the westward instead of to the eastward, and then doubling back through the Straits under cover of night, but even this stratagem was of somewhat doubtful value when dealing with an enemy who was perfectly well aware of the vital necessity of Malta being reinforced and supplied.

Syfret sailed with his convoy on July 20th, with Somerville's covering force keeping ahead of him and to the northward of his track. By the morning of July 22nd the convoy was within the orbit of the enemy's air reconnaissance, and "snoopers" and shadowers duly appeared.

That night the convoy was attacked by a U-boat. None of the torpedoes hit a ship, and the U-boat was at once so strongly counter-attacked with depth charges that even the ultra-conservative Admiralty conceded that: "It is possible that this U-boat was destroyed." In any event, the U-boat did not return to the attack.

By the following morning the convoy was within attacking range of the enemy air bases in Sardinia, and the first air attacks duly developed. An attack by six torpedo-carrying aircraft was cleverly synchronised with a high-level bombing attack by a large number of aircraft. The defence, however, was ready for them. Naval fighter aircraft tore into the formation of bombers and broke them up so that they had to abandon any thought of accurate pattern bombing. Then the fighters went after the individual bombers, and so harassed them that they were put off their aim. Two of the enemy bombers were seen to come down in flames. Three others were hard hit and had to jettison their bomb loads in the hope that, unladen, they might be able to reach their base.

While the fighters were dealing with the high-level bombing attack the torpedo-carrying aircraft were dealt with by the barrage from the guns of the escorts and convoy. Three of the six aircraft were shot down into the sea. Not one of those immensely valuable ships in the convoy was hit, but a torpedo hit the stern of the destroyer *Fearless*. She was disabled and on fire, and although she was in no immediate danger of sinking it was obviously impossible to attempt to tow her either to Malta or back to Gibraltar, so she had to be sunk by our own ships.

During the afternoon the enemy returned to the attack, again making use of synchronised high-level bombing and torpedo-bombing attacks. Again, however, the attacks were driven off without any ships being hit.

As night fell Syfret altered the course of the convoy and took bold action in the hope of throwing out the enemy's calculation. His move was highly successful. In the words of the official Admiralty communique, the convoy "evaded the enemy's air forces by determination and skilful handling." One would have thought it impossible to hide a big convoy and its escorts in the narrows between Sicily and the Tunisian coast in clear weather, but this is what Syfret achieved, and during the night the men in the ships were able to watch enemy aircraft dropping flares and searching for them.

During the night, however, some E-boats found and attacked the convoy with torpedoes, and one of the supply ships was hit. She was, however, able to continue with the convoy under her own steam. One of the E-boats was certainly destroyed, and others his and damaged.

Early next morning two Cant flying-boats on reconnaissance picked up the convoy and began shadowing it, taking care to keep out of the range of the ship's guns. The naval fighters promptly went after them and shot them both down into the sea.

The convoy was then approaching Malta, and the enemy realised that his last chance of stopping it, or of sinking its ships, lay within the next few hours. He accordingly threw in everything he had in a last desperate effort.

Between 6.30 in the morning and 10 o'clock three separate air attacks were launched against the convoy, and the enemy now used German dive-bombers as well as his high-level bombers. A cruiser and a destroyer were slightly damaged in these attacks, but so efficient was the work of the escorts and of the merchantmen in the convoy that not one of the all-important supply ships was hit.

Shortly before noon the convoy steamed into the Grand Harbour at Valetta. Every one of the supply ships which had left Gibraltar had arrived at Malta. It was a triumph which seemed almost a miracle. Certainly neither Syfret nor Somerville could have expected to get that convoy through without the loss of a ship. Our losses, apart from the destroyer *Fearless*, were six naval fighter aircraft, but the crews of four of these had been saved. The enemy's abortive attempts to stop supplies and reinforcements reaching Malta had cost him at least a dozen aircraft shot down and many others damaged, and a U-boat probably sunk.

Some time later the *London Gazette* announced that "Rear-Admiral Syfret had been appointed a Companion of the Order of the Bath for courage, resolution and leadership in operations in the Mediterranean waters."

October, 1941, found Rear-Admiral Syfret's flagship in northern waters. The Malta convoy season for that year had drawn to a close and, after taking part in one more operation and making a brief visit to the Cape, on duty with another convoy, he was ordered to rejoin the Home Fleet, where his cruiser squadron properly belonged.

The life in a cruiser in war is normally one of constant movement, and H.M.S. *Edinburgh* was no exception. After a month or two of patrol activity, Syfret was ordered, early in December, to take a small convoy to North Russia. There were only seven merchant ships and for them the *Edinburgh* and two destroyers were a sufficient escort. No enemy was sighted as the little force crawled northwards at 7 knots through perpetual darkness. As they neared the North Cape a signal was received in the flagship, informing the Admiral that he had been selected to succeed Sir James Somerville in command of the famous Force "H," which had long been playing an aggressive rôle in the western Mediterranean. At that time command of Force "H" was the cherished ambition of nearly every Rear-Admiral on the Flag List, and Syfret would have been less than human if he had not been overjoyed at the choice falling upon him, for he was at that time still comparatively junior in his rank.

The convoy for North Russia duly arrived at Kola Inlet, on the Russian Arctic coast, but it did not do so entirely without incident. At about midday on the last day, as the ships were steaming slowly towards the estuary, two enemy aircraft appeared on the scene and dropped six bombs before being driven off by the ships' anti-aircraft fire. Four bombs exploded harmlessly in the sea, but the remaining two hit a merchant ship, one landing on the bridge and one in her Number 4 hold. Neither exploded, and Syfret detached a destroyer to shepherd the vessel and her valuable cargo into harbour. On arrival a bomb disposal squad boarded her and the bombs were safely removed and thrown into the sea.

On the morning of Christmas Day, in a snowstorm, Syfret said good-bye to his friends and ship's company in the *Edinburgh* and transferred to H.M.S. *Kent* for passage to England on his way to take up his new appointment.

Mr. Anthony Eden, the British Foreign Secretary, had just paid an official visit to the Kremlin, and the *Kent* had been detailed to take him, M. Maisky, the Soviet Ambassador to London, and other members of the Russian delegation, to England. These distinguished passengers embarked in the *Kent* on Christmas evening and the ship sailed soon afterwards, being escorted for the first part of her journey by a Russian destroyer.

On 12th January, 1942, Rear-Admiral Syfret hoisted his flag in the battleship H.M.S. *Malaya* at Gibraltar as Flag Officer Commanding Force "H."

Although the next two months were occupied in small operations, these were none the less important. Malta at this time was being subjected to heavy air attack and her reinforcement by fighters presented a recurring problem of immense importance. On three occasions Force "H" sallied forth into the Western Basin with numbers of R.A.F. Spitfires ranged on the flight decks of aircraft carriers. On arrival at a prearranged point within fighter flying range of Malta, these aircraft were flown off to their destination. All arrived safely.

Meanwhile bigger events were pending. The disastrous sequence of events in the Far East at the end of 1941 and early in 1942 had led to Japanese naval supremacy in the Bay of Bengal as well as in the waters farther east. Ceylon was in danger, and the whole of the intricate British convoy organisation in the Indian Ocean was in deadly peril. At the northern tip of Madagascar the fine land-locked harbour of Diego Suarez, then held by the Vichy French, dominated the thousands of miles of sea to its north and east. Had a determined enemy seized possession of this base he could have caused immense harm to our shipping throughout the Indian Ocean.

The risk of Diego Suarez falling into Japanese hands was too great to be accepted, even though the prevention of such a danger meant carrying out an extensive operation against our erstwhile Allies and at a great distance.

On the last night in March, 1942, Rear-Admiral Syfret sailed from Gibraltar in H.M.S. *Malaya*. The reason for the departure was a closely guarded secret, shared only by the Admiral and two or three of his staff. Naturally, rumour was rife on board and there were high hopes that the move meant a return to England. Next morning, however, the Engineer Commander came on deck soon after daylight and, with a glance at the rising sun, grunted disgustedly: "It looks more like whites than winter woollies." The *Malaya* was southward bound.

At Freetown the *Malaya* met the troop convoy, which had sailed direct from England, and there Rear-Admiral Syfret conferred with Major-General R. G. Sturges, Royal Marines, who had been selected as the Military Force Commander under Syfret. The object of the expedition was still a close secret, although it was no longer possible to conceal from officers and men that some kind of combined operation was in prospect.

Two days at Freetown were barely sufficient to settle the details of the assault between the Naval and Military Commanders before the force, accompanied by the troopships, and with an augmented screen, sailed again on its journey south.

As night fell on 19th April, the *Malaya* and her charges entered the harbour at Cape Town, and the Admiral landed to discuss the forthcoming operation with General Smuts. During his absence his staff and gear were moved to the aircraft carrier *Illustrious*, in which he hoisted his flag early the following morning and sailed at high speed for Durban. There his flag was again transferred, this time to the battleship *Ramillies*, for the assault.

The force spent a week at Durban in making and perfecting, as far as possible, the final arrangements for the operation. During this period there was considerable anxiety on the score of security. The South African press was discussing the strategic importance of Diego Suarez in articles and published letters, and it seemed to Syfret that it would be impossible to keep secret the destination of the assault convoys.

In the event, however, complete surprise was achieved. This was the more remarkable because after leaving Durban unexpectedly strong favourable currents and fine weather brought the convoys to the rendezvous off the north-west tip of Madagascar some hours earlier than had been planned. As a result, the convoys had to waste time in waters where air or submarine observation was to be expected. Neither the Japanese nor the Vichy French authorities of Madagascar apparently had any idea of what was afoot. No reconnaissance aircraft was seen and no part of the force was reported by a submarine. The junction of Rear-Admiral Syfret's forces with those of Rear-Admiral Boyd, who had brought two aircraft carriers south from Kilindini to provide the initial air support for the assault, was safely and secretly accomplished.

The landing of the troops which were to attack Diego Suarez took place on the opposite side of the island of Madagascar—the west side. The troops were then to advance across the narrow part of the island to Diego Suarez and Antsirane, in order to take the strong defences of the port on the rear. The places selected for the landings were in two bays, called Courrier Bay and Ambararata Bay.

As was stated in the communique issued jointly by the Admiralty and War Office, the British force "arrived off Courrier Bay at dawn on May 5th. The entire force, both naval and military, and its supplies were conveyed safely over a very long distance and arrived off Courrier Bay at the appointed time without any loss." The conveyance of the force had in itself been a considerable naval operation, calling for much careful organisation.

The first task facing the naval forces was the carrying out of a considerable minesweeping operation, for Courrier Bay and its approaches were found to be heavily mined. Not only did this minesweeping have to be done efficiently, it had to be done quickly, for delay in landing the troops would have removed the element of surprise from the whole operation. In the event, the landings took place up to time, but during the minesweeping the corvette *Auricula* struck a mine and was seriously damaged. Great efforts were made to save the ship, but they were fruitless and she subsequently sank.

Major-General Sturges wrote in his despatch: "The approach of the transports and the minesweeping, escorting, and covering warships was a difficult and dangerous operation. The French, in fact, considered approach from this direction to be impossible by night, and written instructions to this effect were found. There is no doubt that the success of the whole operation and the comparatively low casualties sustained by the Army were largely due to the acceptance of this risk by the Naval Commanders concerned, and the skill and seamanship displayed by the Royal Navy and Merchant Navy in executing this part of the plan."

To distract French attention from the west side of the island the cruiser *Hermione* created a diversion just before dawn on the east side of the island, making smoke and firing starshell in the vicinity of Ambodivahibe Bay, the most probable landing place on the east coast, south-east of Antsirane. At daybreak naval aircraft dropped parachutes with dummies in the inaccessible country round Mahagaga, on the route from Ambodivahibe Bay to Antsirane. It was subsequently learnt that these diversions caused the French authorities to send troops to the Mahagaga area long before troops were sent in the direction of the real landings in Courrier and Ambararata Bays.

Other precautions had to be taken by the naval command. It was known that there were Vichy submarines in the vicinity, and one of these tried to attack and was sunk. There was also the possibility of meeting with Japanese submarines.

While the minesweepers were sweeping the landing craft into the beaches, naval aircraft, operating from Rear-Admiral Boyd's aircraft carriers, attacked the aerodrome south of Antsirane. This was a very important move, for it deprived the enemy of all air power, both for reconnaissance and attack purposes, at the very outset. In his despatches Syfret paid high tribute to the way in which the naval airmen responded to every call made upon them both in this initial attack and subsequently in giving support to our ground forces. They also accounted for the French sloop *D'Entrecasteaux*, which was in Diego Suarez harbour.

Madagascar is one of those places where a strong wind gets up every day and blows steadily all day, dying away in the evening. This wind did nothing to assist the difficult work of landing troops, vehicles and stores. As the official account said: "The task of putting ashore the troops, their vehicles and their stores was carried out speedily despite deteriorating weather conditions, and great credit is due, not only to the naval personnel and the troops, but also to the high standard of seamanship of the officers and men of the Merchant Navy in the troop and supply ships."

By 6 p.m. on May 5th our forward troops were in contact with a strong enemy defence position running across the isthmus a few miles south of the town of Antsirane. This position was attacked at dawn next morning, but without success. Our troops were held up and casualties began to mount up.

That afternoon Major-General Sturges, Royal Marines, who was commanding the troops, held a conference with Rear-Admiral Syfret on board his flagship. As a result, it was decided that a diversion should be created to the northward during the night and timed to coincide with a night attack on the French positions across the isthmus. Both this attack and the diversion had to take place after dark but before the rising of the moon, which was at the full.

The diversion was to take the form of a landing in the town of Antsirane itself, the landing party to consist of fifty Royal Marines from H.M.S. *Ramillies* under the command of Captain Price, Royal Marines.

This force was to be taken into Diego Suarez harbour and landed on the jetties of Antsirane by a destroyer. The destroyer selected was H.M.S. *Anthony*, commanded by Lieutenant-Commander John Hodges, a son of Admiral Sir Michael Hodges.

It was a desperate venture, bold in conception and boldly carried out. The *Anthony* embarked the Royal Marines and sailed to the northward to round the northern end of Madagascar. It was extremely hot and most uncomfortable in the crowded destroyer. There was quite a heavy sea running, and the temperature on the *Anthony's* engine-room floor plates reached 146 degrees Fahrenheit, so that no man could remain on watch for more than a few minutes.

As night fell H.M.S. *Anthony* was approaching the entrance to the great landlocked harbour of Diego Suarez. This entrance is less than a mile wide, and was guarded by several batteries of heavy coast defence guns mounted on the Orangeo Peninsula.

At the appointed time the *Anthony* rushed the entrance. She was heavily fired on but, miraculously, was not hit, and she replied to the enemy's fire with every weapon she had.

From the harbour entrance to the jetties of the port of Antsirane is nearly four miles. It must be remembered that it was a pitch dark night and there were no navigational facilities in the way of lighthouses, beacons or light buoys. Hodges had to perform a considerable feat of navigation under fire and with his ship proceeding at high speed in confined and unfamiliar waters. Just as he approached the jetties he saw a blue light flashing ahead of him. He thought this might be a signal from the Commando troops who, it was thought, might have succeeded in crossing in boats from the village of Diego Suarez. Just in time Hodges realised that it was a navigational warning light, and with a magnificent display of seamanship he laid the *Anthony* stern first alongside the jetty.

The Royal Marines dashed ashore. The diversion was a great success. Not only did it confuse the enemy and paralyse some of his defence organisation, for the Marines captured the artillery headquarters; it saved subsequent street fighting with inevitable casualties and damage to the town. French resistance in the Antsirane virtually collapsed, and the forces on the Orangeo Peninsula surrendered on the following day, after a short bombardment by the 15-inch guns of H.M.S. *Ramillies*.

On the afternoon of May 7th Rear-Admiral Syfret's force, preceded by minesweepers, entered Diego Suarez harbour. Syfret then had to tackle the difficult problem of diplomacy involved in the settlement of terms of surrender.

On the morning of 8th May the Admiral landed with members of his staff and met the Vichy French commanders to inform them of the terms to be enforced by the British Government. Behind the Admiral, at the conference table, was an enormous coloured poster of Marshal Petain. The Vichy French delegates were seated opposite

Crown Copyright Reserved

Vice-Admiral Sir Neville Syfret holds a conference with
Brigadier Festing, Major-General Sturges and Captain Howson
on board his flagship after the surrender of Madagascar.

and possibly drew encouragement from this picture for they were disposed to be argumentative. The negotiations were, however, firmly handled by Rear-Admiral Syfret and all the points stipulated by the British Government were rigidly enforced.

After these diplomatic problems had been dealt with, the no less troublesome difficulties of administration remained. Major-General Sturges was duly installed ashore as Fortress Commander and, as such, took over the military command of the port area, but there were numerous problems connected with the unloading and sailing of ships, the defence of the anchorage, the installation of efficient communications and the taking over of the dockyard and naval base. These measures necessitated frequent conferences on board and ashore, and were not facilitated by the high wind which always blew during the day and made boat work difficult and sometimes hazardous.

As the month of May drew to a close, however, Syfret felt that his work in Madagascar had come to an end, and he obtained permission from the Admiralty to turn over his responsibilities in that area.

Rear-Admiral Neville Syfret was subsequently mentioned in despatches "for bravery and enterprise in a successful operation which led to the surrender of the important base of Diego Suarez."

After a fortnight in Durban, Rear-Admiral Syfret left the *Ramillies* and travelled by rail to Capetown where he hoisted his flag in the armed merchant cruiser *Canton*, in which ship he took passage for Freetown. For a brief space Syfret relaxed from the responsibilities of high command in a difficult operation, and spent most of his time in the *Canton* in reading and playing deck quoits.

The respite was short. During the passage north up the west coast of Africa a signal was received from the Admiralty directing Syfret to report in London as soon as possible in order to discuss the plans for another important operation. In order to save time the *Canton* put into Takoradi, from which port Syfret travelled by air to London—and a most uncomfortable flight it was.

Neville Syfret was promoted to the rank of Acting Vice-Admiral on July 14th, 1942, almost at the same time as he learnt that the next operation with which he was to be concerned was the fighting through to Malta of the famous convoy of August, 1942.

The passage of this convoy to Malta was so important that greater steps than ever before were taken by the Admiralty for its protection. Its safe arrival at Malta was vital to the continued resistance of that indomitable island.

Vice-Admiral Syfret sailed on August 2nd, 1942. His flag was flying in the battleship *Nelson* and he had with him the battleship *Rodney*, several cruisers, and a considerable number of destroyers. In the Atlantic off the west coast of Spain Vice-Admiral Syfret met Rear-Admiral Lyster, commanding the aircraft carriers. The close escort of the convoy was commanded by Rear-Admiral H. M. Burrough, with his flag flying in the cruiser *Nigeria*.

On August 10th the whole armada passed through the Straits of Gibraltar. It was a powerful force, with two battleships, five aircraft carriers, several cruisers and numerous destroyers, and two fleet tankers from which to fuel the destroyers at sea, as well as the all-important merchant ships with their precious supplies for Malta.

As the Rock faded astern, each commanding officer opened a sealed envelope telling him the details of the operation. As with all previous Malta convoys, the covering force of heavy ships and carriers was to remain with the convoy until they reached the vicinity of Cape Bon, and the close escort would then protect the merchant ships on their passage through the Sicilian narrows.

Concurrently, two important subsidiary operations were to be carried out. One was the reinforcement of the R.A.F. in Malta by twenty-seven Spitfires which were to be flown off the aircraft carrier *Furious*. The other was to cover the passage westwards from Malta of four British merchant ships, who were to take advantage of the fact that the enemy's staff was likely to be fully employed with the main convoy operations to slip through, trying if necessary to pass themselves off as Italian ships.

All went well until the early afternoon of 11th August. At about 1.15 p.m. on that day a U-boat managed to penetrate the destroyer screen and deliver a brilliant attack. The aircraft carrier *Eagle* was hit by four torpedoes and sank in six minutes. Fortunately her ship's company were all moving to their action stations at the time, with their lifebelts on, so that loss of life was extremely small. Nevertheless, apart from the loss of a fine ship, the fighter cover which she could have provided was to be badly needed on the following day.

The torpedoing of the *Eagle* occurred while the *Furious* was flying off Spitfires and was therefore committed to a steady course and speed—a matter which caused a few minutes of anxiety, but the strenuous efforts of the screening destroyers successfully kept down any U-boats, which might have been in the vicinity and prevented them from again attacking.

During the day, apart from numerous U-boat alarms, there were several enemy aircraft "snooping" around the fleet, and it was quite evident that the enemy was fully aware of the situation. At dusk the expected air attack developed. No doubt the enemy would have attacked earlier, but he had a healthy respect for the strong fighter cover put up by the aircraft carriers, who did a great job during daylight, many "snoopers" and potential raiders being shot down. As daylight faded, however, the fighters were landed on the aircraft carriers and the enemy's chance came. Just before nine o'clock he threw in his high-level bombers, and the ships opened fire with every anti-aircraft gun they had. Anti-aircraft fire, though seldom lethal in this kind of action, has a most disconcerting effect on the bomber's aim, and this particular barrage was one of the heaviest of the war. The enemy persevered for about half an hour, and was then obliged to withdraw, discomfited, without having caused any damage whatever. The convoy steamed on serenely through the welcome cover of night.

Wednesday, 12th August, dawned clear and warm, with a faint heat-haze on the horizon. The fleet was ordered to be at immediate notice for air attack. Every one expected fireworks and they were not long in coming. The first attack developed at about 9.15 a.m. and from noon onwards until nearly 7 p.m. attacks were almost continuous. High-level bombers, dive-dombers and torpedo-bombers were employed and—a new departure—aircraft dropped mines on parachutes immediately ahead of the convoy in an effort to cause confusion. At the same time there was plenty of evidence that U-boats were very active. Several torpedoes narrowly missed their marks. One submarine, rather too venturesome, was brought to the surface and destroyed by the united efforts of the destroyers *Pathfinder* and *Ithuriel*.

The Fleet Air Arm fighters again did magnificent work. During the operation, they destroyed for certain not less than seventy aircraft, and it was undoubtedly largely owing to their efforts that the fleet and convoy came through that strenuous day almost unscathed.

That day Syfret never left the bridge of his flagship. The

strength and continuity of the enemy's attacks made it necessary
for the Admiral to make an almost continuous succession of lightning decisions, a mistake in any of which might have had the most
serious consequences, and which called for the most skilful handling
of the fleet and the convoy for which it was responsible. Syfret
remained tireless and unperturbed throughout.

Just after 6.30 p.m. a most vicious air attack developed. It was a
high-level bombing attack combined with mine-dropping aircraft,
and skilfully synchronised with an attack by torpedo-bombers
which, coming in on the disengaged side, hoped to catch the fleet
off its guard. In this they were unsuccessful, but some half-dozen
Stuka dive-bombers, appearing suddenly out of the setting sun,
scored a hit on the aircraft carrier *Indomitable*. Flames appeared on
her flight deck and with a few moments she was enveloped in smoke.
Shortly afterwards the air attack ceased. The fleet was now getting
close to the Narrows and it was time for the covering force to retire.
Accordingly, at five minutes to seven, Syfret made a signal to Rear-
Admiral Burrough to proceed with the convoy, while he himself
turned back to the westward, keeping as he did so an anxious eye
on his damaged aircraft carrier. Her Commanding Officer, Captain
T. H. Troubridge, rose magnificently to the occasion and within a
matter of minutes he reported that the *Indomitable* was able to
steam at 22 knots.

Syfret's fleet steamed westward with the knowledge of duty well
done so far as it lay with them, but for the convoy and its close
escort the worst was yet to come. As they entered the Narrows,
E-boats delivered an attack and U-boats were again active. The
cruisers *Nigeria* and *Cairo* were damaged and the cruiser *Manchester*
and destroyer *Foresight* subsequently sunk. Nevertheless, although
heavy casualties were sustained, vital supplies were successfully
fought through to Malta.

As soon as the signal reached him that *Nigeria* and *Cairo* had
been damaged, Vice-Admiral Syfret detached the cruiser *Charybdis*
and two destroyers to their assistance. The damaged *Indomitable*
was sent on ahead to Gibraltar, and the remainder of Syfret's
force cruised in the Western Basin without molestation, ready to
support Rear-Admiral Burrough's force in its dangerous return
journey.

At one stage even the main surface forces of the Italian fleet
made an attempt to interfere with these operations, but the attempt

was scotched by the efficiency of our forces and one of our submarines.

The Italian forces consisted of both 8-inch and 6-inch gun cruisers, which joined forces in the Tyrrhenian Sea and then steered south towards the line of advance of the convoy. This force was sighted and reported by one of our reconnaissance aircraft, and an air striking force was at once sent to attack them. The attack developed off the north-west point of Sicily. Its results could not be observed, but it had the effect of discouraging the Italians, who at once put about and made for the shelter of Palermo. On their way there, however, they were intercepted by one of our submarines under the command of Lieutenant A. C. G. Mars, R.N., who scored two torpedo hits on the Italian cruisers.

Meanwhile the passage of the four west-bound merchant ships from Malta had achieved an unexpectedly complete success. While the main air battle was going on to the north of Cape Bon on 12th August, they slipped past to the southward. They were not entirely undetected, but a combination of bluff and good luck enabled them to escape without even being attacked.

On the afternoon of August 14th Rear-Admiral Burrough's force rejoined the main body of the fleet. It had done its work superlatively well and seen to it that Malta received the sinews of further resistance, but it had had a gruelling time. Even that morning, when it was west-bound after seeing the merchant ships into Malta, it had sustained a most determined attack. The enemy had freely used bombs, torpedoes and parachute mines in a last desperate effort, but, with the exception of slight damage to one ship, the squadron had miraculously come through without harm.

After the rejoining of Rear-Admiral Burrough's force, Vice-Admiral Syfret set course for Gibraltar, where he arrived on the following day.

On September 8th, 1942, Neville Syfret was created a K.C.B. "for bravery and dauntless resolution in fighting an important convoy through to Malta."

In the early hours of November 8th, 1942, there took place the initial landings of the Allied troops at Algiers, Oran and Casablanca. It was a day which was to alter the whole course of the war. Under General Eisenhower, the Supreme Allied Commander in the North African theatre of operations, all naval forces employed were commanded by Admiral Sir Andrew Cunningham who was designated

Allied Naval Commander, Expeditionary Force. His command included the American Naval Forces employed in the Casablanca landings, the British warships and landing ships and craft for the assaults at Algiers and Oran and Force "H" which was the main covering force in the Mediterranean and under the direct orders of Vice-Admiral Sir Neville Syfret.

In the words of the communique issued by the Allied Head-quarters in North Africa after the landings: "The Navy's responsibility consisted in ensuring the safe, timely arrival of a large expeditionary force, comprising many ships of varying tonnage and speeds, running from liners to trawlers, which had to be moved across more than 3000 miles of submarine-infested waters. Never before in history have seaborne amphibious operations been launched so far from their points of departure without secondary advanced bases."

The safe conduct of that force in convoys consisting of several hundred ships without the loss of a single vessel, and the preservation of secrecy, even during the passage of the Straits of Gibraltar, was one of the greatest maritime feats of all time.

Vice-Admiral Syfret had sailed on October 30th, flying his flag in the battleship H.M.S. *Duke of York*, and on the night of November 5th, after carrying out many exercises on passage in order to ensure that all personnel and material were at the peak of efficiency, he anchored in Gibraltar Bay to fuel and receive final instructions from Admiral Cunningham, who had set up his temporary headquarters in the Rock.

Before daylight revealed the ships to the prying eyes of enemy agents on neutral territory, Syfret and his Force "H" left Gibraltar Bay and sailed eastwards into their familiar waters of the western Mediterranean.

An overseas expeditionary force is always at its most vulnerable when it arrives at its destination; while ships are lying stopped and landings are taking place and other ships are lying off waiting their turn to disembark their troops, equipment and stores. The danger to the easternmost landings was great, for Italy had at her disposal very fast modern capital ships and cruisers seemingly ideal for attacking an expedition at the most critical stage in its progress. But between Italy's navy and the Allied landings lay Vice-Admiral Sir Neville Syfret, with his covering force of battleships, cruisers, destroyers and aircraft carriers.

It seems obvious that the existence and presence of this force was known to the enemy even before it was mentioned in the communiqué issued by the Allied Headquarters a week after the first landings, and that this knowledge persuaded the Italian naval commanders that a supine rôle was for them the safest; for they made no attempt to interfere.

Before daylight Force "H" was again on the move towards its familiar patrol area in the Western Basin.

After the complete success which crowned the North African landings and the U-boat counter-attack had been broken, a period of comparative quiet descended on the naval scene in the Mediterranean. Syfret again transferred his flag to *Nelson*, and for the next two or three months "Force "H"", in the intervals of patrolling south of the Balearic Islands, divided its time between Gibraltar and the new Allied naval base of Mers-el-Kebir, close to Oran, which was administered by the Americans. This period brought to Syfret much hard administrative work but little action, and to the Admiral and his staff it must have seemed rather an anti-climax after the tremendous events of the past year.

Syfret's eventful period of command at sea was nearing its end. Early in the New Year, 1943, he was offered the important appointment of Vice-Chief of the Naval Staff at the Admiralty in succession to Vice-Admiral Sir Henry Moore, and about a month later he relinquished the command of Force "H" and sailed for England. After a month or two of well-earned rest, he took up his new appointment at the Admiralty at the beginning of June.

The appointment of Vice-Chief of the Naval Staff has been described as one of the most exacting posts in the Admiralty. Under the First Sea Lord, the Vice-Chief of the Naval Staff superintends all British naval operations and presides at the daily staff meeting where current operational matters are discussed. In addition, as one of the Vice-Chiefs of Staff, he attends meetings once or twice a week with his counterparts in the War Office and the Air Ministry, and deals with numerous inter-Service problems "on the Vice-Chiefs' level." His duties necessarily make him conversant with current problems of State on the Ministerial plane, for in the absence of the First Sea Lord the Vice-Chief deputises for him at the daily meetings of the Chiefs of Staff Committee, which is concerned with the higher direction of the war.

Sir Neville Syfret on several occasions shouldered this additional responsibility. The longest period was for about two months in 1943. At the Quebec Conference in August of that year Admiral of the Fleet Sir Dudley Pound, the then First Sea Lord, was taken ill, an illness which was unhappily to prove fatal. Admiral of the Fleet Sir Andrew Cunningham succeeded Sir Dudley Pound on 15th October, but until that date Vice-Admiral Sir Neville Syfret was in supreme control of the Naval Staff.

THOMAS HOPE TROUBRIDGE

D.S.O.

Rear-Admiral in His Majesty's Fleet

IN THE year 1798 Lord Nelson wrote to Earl St. Vincent of Captain Troubridge of the *Culloden*:

> "He deserves every reward which a grateful country can bestow on the most meritorious sea-officer of his standing in the Service. I have felt his worth every hour of my command."

Born at Portsmouth on February 1st, 1895, Rear-Admiral Thomas Hope Troubridge is a direct descendant of Nelson's captain, and the same words might well apply to him. It is doubtful, however, if any Commander-in-Chief in this war could write them of him because he has not served for long periods in one appointment. His service has, in fact, been varied and ubiquitous, for he has been much in demand. The waters of the Arctic Ocean know him. So does the Bay of Bengal. He commanded one of the Task Forces during the invasion of North Africa, one of the Task Forces during the invasion of Sicily. He was in command of the naval forces off the Anzio beach-head in Italy, where great issues hung perilously in the balance for days and weeks, and the British and American troops, in terrible minority against Kesselring's best German troops and equipment, had to rely upon the naval forces to avert disaster. He commanded the aircraft carriers which provided practically the sole air cover for the landing of General Patch's troops during the invasion of Southern France. And between all these active fighting appointments he has been in the curious position of being appointed by the British Admiralty to think as a member of the German High Command.

Naturally that very unusual appointment was not publicised. The official records will tell you only that Captain T. H. Troubridge served at the Admiralty from December, 1940, to June, 1941, his appointment being to "H.M.S. *President*, additional, for duty inside the Admiralty with N.I.D." (Naval Intelligence Division). The official wording was in no way unusual, but Troubridge's job was very unusual.

At the end of 1940 there was set up a committee of senior officers, one from each of the Fighting Services, one from the Foreign Office, and one from the Ministry of Economic Warfare, all of whom were chosen for their knowledge of Germany and the Germans. This committee, of which Troubridge was the naval member, was called upon to examine and appreciate situations *from the German point of view*.

Concurrently with this work Troubridge broadcast several times in German, addressing his talks to the Wehrmacht and concentrating on themes which, it was hoped, would tend to discourage the crews of the U-boats.

Captain Troubridge did much to make our naval propaganda to Germany a potent weapon. It was a conception of warfare new to the British Admiralty, especially when it was appreciated that cunning propaganda might cloak an operation to "jockey" the German naval command into undertaking some movement which was fundamentally unsound and of which we were ready to take full advantage.

Fortunately the Admiralty had in Tom Troubridge an officer capable of assessing the probable effects of our propaganda moves and of judging whether our propaganda ammunition was of the best possible design to penetrate the German psychological armour. Troubridge had an intimate personal knowledge of Grand-Admiral Raeder, the head of the German Navy, and of most of the other personalities at the head of the Nazi hierarchy, and he knew more than any other Englishman of the problems, strengths and probable weaknesses of the new German navy. He was the one British officer who was capable of playing these grim charades to perfection.

Troubridge had gone to Berlin as British Naval Attaché in July, 1936, and had left there three years later, when it became all too apparent that to keep a Naval Attaché in the German capital would merely mean the internment of a valuable officer on the outbreak of the war, which was by then recognised on both sides of the North Sea as inevitable.

As Naval Attaché in Berlin Tom Troubridge was a tremendous success. He is a big man—not so much in height as in solidity. No man would have called him fat, yet the scales would show him as a man far heavier than is to be expected from his height.

His shoulders are, in fact, monumental, and give him a presence which is in keeping with the German conception of the British Navy. He has a bulk and solidity—there is no better word for it—which was entirely in accordance with the German idea—and ingrained fear—of the unshakable influence of British sea power. Add to this Troubridge's immense sense of humour and of the ridiculous, and his utter fearlessness, and one can well appreciate the fact that the Germans always found themselves at a loss when dealing with him. He has a love of directness which they found profoundly disconcerting, and a rumbling fearless laugh which could shake even the foundations of the vast new Reich Chancellery.

Troubridge was a thorn in the flesh of the Nazis, but he was probably the best Naval Attaché whom Britain has ever sent to Berlin. Yet no former British Naval Attaché could have had so difficult a job.

Troubridge's reports, viewed in retrospect and in the light of subsequent experiences, are gems of realism. Anybody reading them now cannot help wishing that they could have been acted upon at the time. They are as factual and as uncompromising as some of the statements on German rearmament made by Mr. Winston Churchill in the days when he worked untiringly as the keeper of our future although he was regarded as a political outcast. Yet in those reports from Captain Troubridge one detects an amused and slightly contemptuous approach to the German problem-children. That may have been unduly kind to the Nazis, but it reflects the mental stature of Tom Troubridge. Big in frame and big in mind, he could not help regarding many of the antics of the Nazi "high ups" as the slightly ridiculous exuberance of adolescence. At the same time he was very conscious of the desire of many Germans to be "correct" and to avoid any suggestion of conduct unbecoming in a naval officer. Even in the years immediately before this war, and long after the Nazi party had seized power, the standard of conduct and behaviour in the German navy was based upon that ruling in the Royal Navy. The new German navy was imitative of the best and apprehensive of the least lapse in etiquette. It was a case of inferiority complex running riot.

Troubridge found that the German naval officers were invariably exceedingly civil, despite the fact that during his tenure of office in Berlin Great Britain and Germany were as close to war as any nations have ever been without burning powder.

When Troubridge arrived in Berlin in 1936 the Nazis had already come into power and they were just beginning to feel their strength in the international sphere. Hitler had been in power for three years. In those three years there had taken place the remilitarisation of the Rhineland, the Anschluss with Austria, and the Anglo-German Naval Agreement. Every one of these steps represented a bite out of the provisions of the Treaty of Versailles designed to prevent Germany from again throwing the peace of the world into the cauldron of her own ambition. Every one of these steps had been taken tentatively and rather fearfully, but after each one Germany had found herself emboldened by the acquiescence of the other nations. The new Nazi system was strengthened, and each fulmination against the disarmament clauses of the Treaty of Versailles carried more weight than the last.

The German Navy had backed the Nazi Party. It had not done so because it wished to take part in politics. The German Navy, in fact, was as reluctant to play politics as the British Navy always has been. German naval officers of the old school, however, were quick to see that the Nazi programme of the repudiation of the disarmament clauses of the Peace Treaty meant, in effect, a chance for them to build up the navy of their dreams.

On his arrival in Berlin, Tom Troubridge found that the vast majority of German naval officers were very busy thinking of the re-birth of a German Navy worthy of the name, and that they had no thoughts of war against Great Britain in the near future. They would, in fact, have been aghast at such a prospect, because it would have meant the inevitable destruction of all their plans. The intelligent German naval officer, Troubridge found, was opposed to the idea of war and to any step by the Nazi Party which might provoke war, because he realised only too clearly that the inevitable result of challenging the British Empire at that juncture would be the defeat of Germany and the extinction of the German Navy, upon which they had pinned their hopes for the future. At the same time, the average German naval officer was perfectly frank in professing his belief that the German Navy would challenge the British Navy in due course, when the former had built up its strength and, above all, its reserves.

Such was the attitude of the German naval officer when Tom Troubridge went to Berlin as Naval Attaché in July, 1936. As time went on, however, and the political situation deteriorated, Troubridge noticed that many German naval officers, who had up till then been concerned solely with their profession and with the building up of the new German Navy, began to believe the propaganda disseminated by the Nazi Party. Even Grand-Admiral Raeder, father and chief of the new German Navy, whom Troubridge had always found an exceedingly intelligent and level-headed man, began making political speeches. Knowing Raeder well, Troubridge felt quite sure that the Grand-Admiral could not really have believed the theories which formed the burden of many of these political speeches. Moreover, during the last year before the war, when the chances of avoiding conflict were obviously becoming more and more remote, Raeder gave Troubridge the impression that he was a very sad man, who realised in his heart of hearts that the chances of Germany winning a war against the British Empire—weak as it was in all respects except sea power—were exceedingly slender. Raeder himself told Troubridge that he had no faith in the submarine war as a decisive factor, and that statement was certainly not intended to deceive. Raeder, too, did not share the belief of Hitler, Goering and others that the Luftwaffe was the overriding weapon which would wrest the command of the seas from the British Navy. It is interesting to note that when the Luftwaffe had failed in its struggle against British sea power Raeder was superseded as Commander-in-Chief of the German Navy by Doenitz, who was a U-boat man.

Tom Troubridge continued to "get on" very well with most of the German naval officers, though he got many a good laugh out of playing off some of the pompous and desperately serious Nazi Party men one against the other. He was, in fact, the perfect Naval Attaché for what was quite the most difficult post to which a Naval Attaché had ever been assigned.

Troubridge left Berlin in July, 1939, having been there for almost exactly three years. Before he left, the German Navy gave a farewell dinner in his honour. Grand-Admiral Raeder interrupted his leave in order to attend the dinner, at which a piece of plate was presented to Troubridge and at which Raeder made a speech in which "he said some very civil things."

Just before he left Berlin, Troubridge was asked by the German naval liaison officer to take to England the Hindenburg Cup, which had been won in the international naval sailing races at Kiel in July, 1939, by the British naval team. The German officer, in asking this, was most insistent that Troubridge should ensure that the cup would be returned to Germany in good time before the sailing races of 1940. Troubridge assured him that, if the worst came to the worst and he could get it back no other way he would have the cup melted down and fired back as a bullet. The pompous German officer did not take the jest at all well! In Troubridge's words, "he was rather shocked at that crack."

Tom Troubridge was in the Admiralty when war broke out. During the months which were characterised as the "phoney war" phase, it was of considerable importance to counter the influence of Nazi Germany in allegedly neutral countries and to try to prevent even those within the German sphere of influence from becoming Germany's satellites. To prevent this, during the period when such military activity as existed seemed to point to the "sitz kreig" as an admission of weakness on the part of the Allies, was a task beyond the capacity of even the most adroit diplomats.

This was the" set-up" with which Tom Troubridge was faced when he was told by the Admiralty to go to Budapest and explain to Admiral Horthy, the Regent of Hungary, that Great Britain and her Allies were undoubtedly winning the war, despite all the available facts and appearances to the contrary.

Troubridge was very far from happy about his mission when he left London, but circumstances came to his rescue. To use his own words, "It was what the Americans would call a ' tough assignment,' but happily whilst I was on my way the news came through of the Battle of the River Plate, and that gave me some much-needed ammunition. I tried to convince Horthy that in the fullness of time the German nation would act in a similar manner to the *Graf Spee* and scuttle."

This preoccupation with the diplomatic side of naval affairs was very interesting, but it did not satisfy Troubridge. He was first and foremost a naval officer and there was a war on. He felt very strongly that his place was at sea, and he put this point of view to the Admiralty with his usual devastating directness. The result was that on New Year's Day, 1940, he took command of the aircraft carrier *Furious*.

The *Furious* was no chicken. She had been built during the last war as one of the freak "super cruisers" evolved by Winston Churchill and Jackie Fisher. She had been the only ship ever to mount an 18-inch gun, and to this day one can see the great stiffening structure installed between decks for this purpose. She had, at the end of the last war, been fitted with half a flight deck as a hybrid aircraft carrier. It had been from the *Furious* in this guise that the first experiments in take off and deck landing of aircraft had taken place. The first deck landing of a land plane was on the *Furious*, carried out by Squadron Leader Dunning, who in August, 1917, succeeded in skidding his Sopwith Pup to a standstill on the flight deck of the *Furious*. A few days later Dunning tried to do it again, went over the bows and was killed. The *Furious* had been altered more frequently than any other ship. She was the ugliest "flat iron" afloat, and had been for so many years that she was something of a sea-mark. Yet she has, for all her years, done magnificent service in unspectacular rôles in this war.

In the first months of the war the *Furious* had covered many thousands of miles while her aircraft helped to protect convoys; she had escorted the first Canadian troop convoy across the Atlantic. When the *Graf Spee* was in Montevideo after the Battle of the River Plate it was the *Furious* which suddenly appeared at Pernambuco with urgent demands for fuel; and in the meantime she had been used for deck-landing training off the Firth of Forth and as an ubiquitous aircraft transport.

In the spring of 1940 the *Furious*, under the command of Captain Troubridge, played a considerable part in the Norwegian campaign, during which ships at sea and troops ashore were almost entirely dependent upon such air support as could be afforded by the few aircraft carriers then at our disposal.

On April 11th our forces landed at Namsos, in Central Norway. On that day the *Furious*, which was the only aircraft carrier available, flew off a striking force to attack German cruisers reported in Trondheim Fiord. When the striking force arrived they were disappointed to find no cruisers and only two small destroyers, and those in water too shallow to allow of a torpedo running with certainty. Only one "possible hit" was scored, but history was made. It was the first time in war that a torpedo attack had been launched by aircraft from a carrier. That "possible hit" at Trondheim was the "shadow cast before" the victories of Taranto, Matapan, and many others in the Pacific.

After the landings at Namsos, Troubridge was ordered to take the *Furious* north to the Narvik area. There he worked for the next fortnight, with his Swordfish aircraft constantly in the air carrying

out reconnaissance and anti-submarine patrols, and attacking such
targets as enemy troops, aircraft parked on frozen lakes, quays and
harbour works, and German destroyers and other ships. The
Swordfish from the *Furious* were a very real scourge to the enemy
in those days, and they worked in defiance of conditions which
would have "grounded" any ordinary airmen. In fourteen days
Troubridge's Swordfish flew a total of 23,870 miles—a distance
equivalent to girdling the world—in weather which would have
been regarded as impossible by lesser men. At times blizzards
reduced the "ceiling" to 200 feet and the visibility to a few yards,
and they were flying in an area of high mountains, cliffs and rocky
ravines. They had to fly up and down fiords only a few hundred
yards wide with scant certainty that they would see its sides before
they crashed into them. Sometimes they had to "forced land" in
snowdrifts or on frozen fiords when visibility and ceiling suddenly
came down to "zero." Their maps were not accurate, and they had
to regain their carrier in fog and snowstorms and land on her
pitching deck while the Arctic gales swept across it in gusts of fifty
miles an hour.

No wonder that Tom Troubridge in his despatch to the Admiralty wrote: "It is difficult to speak without emotion of the pluck
and endurance of the young officers and men, some of them midshipmen, who flew their aircraft to such good effect. Once they
had undergone their baptism of fire their morale and spirit rose as
each obstacle was in turn successfully surmounted. All were firing
their first shot in action, whether torpedo, bomb, or machine-gun;
many made their first night landing on the 11th of April; and,
undeterred by the loss of several of their shipmates, their honour
and courage remained throughout as dazzling as the snow-covered
mountains over which they so triumphantly flew."

Nobody who knows Tom Troubridge would ever accuse him
of being given to extravagant praise or flights of poetic fancy.
They will realise that those words were literally wrung out of
him in his whole-hearted admiration for the youngsters whom he
commanded.

Troubridge had plenty of anxieties. It was always difficult in
those waters and in the uncertain Arctic weather to know when
to send aircraft off. It was even more difficult to manœuvre the
aircraft carrier in order to facilitate their return. For aircraft to
land on a carrier's deck the carrier must be headed dead into the

Crown Copyright Reserved

Rear-Admiral Troubridge
with Vice-Admiral Lord Louis Mountbatten

wind and her speed adjusted to that of the wind so that the wind up the deck will be neither too strong nor too light for a controlled landing in a very short distance. That was no easy matter in the Arctic fiords, where the gales were heavy and sudden and accompanied by unpredictable squalls, and where the winds blew round the fiords in every known direction. It posed a problem in seamanship and ship handling to the captain of an aircraft carrier such as few sailors would be called upon to face, and men's lives hung on that problem. For Troubridge it was doubly difficult because the *Furious* had a damaged "A bracket"—the bracket supporting the propeller shaft immediately before the screw—which would have been repaired some time before if it had been possible to spare the ship for refit. Such was the shortage of aircraft carriers, however, that the *Furious* could not be spared from active duty, so Troubridge had to do his best with a ship which was always unhandy in strong winds and which was made far more unhandy by her damaged "A bracket." Nobody but a seaman can realise quite what that meant to Troubridge or the degree of skill which he had to display in handling the *Furious* during flying operations in Arctic weather and narrow waters.

There came a day when the enemy, worried by the attention of the Swordfish, succeeded in discovering the *Furious* in her "hide-out" to the north of the Lofoten Islands. The German reconnaissance aircraft was quick to report her, and the Luftwaffe was sent off to sink her and thereby end the Swordfish scourge to which the Germans had been subjected in conditions such that even the Luftwaffe's crack pilots of those days seldom braved the air. Mad dogs and Englishmen may go out in the midday sun, but only the Fleet Air Arm pilots in Swordfish would have gone up in those squally blizzards.

Fortunately, the snow squalls so shrouded the aircraft carrier that the German striking force did not succeed in locating it. Instead, a single reconnaissance aircraft appeared and attacked. Troubridge did his best to avoid the bombs, but his manœuvring was hampered by the narrowness of the fiord and the damaged "A bracket" of the *Furious*. The aircraft dropped a "stick" of bombs. No bomb hit, but two of them fell sufficiently close to do damage to the machinery as well as to the hull of the ship. The delicate blades were stripped off her port turbines.

It was recognised that the *Furious* could no longer usefully operate in the face of the enemy, and she was therefore ordered back to England. That was on April 25th, and by that time the aircraft carriers *Glorious* and *Ark Royal* were available to take over her duties off the Norwegian coast.

Although the *Furious* was incapable of facing the enemy, she was still fit for sea. So desperate was the shipping situation at that time, and so important the transport of aircraft produced in the factories of the United States, that the *Furious* was kept out of the dockyard and employed as an aircraft transport in her damaged condition. Troubridge remained in command of the ship. He took the *Furious* across the Atlantic, loaded her with the products of the American aircraft factories, and brought them over to England.

That transport trip was just completed when there was imperative need for an operational aircraft carrier in Norwegian waters once more. No other carrier was then available, so the lame old *Furious* had to be used.

Three operations were carried out in the Arctic by the *Furious* during that autumn. These were against Andalsnes, against Trondheim, and against Tromsoe. All three of these operations had the same objects. They were to attack and destroy as much German shipping as possible off the Norwegian coast and to force the Germans to move squadrons of the Luftwaffe up to Norway to protect this shipping and so relieve the pressure of air attack on Great Britain.

Even after those operations had been successfully carried out, there was no rest for the gallant old *Furious*. Like all good sailors, Troubridge was deeply attached to his ship, but for all that he would have moved heaven and earth to leave her if there had been any suggestion that she should "prop up the dockyard wall." Damaged as she was, and capable of only a fraction of the performance of a modern aircraft carrier, she was useful, and " T. T." saw to it that her usefulness was most fully exploited.

Thus it was that November saw Troubridge on what passed for a bridge in the *Furious*, heading south. The ship was stuffed with Hurricane fighters of the Royal Air Force, while on her flight deck she carried four Skuas of the Fleet Air Arm for reconnaissance and for the protection of the ship. The *Furious* was not working as an aircraft carrier, but as a very efficient aircraft transport. In her Troubridge was taking to Takoradi a goodly load of Hurricanes of the Royal Air Force. Those Hurricanes were landed in West Africa from the *Furious*. From there they flew by stages across Africa to Cairo, and arrived in the Western Desert in time to play a very important part in General Wavell's offensive against Graziani's armies.

The world has almost become drugged into indifference by the repeated use of phrases such as "total war" and "global war." Nevertheless, when one is concerned with hard facts it is a matter of wonder as well as importance that a military victory on one side of a continent should have owed so much to air power brought to the scene through the influence of sea power many thousands of miles away. The "Desert Rats" probably thought themselves very far away from the Atlantic, yet the Royal Air Force fighters which gave them so much help and support had come from the Atlantic and from an old and damaged ship which had given air support to their soldier friends in the Arctic under very different conditions. It was just another illustration of the invaluable flexibility which the possession of sea power gives to all our armed forces.

After that air-transport trip to West Africa H.M.S. *Furious* returned to England. It was more than high time that she was repaired and refitted, and Troubridge left her in December, 1940.

It was then that he was appointed to the Admiralty to serve on the Committee of Senior Officers. It was a job that he could do by reason of his knowledge of the German personalities who directed the enemy's strategy, and there was nobody else who could do it half as well. Troubridge realised this and threw himself into the job with his customary enthusiasm and drive. Nevertheless, he was far from happy. He was a naval officer with a great and natural desire to serve at sea in time of war, and it was inevitable that he should dislike such an appointment. He hated it, but he did everything that was asked of him and a bit more. That was in the Troubridge tradition.

In June, 1941, however, his patience was rewarded. He was appointed to command the battleship *Nelson*. Very soon after Troubridge had assumed command of this ship she was ordered to the Mediterranean, where she formed part of the famous "Force H" which dominated the Western Mediterranean. Admiral Sir James Somerville then commanded "Force H," and he hoisted his flag in the *Nelson*. Three times vital convoys were run through from Gibraltar to beleaguered Malta under the cover provided by "Force H," and in each one of these tricky operations James Somerville commanded the covering force from the *Nelson*, which was commanded by Troubridge. Thus the Troubridge of 1941 learnt to wage war in the waters in which his ancestor had made war with the *Culloden* as one of Nelson's most valuable ships.

On the last of H.M.S. *Nelson's* trips into the central Mediterranean as cover for a Malta convoy she was unlucky enough to be hit by a torpedo dropped by an Italian aircraft. It was one of those freak attacks in which an Italian pilot demonstrated the almost incredible courage of which his race is capable when embarked upon an individual effort. Several torpedo-carrying aircraft had come in to attack. Many of them had been shot down—others had dropped their torpedoes at a distance which gave even the big ships plenty of time to take avoiding action. Troubridge had swung the *Nelson* away to avoid some of these torpedoes dropped at a distance when a lone Savoia came in low, surviving by some miracle the terrific barrage put up by the short-range anti-aircraft guns of the ships, and dropped a torpedo close to the *Nelson*. The Italian aircraft paid the penalty, but the *Nelson*, even under full helm, could not turn in time. She was hit forward, below the thickest of her armour and under-water protection.

The *Nelson* was not very badly damaged, but her speed was considerably reduced, and, what was worse, the damaged forepart of the ship sagged, and jammed the foremost 16-inch gun turret so that a proportion of her main armament was rendered useless. The ship was turned back towards Gibraltar. There was anxiety about her in the Admiralty in London, but no anxiety on board the ship. James Somerville, it must be admitted, was momentarily out of sympathy with Tom Troubridge, whose estimate of the damage was concerned chiefly with the fact that he had in the foremost refrigerator, which was flooded as a result of the explosion, a dozen chickens and a lot of eggs.

James Somerville, however, has a sense of humour only matched by those of Tom Troubridge and Andrew Cunningham, who was then Commander-in-Chief in the Eastern Mediterranean. Between Cunningham and Somerville there had long been an interchange of pleasantries which made the signal logs of their respective flagships a joy to read. On this occasion Cunningham, on receiving the report of the hit on the *Nelson* and being assured that no serious damage had resulted, sent a signal to Somerville commiserating with him on his "slap in the belly with a wet fish" (a torpedo is known in the

Royal Navy as a "fish," among other terms). Without a moment's hesitation James Somerville replied to Andrew Cunningham: "Thanks very much, but a hit below the belt at my time of life does not hurt."

Somerville and Troubridge took the *Nelson* back to Gibraltar, and the fact that there were no eggs for breakfast was mitigated by the feeling that for once they had got the better of an exchange of signals with "A.B.C."

The damage to the *Nelson*, although not serious, made it necessary for the ship to return to the United Kingdom for docking and refit. Troubridge brought her safely home and was then available for another appointment.

He was not kept waiting. He had enjoyed only a few days' leave when he was appointed to command the aircraft carrier *Indomitable*. This was one of the new big "fleet" aircraft carriers, and very different to the old *Furious*, although the spirit of the Fleet Air Arm was the same in both ships. In the *Indomitable* Troubridge went to the Indian Ocean, where he combined his appointment in command of the aircraft carrier with that of Chief of Staff to the Rear-Admiral commanding the aircraft carriers of the Eastern Fleet. Troubridge was in the Far East for six months. On his own admission they were very grim months because, for the first time for over a century, the British Navy was then "on the run" in that theatre of war.

It was a situation which was full of difficulty—one in which the personality of a commander could go far towards outweighing the depressing facts of the situation. At that time the Japanese Navy was steaming in the Indian Ocean with comparative impunity, and the situation demanded the highest standards of service and morale from the men who had, for the most part, borne the brunt of war against odds in the Mediterranean before being suddenly called upon to face seeming disaster in the Far East instead of the home leave which they had expected.

It was another "tough assignment," but there was little time to brood. Almost immediately Troubridge and his men were involved in an operation which called for offensive action, although it was unfortunately directed against our former French Allies.

The Japanese Navy had taken advantage of British naval weakness in the Bay of Bengal and the Indian Ocean to spread its operations halfway to Africa. Off East Africa lay the great island of

Madagascar, with the enormous harbour of Diego Suarez at its northern end. Diego Suarez was the Scapa Flow of the Indian Ocean, and it was essential to deny its use to the Japanese fleet. Japanese naval encroachment in the Indian Ocean underlined the danger, which was far greater than the mere possession of a harbour; for an enemy fleet established at Diego Suarez would be in a position to cut our lines of communication from the Cape of Good Hope to Suez, and therefore prevent our Eighth Army from receiving the reinforcements and supplies necessary to fight the great battle of Alamein. Here was yet another instance of the influence of sea power upon military history at a great distance from the naval action.

Madagascar was a French colony which had declared its allegiance to the Vichy Government of Occupied France. Great Britain had done everything possible to respect French sovereignty, but we could not acquiesce in the tendency of the Vichy French authorities to collaborate with Germany and Japan.

In the circumstances, it was decided that Diego Suarez should be taken over by the British Eastern Fleet. A combined operation was therefore planned and organised. It was the first invasion upon which the United Nations embarked. The air cover for this invasion was provided from the aircraft carriers *Indomitable* and *Illustrious*. Its first job was the eradication of French air power just before the landings took place. The work of the Fleet Air Arm at Madagascar was difficult and distasteful, but it was brilliantly carried out, and there is no doubt that it contributed to the shortening of the hostilities, and therefore to a reduction in the number of casualties both among our troops and among those commanded by the Vichy French authorities.

By August, 1942, Troubridge, in the *Indomitable*, was back in the Mediterranean, and this aircraft carrier played a prominent part in fighting through to Malta the most vital supply convoy of the war.

The air cover for the passage of that convoy was to have been provided by the aircraft carriers *Victorious*, *Indomitable* and *Eagle*, under the command of Rear-Admiral Lyster, whose flag flew in the *Victorious*. The *Eagle*, however, was torpedoed and sunk by a U-boat very soon after the convoy had left Gibraltar, so that the responsibility for air cover falling upon the *Victorious* and *Indomitable* was greatly increased. Fortunately Troubridge had the Navy's best fighter squadron embarked in the *Indomitable*. Although this squadron was equipped only with Hurricane I's, it did great execution during that operation, and played an important part in the relief of Malta at that critical moment in the island's history. The squadron shot down twenty-nine enemy aircraft and scored at least twenty-five "probables" and "possibles." A high proportion of the latter are likely to have crashed out of sight of the fleet.

Towards the close of the last exciting day of that convoy battle the *Indomitable* was set upon by a squadron of Junkers 87's. They delivered a series of most determined dive-bombing attacks on the aircraft carrier, and succeeded in hitting her with a number of heavy bombs. The ship was never in any danger of sinking, but she was badly damaged. Malta had been relieved, but it had cost the Navy one aircraft carrier sunk and another so damaged that she ceased to be an effective unit for the next six months; as well as loss and damage to smaller ships. It was a heavy price to pay, but it was more than justified by the relief of Malta at a time when the island had very little food, and when the guns had to be severely rationed owing to shortage of ammunition, and aircraft had to be kept on the ground for lack of petrol. History will assuredly rank the passage of that convoy among the operations which have had a far-reaching effect on the course of the war.

Tom Troubridge brought the damaged *Indomitable* safely back to England, and then promptly took up another appointment which again brought him into action in the Mediterranean. Once again he was to have to fight against Frenchmen who gave allegiance to the collaborationist government at Vichy.

It had been decided to invade French North and West Africa, and thereby lay the foundations for a tremendous movement which was to drive the enemy out of Africa, open the Mediterranean to shipping, and provide the United Nations with a land mass upon which to base operations against "the soft underbelly" of Europe.

In West Africa the operation was to be aimed at Casablanca from the opposite side of the Atlantic, and was therefore an American commitment. In North Africa the troops to be landed in the initial phases were, for political reasons, to be American, but the naval forces were to be British. There were to be two main immediate objectives in North Africa—Algiers and Oran—and each landing was to be conducted by a Task Force Commander, under the supreme command at sea of Admiral Sir Andrew Cunningham.

The Algiers Task Force was put under the command of Rear-Admiral Harold Burrough, and the Oran Task Force under Troubridge, who was made a Commodore First Class.

The landings took place just before dawn on November 8th, 1942, and, although at Oran there was little opposition ashore except in the outskirts of the town, the French naval forces fought bitterly, and the Oran operations gave rise to one of the most gallant naval actions of the war.

All the troops in the initial landings, including the Rangers—the American equivalent of the British Commando troops—were to be landed over the beaches, but these were to assault the "back door" of Oran. At the same time it was considered essential that the direct approach should be undertaken with the idea of seizing the harbour and port by a sudden *coup de main*, and so preventing the destruction of the harbour works or the blocking of the port.

This, of course, meant that the boom guarding the harbour entrance would have to be smashed open as a necessary preliminary to the direct assault on the harbour and the port. It was decided to break the boom by charging it with ships, and subsequently to blow up its remains with special mobile mines. The *Walney* and *Hartland* were chosen for this task. The *Walney* was commanded by Lieutenant-Commander P. C. Meyrick, R.N., and had on board Captain Peters, R.N., who was the senior officer and in charge of the operation, and the *Hartland* was commanded by Lieutenant-Commander J. P. Billot, R.N.R. Both ships had formerly been United States coastguard cutters, and had been transferred to the British Navy to help as convoy escorts during the worst phase of the Battle of the Atlantic.

At one minute past midnight on November 8th the *Walney* and *Hartland*, having separated from the rest of the naval forces approaching Oran, made final preparations for charging the boom and carrying out the direct assault on the port. Each ship had on board 200 United States Assault Troops, between decks so that they were given as much protection as possible. With 200 troops between decks there was no room to move, and it would have been quite impossible to supply the guns with ammunition from the magazines. Ammunition for all guns had therefore to be stacked on deck. There were also canoes and special mobile mines on deck. The scheme was for the ships to break through the boom by ramming it at speed, and then to lower the canoes inside the harbour.

These would launch the mobile mines, which were designed to destroy and clear away all remaining obstructions at the harbour entrance.

The cutters made a landfall off Pointe d'Aiguille and crept westwards towards Oran at slow speed. They were only a quarter to half a mile off-shore, and slow speed was therefore necessary to avoid bow-waves and wakes which could easily have been seen from the shore. Between the cutters and the shore were two motor launches—M.L.s *483* and *480*—which were to lay a smoke screen to cover the final dash of the cutters when about to ram the boom.

As the cutters approached the entrance to Oran harbour and circled to seaward before making their dash for the boom, they were seen from the shore. The Vichy destroyer *T.73* and the batteries at Gambetta and Ravin Blanc opened a hot and accurate fire. This was directed chiefly at the *Hartland*, as the *Walney* was already getting some cover from the smoke screen laid by the motor launches.

The *Hartland* was badly hit by the opening salvoes. Several fires were started on board and there were a large number of casualties. These included most of the guns' crews, so that the ship was unable to fight back strongly. The commanding officer of the *Hartland* was blinded in one eye by a shell splinter, and in the very short time before he was able to resume command the ship became out of control and hit the jetty. In spite of all this, Lieutenant-Commander Billot succeeded in manœuvring his damaged and burning ship into her appointed place and gave the order for the canoes with their mines to be dropped, but this order could not be obeyed as all the canoes were riddled and most of the gear shot away. The First Lieutenant made a gallant attempt to make the ship fast to the jetty in order to hold her in position, as her engines were by this time out of action. But it proved impossible to secure the ship, since practically every man had been killed or wounded and the jetty and the ship's decks were being swept by machine-gun fire at point-blank range. The *Hartland* could do nothing to keep down the volume of fire, since none of her guns were able to fire. Nor could she manœuvre so as to render it less effective.

With nearly all his men killed or wounded and with the ship so badly on fire that the flames rose higher than the top of the funnel and ammunition was exploding in all directions, Billot gave the order to abandon ship. Although he was himself seriously wounded, he personally supervised the removal of the wounded from the burning ship, which was likely to blow up at any minute. The *Hartland's* battle ensign still flew, but the French nevertheless ceased fire and thereby put an end to the slaughter.

Meanwhile the *Walney* was also suffering severely. She had duly rammed the boom at 15 knots and broken through it quite easily. She had then reached her appointed position and dropped her canoes in less than one minute, despite the fact that she was by that time under heavy fire at close range. Fortunately, however, the fire was not at that stage very accurate. Having dropped her canoes, the *Walney* went on up the harbour to land her assault troops. She had boarding parties ready in her boats and sixteen American grenade throwers ready on her forecastle. Peters intended to board the big French destroyer *Epervier*, which was lying alongside the Quai de Controle. He intended to lay the *Walney* alongside the Frenchman, with her port side to her. Just before this could be done, however, another French destroyer appeared. This ship passed up the starboard side of the *Walney*, so that the cutter was simultaneously engaged from both sides at a range of a few yards. She was also engaged by gunfire from two submarines, which were lying farther up the harbour.

Caught in this point-blank cross-fire from guns ranging from about 5-inch down to light automatic weapons, the *Walney* was disabled in a few minutes. Her engines and steering gear were put out of action and so heavy were the casualties among the exposed personnel of the guns' crews that the ship was virtually silenced. There was one exception. The after machine-guns, by some miracle, were kept in action, their crews surviving through the hail of shells and bullets. Captain Peters survived and was awarded the Victoria Cross, but was tragically killed in an air crash on his way back to England—Lieutenant-Commander Meyrick was killed. Well over half the crew and the troops on board were killed or wounded, but still the *Walney* fought back with her after machine-guns, although it was rather like going into action with a pea-shooter against a herd of elephants.

Worse was to come. The *Walney* drifted helplessly until she was at right angles to the *Epervier*, so that the latter's fire raked her fore and aft and had an increasingly devastating effect. Yet those after machine-guns in the *Walney* were kept in action, and spat back defiance for nearly an hour. By that time the *Walney* was nothing but a burning hulk, with more than 50 per cent of her crew and passengers casualties and with her own ammunition exploding in all directions. Lieutenant W. D. Mosely, R.N. was the senior surviving officer of the ship, and he gave the order to abandon ship. He and others were picked up by the crew of the *Epervier* and were very well treated by the French on board that ship. The officers and men of the *Epervier* had fought bitterly and determinedly, but they were impressed by the magnificent fight which the *Walney* had put up against impossible odds.

Although the boom across the harbour entrance had been broken, the direct assault on the port had not taken place, and unfortunately the resistance put up by the Vichy navy was not at an end. On November 8th, a few hours after the actions of the *Hartland* and *Walney*, some French naval forces made a sortie from Oran against Commodore Troubridge's Task Force. This resulted in the sinking of a French destroyer of the *Alcyon* class by H.M.S. *Aurora*, and the French escort vessel *La Surprise* being sunk by H.M.S. *Brilliant*. On the following day—November 9th—there was another skirmish, during which a French destroyer of the *Canard* class was set on fire by H.M.S. *Aurora* and H.M.S. *Jamaica* and was beached by her crew. On that day, and on November 10th, the 16-inch guns of H.M.S. *Rodney* were used to bombard Fort Santon, the guns of which dominated the entrance to the harbour of Mers-el-Kebir. By the middle of the afternoon of November 11th Admiral Darlan issued orders from Algiers which led to the cease-fire being sounded by the French throughout North Africa.

The invasion of French North Africa was an accomplished fact, but that did not mean that there was rest and relaxation for either of the Task Force Commanders. The French had ceased to resist, but the Germans were reacting strongly and were making good use of the Luftwaffe based on Sardinian airfields. They were also collecting packs of U-boats to operate against our transports and supply ships and their covering forces off North Africa. It has been authoritatively stated that the Germans were able to mass a minimum of fifty U-boats off the North Africa coast within a few days of our landings. The greater weight of the German counter offensive fell, inevitably, upon Rear-Admiral Burrough's Eastern Task Force off Algiers, but Commodore Troubridge's Western Task Force was far from being unmolested. With hundreds of ships, carrying tens of thousands of troops and their equipment and supplies in his charge, there was need in Troubridge's force for constant vigilance and readiness to meet any move which the enemy might make. It is as well to remember that the Italian Fleet was at that time still an Axis instrument and, on paper at all events, a very powerful one, and surface attack also had therefore to be guarded against.

In those days Troubridge came into close association with the American Army. In that association he found compensation for having had the distasteful task of quelling French resistance. So much so that he wrote afterwards: "This was a very enjoyable experience, and I found that the American Army, whom we had to land, were extremely easy to work with and a particularly friendly crowd."

Troubridge wears the red and white ribbon of the United States Army Distinguished Service Medal for his part in the Oran landings.

It was some weeks before Troubridge came home from the invasion of French North Africa. When he did he was attached to the Combined Operations Command during the preparatory phase of the next invasion. Ever since commanding that Task Force at Oran he has held appointments intimately concerned with combined operations against hostile coasts; and ever since his command of the *Furious* in 1940 his connection with aircraft carriers seems to have played an important part in the appointments for which he has been selected. Invasions and aircraft carriers seem to have been harnessed to his recent career.

Tom Troubridge was promoted to the rank of Rear-Admiral in January, 1943, and at the same time he was chosen to command one of the British Assault Groups for the invasion of Sicily. There were three of these British Assault Groups and three United States Assault Groups. The three American groups were to land troops on the southern shore of Sicily, while the British landings were to be made around the south-east corner of the island and along its east coast.

The latter was at once the most important and the most dangerous in which to carry out amphibious operations. The east coast of Sicily flanks the approaches to the Straits of Messina. It was heavily fortified and the waters thickly mined. Moreover, ships operating in that area would be tempting targets for air forces operating from the Italian mainland as well as from Sicily. There was also increased danger from U-boats and E-boats, and even the possibility of sorties by the Italian surface ships either from Taranto or through the Straits of Messina. These dangers did not exist in anything like the same degree off the southern coast of Sicily, yet it was the southern part of the east coast which was the key to the invasion. It has been said with truth that no invasion can be considered successful until the invading force has at its disposal at least one adequate port at which reinforcements and supplies can be landed irrespective of weather conditions. In the invasion of Sicily this meant the capture of a port, for there were not available any of the artificial harbours and other devices which were so successfully employed during the invasion of Normandy.

The only feasible ports in the whole area of the Allied landings in Sicily were Syracuse and Augusta, both on the southern part of the east coast of the island. Both were naval bases and strongly defended by heavy coastal batteries, minefields and other defences.

Tom Troubridge was allocated that most important and the most dangerous sector in the invasion of Sicily—the landing of troops in the neighbourhood of Syracuse and Augusta and the capture of these two ports. It was an anxious task, although he knew that his force would be screened by destroyers and small craft against U-boats and E-boats, while to seaward he was to be covered against attack by the Italian Fleet by a force of battleships and cruisers, and would be given air cover from a force of aircraft carriers. Moreover, he knew that he would have plenty of naval bombarding power on which he could call for the reduction of enemy shore batteries.

In the spring of 1943 the force which Rear-Admiral Troubridge was to command during the invasion of Sicily sailed from England to Suez by way of the Cape of Good Hope. Troubridge himself flew direct to Cairo, where he spent a fortnight working on the final plans with Admiral Ramsay. Then he joined his large amphibious force on its arrival at Suez and hoisted his flag in the headquarters ship *Bulolo*. During the passage of that force round the Cape of Good Hope and up the east coast of Africa one can well imagine that Troubridge was thankful that, as a result of operations in which he had taken part, Madagascar was no longer in the hands of the Vichy authorities and capable of being exploited by the enemy.

At Suez, Troubridge's force stretched their legs after their long voyage. They did a great deal more than stretch their legs. Tom Troubridge is not a man to leave things to chance, and he knows very well the importance of fitness and of training before undertaking a dangerous operation. He therefore trained his force hard at Suez for two months before embarking again, this time for the real thing—the first invasion of the European "fortress."

Troubridge landed the Thirteenth Corps of the Eighth Army close to Syracuse just before daylight on July 10th. The Thirteenth Corps was then commanded by General M. C. Dempsey, who now commands the British Second Army in Western Europe. Despite a last-minute postponement of the time of the landings owing to bad weather conditions during the approach, the landings were successfully carried out, and it became apparent that surprise had been achieved everywhere along the British and American sectors, since the enemy considered the weather too bad for landings to be attempted. In Troubridge's words: "The proceedings went with a swing." This was in spite of the minefields and repeated attempts by the enemy to interfere with U-boats and E-boats, as well as sporadic attacks by aircraft. As ever, the minesweepers did a magnificent job of work, frequently continuing imperturbably to sweep up the mines despite heavy and accurate shelling by the shore batteries. These, however, were soon silenced by a series of bombardments from destroyers, cruisers and even the 15-inch and 16-inch guns of battleships. By night a whole series of swift but gallant and successful actions were fought against U-boats and E-boats by our motor torpedo boats and motor gunboats. Admiral Sir Bertram Ramsay, who was in general naval command of the British sectors, gave magnificent protection and support to the landing forces and to the troops ashore.

On the day after the landings Tom Troubridge, who had embarked in a minesweeper for the purpose, entered Syracuse harbour. He was thus the first British Admiral to enter an enemy port in Europe under invasion conditions. The entry into Syracuse of that minesweeper, with Rear-Admiral Troubridge's flag flying proudly at its masthead, marked the success of the first phase of the invasion. We had seized a deep water port. From that moment the final success of the invasion of Sicily was assured, although there was much hard slogging ashore, and much small ship fighting, minesweeping and bombarding at sea.

In the early morning of the day after he had been the first to enter the port of Syracuse, Tom Troubridge left that port in order to enter Augusta. Our troops were on the outskirts of the town and it was considered that the arrival in the port of a fairly powerful

British warship flying an admiral's flag would achieve the surrender of the garrison remnants without further fighting.

The ship which Troubridge selected for this duty was the big destroyer *Eskimo*. She was one of the "Tribal" class of destroyers, with an imposing silhouette and eight 4.7-inch guns in addition to torpedo armament and lighter weapons.

Troubridge was, in fact, the first to enter the port of Augusta, but the operation did not go quite according to plan. He left Syracuse in H.M.S. *Eskimo* very early in the morning. Soon after leaving Syracuse the *Eskimo* was attacked by enemy aircraft and one bomb scored a direct hit in the engine-room, putting the ship out of action. Troubridge then transferred to the cruiser *Mauritius*. It was considered, however, unwise to send a cruiser into Augusta because of the great risk from mines and obstructions, so that outside the port Troubridge transferred to the destroyer *Exmoor*.

Troubridge entered the harbour of Augusta in H.M.S. *Exmoor*, but, in his own words: "My progress was not quite so easy. Although I was the first into Augusta, I was also the first out, my departure being hastened by a considerable volume of fire from various unfriendly gents ashore."

Troubridge's main responsibilities in regard to the invasion of Sicily were now discharged, and before long he was ordered away to a very different sphere. His new appointment took him to India, where he had to train Combined Operations forces which were to be used in the Burma campaign. In this duty he was accorded the title of "Flag Officer, Overseas Assault Force." Troubridge's experience at Oran, at Suez, and off the coast of Sicily stood him in good stead, and he made his assault force far more formidable by their training than they were in numbers or equipment.

Christmas, 1943, however, saw him back in the Mediterranean in order to take part in the landings at Anzio and Nettuno and in the subsequent operations off that fiercely contested beachhead. Troubridge brought the assault force which he had been training in India back to the Mediterranean for this operation, it having been decided by those in charge of the higher direction of the war that the Mediterranean theatre should have priority over the contemplated Burma campaign.

In parenthesis, one may regret the fact that Tom Troubridge had been in India at the time of the Salerno landings. Had he not been he would almost certainly have been present during that operation, and thereby followed in the wake of his great ancestor of Nelson's days in the waters off Salerno. It was in 1799 that a blood-thirsty Italian ran a Jacobin to earth in a Salerno alleyway and sent his head to Troubridge with a request that it should be forwarded to Nelson, then at Naples. Troubridge did not send Nelson the head, but wrote of the gift and enclosed the Italian's covering letter, across the bottom of which he scrawled: "A jolly fellow—T. Troubridge." Nelson, in a letter to Lord St. Vincent, wrote of this incident: "Our friend Troubridge had a present made to him the other day of a head of a Jacobin, and makes apology to me, the weather being very hot, for not sending it here."

The Anzio beachhead has already taken its place among the controversial operations of the war. There is no denying the soundness of the conception, which was to turn Kesselring's flank by the presence of a large force behind his position in the so-called "Adolf Hitler Line", and to level a direct threat at Rome and all the communications radiating southwards from it. It is alleged, however, that the beachhead was not fully exploited in the early stages, and that military commanders contented themselves with consolidating the initial objectives laid down when they might well have pushed on to other objectives, thereby confusing the enemy and preventing him from massing for his counter-attack.

Be that as it may; there is no doubt that the naval side of the operation was a complete success. All the troops, equipment and supplies were landed safely at the appointed times and places, and surprise was achieved in these initial landings.

The naval part of the Anzio and Nettuno landing operations were under the command of Rear-Admiral F. G. Lowry of the United States Navy, who had the title of Naval Commander, Amphibious Task Force, and flew his flag in the U.S.S. *Biscayne*. The British component of the naval force was under the command of Rear-Admiral Troubridge, whose flag was again flying in the *Bulolo*. The main American landing was carried out four miles east of Anzio, and the main British landing six miles north of Anzio. Here Troubridge put ashore the British First Division. At the same time United States Rangers and British Commando troops carried out a direct assault on Anzio itself.

So successful was the approach that the convoys reached their appointed beaches at the right time without having been molested.

Surprise had been achieved, and there was consequently practically no opposition on the beaches, although some of these were found to have been mined. For gunfire support, if needed, Troubridge had been provided with the cruisers H.M.S. *Orion* and H.M.S. *Spartan*, while Rear-Admiral Lowry had the cruisers H.M.S. *Penelope* and U.S.S. *Brooklyn* available for similar duties east of Anzio. Additional support was available for the whole force by the presence to seaward of the British destroyers *Faulknor*, *Ulster*, *Tenacious*, *Kempenfelt* and *Grenville*; the American destroyers *Ludlow*, *Plunkett*, *Gleaves*, *Mayo*, *Woolsey* and *Niblack*; and the Dutch gunboats *Flores* and *Soemba*.

The approach and the initial landings were so successful, however, that neither the cruisers detailed to provide gunfire support, nor the destroyers provided for additional support were called upon. What might have been a dangerous and costly landing was virtually unopposed by reason of the successful exploitation of surprise. There is little doubt that a diversionary operation carried out off Civitavecchia played an important part in diverting the enemy's attention from the Anzio-Nettuno area and contributed largely to the initial success of the Allied landings.

The landing of British and American troops in the Anzio-Nettuno area was timed for dawn on January 22nd, 1944, and took place at that time. Some hours earlier the cruiser H.M.S. *Dido*, the British destroyers *Inglefield* and *Loyal*, and the French destroyer *Le Fantasque* had bombarded Civitavecchia, some seventy miles up the coast, and north-west of Rome. This bombardment was followed by a dummy landing, and there is no doubt that the Civitavecchia diversion succeeded in making the enemy "take his eye off the ball" in the Anzio-Nettuno area.

Having carried out this diversion, the *Dido*, *Inglefield*, *Loyal* and *Le Fantasque* moved down the coast and took up stations well to the southward of the beachhead, off the coast road leading from Formia to the beachhead. By 11 a.m. on the day of the landings it was seen that the Germans were moving vehicles along this road towards the beachhead, and the ships began shelling the road. This bombardment of the coast road was continued for twenty-four hours, until nearly noon on January 23rd. By that time it was seen that the road was seriously damaged and it was considered sufficient to leave one destroyer to interfere with such enemy movements along it as were likely to be possible. Further bombardments of the road were, however, carried out during that night and the following day.

By the late afternoon of the day following the first landings the beachhead had been extended and consolidated; practically all the landing craft and landing ships had discharged their cargoes; Anzio had been captured and its small harbour was being rapidly cleared of wrecks so that it could be put into use. This was as well, for the weather, which had been favourable for the initial landings, was deteriorating and threatened to become worse. As it was, landings over the beaches had to be discontinued on January 24th, when there was a strong south-westerly wind and considerable surf, but by that time the initial landings of men, equipment and material had been completed and the port of Anzio was able to handle such further traffic as was essential.

It was on the same afternoon—January 24th—that German aircraft took a hand in the operations and attacked three British hospital ships anchored off the beaches. Of these the 2700-ton *St. David* was sunk, the 4300-ton *Leinster* set on fire, and the 2700-ton *St. Andrew* damaged by a near miss. Needless to say, the ships were clearly marked as hospital ships and could not possibly have been mistaken for anything else.

Week after week the struggle round the perimeter of the beachhead dragged on, and week after week the naval forces and merchant seamen of the Allies did everything possible to succour the hardpressed British and American troops ashore. There was no respite until General Alexander's armies at last broke the "Adolf Hitler Line," relieved the garrison of the beachhead, captured Rome, and set his armies and his air forces to a pursuit of the defeated Germans which carried him quickly to the neighbourhood of Florence and the "Gothic Line."

The Anzio beachhead had not succeeded in turning Kesselring's flank in his "Adolf Hitler Line" positions, and it had been costly, but there is little doubt that it contributed to General Alexander's victory by containing large German forces which would otherwise have been available to strengthen Kesselring in his main positions south of Rome. As for the Navy's task—it had been most faithfully discharged. The military forces were put ashore without loss, and they were kept constantly supplied despite the worst that the enemy could do. Let the figures speak for themselves on the supply task undertaken and performed. The Navy had been told to be prepared to land 1500 tons a day at Anzio and on the neighbouring beaches for a period of fourteen days. In the event, they landed an average of 5000 tons a day for more than a hundred days.

After the Anzio landings the responsibility for the "build-up" and supply of the forces ashore in that area devolved upon the Flag Officer, Western Italy—Rear-Admiral J. A. V. Morse, C.B., C.B.E., D.S.O. Troubridge went to Algiers in the *Bulolo* and there he awaited the next amphibious operation, being engaged meanwhile in the normal training and administration of his force.

Early in April Troubridge deputised for Rear-Admiral Dundas as Chief of Staff to the Commander-in-Chief, Mediterranean, while that officer returned to England for a much needed spell of leave. On Admiral Dundas's return to the Mediterranean Troubridge went to Ajaccio in Corsica to plan and prepare for a combined operation for the capture of Elba.

This operation, which Tom Troubridge describes as one of the most difficult that he has ever been called upon to undertake, was a truly United Nations affair. The naval force was for the most part British, supplemented by a number of American landing craft and two Greek minesweepers. The military force consisted of the Ninth French Colonial Infantry Division under General Magnan, and the Air Force was a mixture of American, British and French under the command of Colonel Dancy of the United States Army Air Force.

A good story is told of Tom Troubridge at this time, which illustrates his directness and his instinctive and unwavering belief in those somewhat high-falutin words inscribed over the entrance to the hall of the Royal Naval College at Dartmouth. Troubridge was presiding at a meeting called to consider the capture of a certain strongly held enemy position through a combined operation. The meeting was dragging on interminably and some of those present seemed to be getting more and more imbued with the possibility of failure. Finally, just as Troubridge's patience was nearing exhaustion, a military officer said that he could not absolutely guarantee the capture of a certain enemy battery. Troubridge banged on the table and rounded on the luckless officer. "In the Navy, sir," he roared, "we do not guarantee things—we *do* them." The meeting broke up in a very different frame of mind and the operation under discussion was carried out without a hitch.

Elba was a tough nut to crack. The Germans had done a tre-

mendous amount of work in fortifying the island, which was small
enough to enable them to concentrate their heavy artillery in the
centre of the island so that all of it could be brought to bear on any
threatened point. Moreover, the shallow waters round the island
were extensively mined.

Success in any amphibious operation depends principally upon
two things—timing and communications—and both of these call
for careful planning and thorough training. If the timing goes
wrong and the landing craft are late in touching down on the
beaches they lose the benefit of the preliminary bombardment, since
the enemy has time to recover and oppose the landing. If communications fail, the Force Commanders are ignorant of the situation
and unable to control the battle.

The place selected for the main landing at Elba was Campo Bay,
on the south-western coast. This was protected by coastal batteries
on the cliffs overlooking the bay, and by numerous batteries covering the beaches. Commando troops were put ashore prior to the
main landing to deal with these coastal batteries, but they had been
able to achieve only partial success when the first wave of the assault
entered the bay.

The landing craft were met by a very hot fire, but they pressed
on with the utmost gallantry, and as they neared the beach the five
rocket craft fired a barrage with such accuracy and devastating effect
that all enemy fire momentarily ceased. The landing craft dashed
forward and, with faultless timing, landed the assault troops while
the smoke and dust of the barrage still hung in the air and obscured
the view of the enemy. The battle was, however, by no means over.
In the darkness several enemy batteries, although overrun by the
first wave of the assault, remained in action and, recovering from
the effect of the rocket barrage, opened fire on the second wave of
the assault, which came into the bay half an hour after the first.
Three of the five large infantry landing craft in this wave were
set on fire, and one of them became a total loss. The survivors were
obliged to withdraw.

Fortunately the communications were as good as had been the
timing of the touch down of the first wave, and as soon as it was
reported that the second wave had been prevented from landing on
the main beach, Troubridge gave orders to switch the second
wave to a "scramble" landing at the entrance to a rocky ravine
on the eastern entrance to the bay. All the remaining infantry were

duly landed at this point, and carried out an attack from that area, which finally overcame the defences of the main beaches some four hours later and enabled the guns and vehicles to be put ashore.

After that the Ninth French Colonial Infantry Division made short work of the remaining defences, and only very few of the 2600 German defenders escaped to the mainland under cover of darkness and thus saved themselves from death or capture. The Allied casualties were not light, but the reduction of this important bastion of the German line enabled the Fifth Army to continue its advance on Pisa and Leghorn. This it did because the capture of Elba freed the port of Piombino, which lies in the narrow strait of that name which separates Elba from the mainland.

As a minor combined operation the assault on Elba was a model, and Troubridge says that he looks back on it with greater satisfaction than he does upon any other such operation in which he has been concerned. The gallantry of the young officers and men on whom the brunt of the fighting inevitably fell was of the usual superb order, and Troubridge wrote in his despatch that it "earned the admiring appreciation of the French Army."

By the early summer of 1944 it had become possible to visualise amphibious operations outside the range of shore-based short-range fighter cover. That seems a simple statement, but in it there lies a reversal of all that had been learnt at such bitter cost during the first years of the war, and appreciation of this was to have an incalculable effect upon the future course and length of the war. In part, of course, the lesson had been learnt in the Pacific, where shore-based air cover was more often than not out of the question, and where massed aircraft carriers had succeeded in providing the necessary air cover for landing operations.

Two main factors combined to make this principle applicable to Europe, where a force would have to reckon with the total available strength of the Luftwaffe, which might be rushed to the danger point, instead of only the air strength of an isolated island or group of islands as was the case in the Pacific. These two main factors were the decline of the Luftwaffe as a result of the war of attrition waged against it so successfully by the Royal Air Force and the United States Army Air Force; and the continued defeat of the U-boats in the Battle of the Atlantic. The latter statement may at first sight seem somewhat far fetched, but it is true.

During the dismal years when the U-boats levied a heavy toll on our shipping and supplies in the Atlantic, orders had been placed for a very large number of "escort aircraft carriers." These were to provide the convoys with short-range air cover throughout their voyages and have a striking force always available to attack the U-boats massing for attack before they could approach within range of the convoys. More particularly, they gave the convoys the benefit of air support in the area which had hitherto been out of range of shore-based aircraft, and which was still out of range of all but a limited number of special V.L.R. (very long range) aircraft. This "gap" in air support had been 300 miles wide, and in it the U-boats had for some time been scoring the majority of their successes.

The "escort aircraft carriers" were only one of the factors which led to the decisive and continued defeat of the U-boats, but it is with them that we are here chiefly concerned. The large programme of "escort aircraft carriers" and the defeat of the U-boats in the Atlantic combined to produce a surplus of these vessels over the reduced requirements for the protection of the great Atlantic trade routes against the U-boats.

Here, then, was material ready to hand—a state of affairs with which we had been all too unfamiliar in the past. The "escort aircraft carriers" could become "assault aircraft carriers," the duty of which was to provide fighter and fighter-bomber support for amphibious assaults outside the range of shore-based aircraft of similar characteristics. There was no necessity to alter the ships for their new duties. All that was necessary was to amend their outfit of aircraft, so that they carried only fighters and fighter-bombers and no torpedo-carrying aircraft or long-range reconnaissance aircraft.

The possession of numbers of these small "assault aircraft carriers" gave the commander of the amphibious force far greater freedom of movement when he had to contemplate an operation at a distance from our shore air bases. The degree of freedom of movement was far greater than if he had been given big "fleet aircraft carriers" with equivalent aircraft carrying capacity. A much smaller number of the big "fleet aircraft carriers" would have been able to deploy the same air strength, but it would have been the case of "too many eggs in one basket." The aircraft carrier force could not be split up, and, moreover, the same risks could not be taken. The loss of an "assault aircraft carrier" could be contemplated, not with a callous equanimity, but with the knowledge that it would not greatly effect the course of the war in other theatres, whereas the loss of a big "fleet carrier" might well do so.

When these factors are considered it is easy to appreciate the profound effect which the advent of these ships had upon the scope of combined operations—and therefore on the course of the war.

One or two "escort aircraft carriers" had been employed during the Allied landings in French North Africa, and one had been lost in tragic circumstances, but they were used far more in the escort than in the assault sense. It was off the beachhead at Salerno that the small aircraft carriers—then still called "escort aircraft carriers"—really came into their own and proved their worth for providing the air component for a combined operation. Apart from the Royal Air Force aircraft operating from Sicily—a distance too great to allow them to work in close support of our troops and respond immediately to requests for the bombing or "strafing" of specified targets—the air support of our troops during the most anxious days at Salerno devolved entirely upon the Fleet Air Arm aircraft. These were mostly Seafires—the naval adaptation of the Spitfire—and to begin with they all operated from their "escort aircraft carriers." In so doing the pilots performed near-miracles, in landing on their short decks in a flat calm—the worst possible conditions for landing fast aircraft on short flight decks. And when the "escort aircraft carriers" were forced to withdraw to refuel, their Seafires landed on a half-built landing strip ashore and operated from it in clouds of dust and flying stones until the landing strip was completed and the Royal Air Force moved in and took over. The Seafires then flew back to Sicily and thence back to their aircraft carriers.

Those Seafires and their "escort aircraft carriers" off Salerno made history. It was after that operation, and in the light of the astonishing performances of ships and aircraft, that the "assault aircraft carriers" became an accepted and indispensable part of any amphibious force called upon to operate at any considerable distance from friendly airfields.

It was the development in affording air cover to amphibious operations at a distance from established air bases that made possible the contemplation of the invasion of southern France—an operation in which Tom Troubridge, with his wide experience of aircraft carrier work and of combined operations, was eminently fitted to play an important part.

The fact that he did so, however, was due to circumstances rather than design on the part of their Lordships of the Admiralty. The "assault aircraft carrier" force had already been formed for the invasion of Southern France under the command of Rear-Admiral La Touche Bisset when that officer was taken suddenly ill and had to be rushed to hospital at Malta. A relief had to be found at once, for there could be no question of postponing the invasion, which, of course, was intimately linked with the progress of the British and American troops which had invaded northern France. Providentially Tom Troubridge was available in that theatre of war, so he was ordered to take over the command immediately.

A lesser man might well have been daunted by the prospect of taking over what amounted to a new arm of the Service on the eve of a great and vitally important invasion operation, the more so since he could expect no "turn over" from the officer whom he succeeded, as the latter was in hospital, unconscious and on the danger list. Tom Troubridge, however, took it in his stride. In truth it was not as difficult a task for him as it would have been for most other naval officers. He had a wealth of experience behind him, and he had watched the evolution of the "assault aircraft carrier" with an interest which might have been called fatherly had it not been so forceful. He had the ships and their aircraft and the duties of each at his finger tips.

To illustrate this one may quote the story of his inspection of one of his "assault aircraft carriers." Tom Troubridge insisted that all officers of the ship should be personally introduced to him, and as this was done by the captain he asked each officer what his duties were. One officer declared that he was the torpedo officer of the ship. Troubridge was perfectly well aware that the whole electric installation of the ship was the responsibility of the so-called torpedo officer, although no torpedo-carrying aircraft were embarked in "assault aircraft carriers," but he could not resist his joke. "Just the sort of job I've been looking for," he said, "torpedo officer of a ship without any torpedoes."

There were, in all, nine "assault aircraft carriers" detailed to provide close air support for the invasion of southern France. All of these were under the command of Rear-Admiral Troubridge as Commander of Task Force No. 88, but they operated in two groups.

One group was under Troubridge's direct orders and the other under the orders of Rear-Admiral Durgin of the United States Navy. Troubridge laid down the policy and the general tasks and orders for both groups of "assault aircraft carriers" and, in fact, they worked in close collaboration throughout the operations, being always in touch by radio-telephony and frequently within visual signalling range of one another.

Rear-Admiral Troubridge had many responsibilities beyond the correct use of the "assault aircraft carriers," of which there were five in his group and four under the direct operational orders of Rear-Admiral Durgin, U.S.N. Troubridge had taken over a tremendous responsibility at twelve hours' notice. He hoisted his flag in the cruiser *Royalist*, and, as if history had to be served, he found that H.M.S. *Troubridge* was one of the escorting destroyers.

Among the other British warships which took part were the old battleship *Ramillies*, which had recently been employed in bombarding the Normandy coast in support of the invasion of northern France, and the cruisers *Orion*, *Aurora*, *Ajax*, *Black Prince*, *Sirius*, *Dido*, *Royalist*, *Agincourt*, *Colombo*, *Delhi* and *Caledon*.

When the invasion of the south of France was "laid on," the assault convoys sailed from Naples through the Straits of Bonifacio, between Corsica and Sardinia. Allied air superiority over the Tyrrhenian Sea could be relied upon to prevent detection of the assault forces until these were to the westward of Corsica. Similarly, support and "build up" convoys sailed from Naples, Taranto, Bizerta and Algiers, and most of these called at Naples before sailing on the final stretch of their voyage to the south of France beachheads. Therein lies a tremendous testimonial to the British and American engineers and salvage men who had in a few months rendered the damaged port of Naples capable, not only of supplying a great advancing army in Italy, but also of mounting an historic overseas expedition.

When the Germans had been forced to abandon Naples they had gone to great lengths with their demolitions, not only of the port, but also of installations in the town. They felt that they had a right to consider that their work of destruction would deny to the Allies any extensive use of the port for many months, if not years. But the Germans were wrong. The Allied engineers and salvage men showed a genius for improvisation as well as an infinite capacity for hard work. The Germans had wrecked the electric light and power supplies of the great town of Naples. The Allies promptly used captured Italian submarines as floating power stations to bridge the gap in supply between the wrecking of the normal plant by the Germans and its rehabilitation by Allied engineers. As to the port—let facts and figures speak for themselves. The Allies entered Naples on October 2nd. By the end of that month 13,000 tons a day were being unloaded in that port. By May the figure was 37,000 tons; and within a comparatively short time the capacity of the port of Naples—with its piers and jetties increased by structures erected on sunken wrecks, was actually greater than the capacity of the port of New York. It seems almost unbelievable, but it is true.

There is little doubt that a high degree of surprise was effected in our landings on the south coast of France in spite of the fact that German propaganda had been screaming about the possibility for weeks and months. Such propaganda, however, was known by experience to work by opposites, when it was not trying to persuade the Allies into an unwary denial. Discount all the propaganda and one finds a belief in the German mind that the Italian ports were hardly capable of supplying our armies in Italy, let alone serving as the main point of departure for an invasion of "Hitler's Europe."

It was undoubtedly due to this over-confidence on the part of the enemy in his demolitions that the convoys destined to invade the south of France were not detected earlier. Despite the distances involved and the proximity of enemy air and submarine bases the assault convoys—which assembled in Naples Bay and sailed by way of the Straits of Bonifacio—were not detected by the enemy until the forenoon before the actual landings.

For the invasion of the south of France "H hour" was later than is usual. It was well after full daylight. This was arranged so that there should be full deployment of the Allied air-power. In the first instance this devolved upon the Twelfth Tactical Air Force, the nearest base of which was Corsica. Then, as the assault neared the beaches, the responsibility for close air support was assumed by the "assault aircraft carriers."

In northern Europe it would have been suicidal to carry out an invasion some twenty-four hours after the assault convoys had been detected by the enemy. Not so in the Mediterranean at that time. It was well known to the Allied Commanders that the bulk of the Luftwaffe had been withdrawn from that theatre of war in a vain attempt to defend the Reich territory against the ever-increasing power of the Allied air onslaught. It was also known that the German U-boat fleet in the Mediterranean had been to a great extent dispersed and that its remnants were based in the Aegean after having been driven out of the western and central Mediterranean. This was an important factor. The invasion of the south of France had necessarily to pass within easy striking distance of Spezzia and Genoa, ports on the flank of the invasion approach which had hitherto been extensively used by U-boats. The surface forces of the enemy could be put in the discount. The Italian Fleet had long since surrendered. The French Fleet at Toulon had been scuttled. Such Italian and French warships as remained in German hands were small and effective only as escorts to small convoys in the Aegean, Adriatic and Gulf of Genoa. Even then, their usefulness was more in the nature of giving a spurious confidence to the men manning the merchant ships than of actual protection against the ever-expanding sea and air power of the Allies.

There were five landing forces in the invasion of the south of France, and these were covered by five groups of naval forces. Most of the British warships taking part have already been detailed, but it may be said here that the total Anglo-American naval forces involved comprised five battleships, twenty-two cruisers, and one hundred and nine destroyers, as well as the nine "assault aircraft carriers." It was an ample force. It had to be. There could never have been any excuse for a failure of the invasion of southern France. It was far more than an isolated operation. It was an integral part of the deployment of the overwhelming strength of the United Nations—using the mobility and flexibility of their sea power—against the vaunted impregnability of the so-called fortress of German-occupied Europe.

This is no place for a detailed account of an operation which was inevitably overshadowed in the public mind by events nearer home in northern France. We are concerned more with the part played by Rear-Admiral Troubridge and his "assault aircraft carriers."

For the first three days of the operation—that is, from the southern France D-day to D plus 3—the aircraft of the Twelfth Tactical Air Force, operating from Corsican airfields—did magnificent work. That is not to say that they did all the work. The short-range fighter cover and fighter-bomber support was even at that stage provided chiefly by the "assault aircraft carriers" operating in an area south of Hyéres. So fast did General Patton's troops advance, however, that by D plus 3—three days after the initial landings—they were operating out of range of the long-range fighters and fighter-bombers from Corsica.

The responsibility for the whole of the air support for the advancing troops devolved, therefore, upon the aircraft from the "assault aircraft carriers." This was a state of affairs which persisted until airfields in southern France had been captured and re-conditioned and land-based aircraft were operating from them. This phase lasted from D plus 3 to D plus 10. For seven days the carrier-borne fighters and fighter-bombers bore the brunt of army support, and most magnificently they did it. They proved up to the hilt the theory that carrier-borne aircraft can support both amphibious and military operations under conditions in which the enemy's shore-based air superiority has been previously reduced.

After the first three days, in which they gave close air support to the landing troops and provided fighter cover for the ships, the carrier-borne aircraft had, for the subsequent seven days, to perform all the manifold duties of an air force working in support of ground troops. They carried out their own reconnaissances, took their own photographs, discovered the places where it would most hurt the enemy to be hit, bombed his strong-points, troop concentrations and communications, and "strafed" his troops on the move.

During the first eight days of the invasion of southern France naval fighters and fighter-bombers operating from the five "assault aircraft carriers" working under Troubridge's direct operational orders, flew nearly a thousand sorties. That meant that on each of the eight days one aircraft, on the average, was taking off from the carriers every six minutes from sunrise to sunset. The fighter-bombers from those five small carriers flew over five hundred and thirty-two sorties; while the fighters flew a hundred and nineteen sorties when spotting for naval bombardments, eighty-four sorties on tactical reconnaissance, a hundred and fourteen in providing fighter cover over the beaches, and a hundred and thirty-two sorties in providing the fighter umbrella over the Task Force. Well over a quarter of a million miles were flown by the aircraft—Seafires, Hellcats and Wildcats—of these five small carriers. Each pilot flew an average of 2300 miles.

In his report Tom Troubridge states that his claims for the damage done by the naval aircraft under his command are conserva-

tive. One can well imagine it. Troubridge is the last man in the
world to make extravagant claims. Yet his assessment of the results
obtained by the fighters and fighter-bombers of his five assault
carriers is that they destroyed 160 enemy motor vehicles and
damaged 190 others; that they destroyed or damaged 147 railway
wagons, 20 armoured fighting vehicles, and 9 bridges. In addition,
14 direct hits and 51 very near misses were scored on enemy coastal
batteries, and other military installations were hit 53 times. There
were 32 hits on roads and railway cuttings, while at sea one supply
ship, one paddle steamer, two E-boats, and three barges were sunk.

As soon as airfields had been captured and the 12th Tactical Air
Force was able to take over, General Saville, commanding the
12th T.A.F., saw for himself what the naval aircraft had accomplished, and he sent the following signal to Rear-Admiral
Troubridge:

"I personally counted 202 wrecked enemy motor-transport on
the road between Brignolles and St. Maximin. This is first-hand
evidence of an outstanding job. I would be grateful if you would
convey to all concerned my congratulations for their excellent
work, which has done much to facilitate the rapid advance of
our ground forces."

One of the most astonishing aspects of this operation, when one
takes into consideration the difficulties and risks involved in operating fast aircraft from small aircraft carriers, is that the serviceability
of aircraft never fell below 85 per cent, and that, throughout those
gruelling days and nights no mission had to be cancelled owing to
unserviceability of aircraft. As Troubridge said in his official
despatch, it was "a magnificent achievement by maintenance crews
and handling parties."

Once the armies of the Twelfth Tactical Air Force were firmly
established in southern France, the "assault aircraft carrier" force
was despatched to the Levant with a view to supporting operations
in the Aegean.

Ever since the black days of 1941 the whole of the Greek mainland and the islands of the Aegean had been in German hands, and
large German garrisons had been maintained on the islands of
Rhodes and Crete and at other important centres. Following the
Italian collapse we had tried to occupy and hold the Dodecanese, but

these operations had proved expensive and abortive owing to lack of air power in that area.

In the autumn of 1944 things were very different. The Russian advance along the Danube and the growing strength of the Yugo-slavs on the main supply routes north of Greece were threatening the enemy's communications with all his forces in south-east Europe. The German forces in Greece and the Aegean were nervous and were showing signs of beginning to pull out. The enemy's few available transports and a number of small vessels, as well as transport air-craft, were engaged in ferrying troops and equipment from the islands to the Piræus and Salonika. If this movement could be stopped the German garrisons would be marooned and would not be available to the enemy for the subsequent defence of the Fortress of Germany.

Early in September a force of cruisers, "escort aircraft carriers" and destroyers was assembled at Alexandria under the command of Rear-Admiral Troubridge—whose flag still flew in H.M.S. *Royalist*—and sailed for the Aegean.

This force remained at sea for twelve days and did its work superbly well. It operated for the most part in the southern Aegean, and at the end of the twelve days the enemy communications with the southern—and more strongly held—islands had been almost completely severed. Five of his dwindling number of transports had been sunk, a U-boat had been sent to the bottom, and a number of small craft had been destroyed. Meanwhile naval aircraft from the carriers had harried the land communications on the islands, shooting up motor vehicles and "strafing" airfields. The naval air-craft also covered minesweeping operations to clear channels to enable our forces to operate against Salonika.

Tom Troubridge also played a part in the destruction of the air transport upon which the Germans fell back when they realised that their sea communications were cut. It was he who suggested that a ship should be kept in the Aegean to act as a fighter directing ship to put the R.A.F. Beaufighters on to their quarries. The system worked extremely well and led to the destruction of a large number of German transport aircraft.

The work of this force in the Aegean paved the way for the subsequent operations and the liberation of Greece. The force earned a special signal of commendation from the Lord Commissioners of the Admiralty.

By that time, however, Troubridge had left it. His appointment to command Task Force No. 88 had been only temporary, necessitated by the sudden illness of Rear-Admiral Bisset. Commodore G. N. Oliver, C.B., D.S.O., had been nominated for the appointment in August, but he did not arrive and take over from Troubridge until early October.

On October 8th, 1944, therefore, Tom Troubridge returned to England after an absence of about exactly eighteen months crammed with very varied and interesting service.

THE END